About the author

FILIP PALDA EARNED his Ph.D. in economics at the University of Chicago.

Dedication

TO MY MOTHER, THE ORIGINATOR AND THE ORIGINAL

CONTENTS

PREFACE

MASTERING ANY DOMAIN OF KNOWLEDGE is hard. Some psychologists estimate it takes about three thousand hours of concentrated study simply to start being able to contribute in a meaningful way to your chosen field. Assuming you could devote a maximum of eight hours a day to perfecting yourself, then under these conditions you would have to study almost three years, and more likely five or even seven. Seven years is the time it traditionally took to pass from being an apprentice to a journeyman in trades such as instrument making, goldsmithing, surgery and barbering. The *Beatles* may just have spent this amount of time performing, and honing their skills before their success.

Becoming a master of economics is not easy, mainly because it is a new science. Pedagogy has been a straggler in the march to understanding. First year economics classes dumb down the subject, and try to make it "accessible" to the many. This has the result of making it accessible to few. That should be no surprise. Have you ever heard of an easy course in bodybuilding? How about *Endurance Running 101* in which you attain the toughness of a marathoner without ever breaking a sweat? The mind is like a muscle. It needs to be stressed before it can grow.

The established sciences are well aware of this. Physics courses the world over pose a challenge. So should economics. There is no short-cut to core concepts, whatever the discipline. The current explosion of wannabe economic best-sellers in popular bookstores turn their faces from this awkward fact. They seek to make economics accessible from the armchair, a topic for midnight reading, sexy, and even freakish. They appeal to the reader's vanity rather than to his or her appetite for knowledge for its own sake.

To be fair, you will also find on a nearby bookshelf popular physics books which try to make that science accessible. But you will also find they are serious works that make little compromise with the reader's demand for instant understanding. Physics books don't expect you to grasp all the intricacies of that science. They seek to help you understand what are the great questions in physics and how physicists go about answering them. How many popular books in economics give you that? By cravenly reducing their expositions to jokes and meretricious anecdotes, economists who try to explain their topic to the wider world are working on the assumption that the topic can only be washed down with beer and popcorn. Such an approach is unfair to the curious.

To the curious, economics may seem a fragmented science. No such confusion existed in the minds of those who founded the field. Economics was a 19th century reaction to rapid social change that made people question the value of the societies in which they lived. Was economic growth worth the upheaval to customs and mores? Did government have a role in moderating the rapid changes taking place? The answers depended on how you weighed the outcomes the modern economic system produced. Put more figuratively, economics came into being as a means of calculating whether social accounts were in balance. Did the capitalist system give workers sufficient reward for their efforts? Did communism promise a better reward system for organizing society? Such questions had seldom been asked with any force because there had been no call for the answers.

For most of history people lived in static economic and social settings. Little changed. The absence of change allowed people to gradually figure out means of balancing social accounts without the aid of worldly philosophers. The need for economics arose when the world started to change too rapidly for governments to really understand where things were going. Those in power turned to economists because they were the only ones who had developed a rough but logically coherent means of thinking about how social accounts added up under different government policies.

A clear and quantifiable idea of the basis of social cohesion is why economics remains the only guide which the mass, anonymous societies of today can use to avoid blundering into depression and even chaos. Economists who think their topic is a tap-dance should seek a calling in the entertainment industry. Economics is a noble undertaking in which there is no place for the intellectual kibitzer, the gag-artist, the purveyor of trivia. If such solemnity strikes you as being excessive, think of "Boozy Barley" Blair in John LeCarré's *The Russia House* explaining in his cups that "today you have to think like a hero to be a merely decent human being."

But does a heroic science call for heroic sacrifice on the part of those who would understand it, at least in its outlines? Just as in physics, there are no shortcuts to mastery in economics. But there are ways to avoid needless confusion. Some people breeze through the study of difficult topics to become masters in a short time. These are the ones we see relaxing at the bistro chatting and laughing with friends while the rest of us toil at our desks in fear of the next examination. Are they so much better than the rest of us? Yes they are. But not because of some otherworldly talent. They are better because they have a knack for getting to the heart of the matter. They know which steps lead to the heights of knowledge. They expend effort, though not needless effort.

What are these steps that can help one to master economics elegantly instead being crushed grossly by the challenge? I believe them to be seven. The first four are basic units: substitution, time, chance, and space. Each has fundamental insights that are applied in all other fields of economics. The way to snap the basic pieces together is through equilibrium analysis, which is the fifth step. Game theory is the sixth step because it draws on the first five steps but itself also makes fundamental contributions from which the first five steps can benefit. Standing seventh, at the top, is the idea of statistical control. Only once we have understood theory of economics, can we then proceed to test these notions. That is what statistical control is about.

Such a list may seem simplistic to some and may even smack of dilettantism to others. What about Ricardo's principle of comparative advantage? Or Say's law? How about the median voter theorem? Deadweight loss? The impression of a café terrace approach to economics mounts as one consults the *Journal of Economic Literature* classifications of economic fields. There are twenty major fields, close to a hundred subfields, and over five hundred fields within the subfields. I won't even attempt to quantify the number of economic journals. Their number blooms like plankton and their nutritional value is about as hearty. How can such a massive archive be reduced to a few hundred pages?

None of that should bother us. Let us take our cue from Nobel Prize winner Robert E. Lucas Jr. When asked how he kept up with all the literature being published in economics he answered that it wasn't really that difficult as there were no more than a handful of articles worth reading. It is a handful upon which I have based the seven steps to economic mastery. Reading original sources is a refreshing surprise. For example, Harold Hotelling's 1929 article "Stability in Competition" is clearer reading than almost anything on the topic that has followed. Sherwin Rosen's "The Theory of Equalizing Differences" is one of the masterpieces of economics and it has kept many an economist busy since it was written in 1986. Even von Neuman and Morgenstern's *Theory of Games and Economic Behavior*, though considered the most quoted but least read work in economics, does in fact have a few passages which are comprehensible to people just marginally below the genius level. Breadth reading is not needed to master economics. Depth reading is the key.

And that is where the book you are holding comes in. You do not need to go back to these original sources to get the basic message of economics. I have distilled these sources for you. You will find the results in the pages that follow. The only thing you need to appreciate is my method. I am not providing a survey of all ideas in economics. Some readers will be shocked to discover that I make no mention of a great many economic giants. My purpose is not to trace intellectual pedigrees. My purpose is to give you what it takes to not only understand what economics is about but to allow you to develop the instincts of the masters who developed this field and whose knowledge is within anyone's grasp.

In my quest to render advanced economic concepts comprehensible to all I have been aided by my conceptual editor Kristin McCahon. Kristin is a prominent editor with over thirty years of experience in being what she describes as an "advocate for the reader". Over the years it has taken to write this book Kristin has been present and has exercised her talents to make the writing clear to all. I owe her an immense

debt of gratitude. I am as usual indebted to my father Kristian
Palda for his help. As a teenager he left the remnants of his
family, devastated by Nazi depredations, and friends behind
and fled Stalin's agents as they encroached upon his beloved
Czechoslovakia and issued warrants for his arrest as an enemy
of the socialist state. His crime being that he was the son of
a capitalist. Under communism, as under Nazism, genetic
circumstances were deemed grounds for prosecution. Nazis
prosecuted Jews and other minorities. Communists had an
aversion to the bourgeois chromosome. I make much of it
but others suffered worse and I never heard my father com-
plain or speak ill of his tormentors. He made his way from
Bremerhaven on a *United Nations* ship to Halifax as a "DP"
or "displaced person", drifting, after a decade of menial work
to Chicago where he earned his *Ph.D.* at the University of
Chicago under Nobellist George Stigler. That training honed
his already superlative intellect to a fine edge. He has used it,
and the unique perspective on life his experiences have given
him, to help me cut away a great deal of superfluous and need-
lessly complicated material. Above all he has reminded me
that economics is not only a science, but is also one of the
humanities. As a humanity it is a tool which should enhance
one's culture and thus aid individuals to improve themselves
and the society in which they live.

I thank Mirja Von Herk who has provided proofreading.
All remaining faults and mistakes remain mine alone. I also
wish to thank the management and staff of Cooper-Wolfling
Publishers for their confidence in this project and their support over the years it has taken to realize it, and the generous use of their facilities and research staff. I thank professor Bernard Kavanaugh of the Latin department of Queen's
University for showing me how to translate "out of games,

honesty and obedience" into "ex ludis probitas et oboedientia". I thank Sébastien Coté for his ideas on bringing this book to a wide public. I especially thank my university the *ENAP* (National School of Public Administration), and its academic director André Bourret, for providing the intellectual environment necessary for the gestation of this project. *ENAP* is a multidisciplinary school which takes a long-term view of research and gives its scholars the latitude to create.

I also thank Jaffer Qamar, a *Ph.D.* graduate from the economics faculty of the University of Chicago with whom I have been carrying on a running economic conversation ever since we met there close on thirty years ago now. He encouraged me, after the positive reception of my earlier book *Pareto's Republic,* to go deep and fill a gap he felt existed in economics. Namely the lack of a survey of the key concepts which was not dumbed down but which at the same time was suited to the curious. That he said was the challenge. Only you may judge whether it has been met.

References

Hotelling, Harold. 1929. "Stability in Competition." *The Economic Journal*, volume 39: 41-57.

Rosen, Sherwin. 1986. "The Theory Of Equalizing Differences." *Handbook of Labor Economics, Volume I.* Edited by Orley Ashenfelter and Richard Layard. Elsevier Science Publishers. 641-692.

Von Neumann, John and Oskar Morgenstern. 1953. *The Theory of Games and Economic Behavior, Third edition.* Princeton University Press.

SUBSTITUTION   2

I F YOU ASK PEOPLE TO state the central problem of economics their answer is "to make money!" How to spend that money seldom comes up. Spending is not a problem. It is a pleasure. You spend on things you like and can afford. Economists see things differently. How to make money is not their domain. They leave that to hedge-fund operators and talking heads on the business segment of nightly news reports. How to spend that money is where all economics starts.

Among the contending definitions of economics, the best known is from Lord Lionel Robbins, who wrote that "Economics is a science that deals with the study of human behavior as a relationship between ends and scarce means which have alternative uses". You have some "ends" meaning goals, such as making yourself as happy as you can, and you have certain "means": namely your income and what it can buy. Showing how to satisfy your ends by adjusting your expenditures within your means is the basis of most economics. It underpins supply and demand. It provides the framework for analyzing government policies as diverse as the minimum wage and taxation. It helps us understand how people invest their money in risky situations and how they spread their expenditures over time.

It took economists from 1838 and the publication of Augustin Cournot's *Mathematical Treatise on Wealth* until 1915 and Eugen Slutsky's definitive mathematical theory of consumer behavior to understand the issues involved in how people substitute one item of interest for another based on their relative prices. Finding the solution was not the hard part. Stating the problem correctly was where the problem lay. The notion of "trade-offs" is where all ruminations began. So let us see what that means from an economic perspective.

The pervasiveness of trade-offs

ECONOMISTS STUDY THE choices people make from a scarce, or limited range of options. Without scarcity, we would have little to study. Infinite abundance means having everything and so never having to make hard choices. If instead, your resources are limited, you can only use more of something by using less of other things. This may sound obvious but the idea is generally absent from debates on public policy. Almost daily we hear calls for government to spend more to "stimulate" the economy, but how often do we hear it said that the money to stimulate must be pulled from some other part of the economy that will then be de-stimulated?

In our personal lives the concept of a trade-off is clear enough if you go into the supermarket with only cash in your pocket. You know that putting a tin of expensive caviar in your cart means you will have less money left to buy beans. Credit cards obscure this constraint on our choices because they push the reality of payment into a dimly perceived future. Financial advisors and even psychologists do a brisk business of reminding us that trade-offs are not just between the here and now but also between the now and then, which is what economists call "inter-temporal constraints on choice". If our advisors fail to convince us to change our behavior, then bill collectors will make sure that we very rapidly come to a complete understanding of trade-offs.

While the need to consume less of something in order to be able to get more of something else is an iron-clad law, there is room for a consumer to seek his or her best purchases within its confines. Economists call this "maximizing utility under a budget constraint". Here is how it works.

If a tin of caviar costs twenty-five dollars and a can of beans costs one dollar, then you have to give up twenty-five cans of beans to get an extra tin of caviar. It also means that if you want an extra tenth of a can of caviar you must give up twenty-five tenths of a can of beans. If you want one thousandth of a can of caviar you must give up twenty-five thousandths of a can of beans. More generally whatever extra part of a can of caviar you want, no matter how minute, the minimum similarly fractionated parts of a can of beans you must give up is twenty-five.

This is what economists are trained to think of when they analyze prices. They are not concerned with the dollar sticker but rather with the relative price of the two commodities. The relative price tells you how that tiniest extra or "marginal" fraction of a good one can be traded off against the other. In more general contexts economists sometimes call this the marginal rate of transformation, but we will just call it relative price. Dollars are important mainly because that is how your budget is measured. If your budget is the fixed sum of a thousand dollars then the relative prices are a guide to how far that thousand can slide you from consumption of one good to the other.

At the going relative price should you increase your purchase of caviar, stay put, or decrease it? Now instead of looking at the rate at which you are obliged to trade off one product for the other, the object of interest becomes the rate at which you are willing to trade them off. Suppose an extra tin of caviar gives you fifty times more pleasure than a can of beans. This means that giving up fifty cans of beans for a tin of caviar would neither increase nor decrease your pleasure, but would leave you indifferent. This is the maximum rate at which you would be willing to trade one commodity for the other. Economists always call this the marginal rate of substitution. "Marginal" to an economists means that extra little bit you give up to get something else. In this situation the consumer is not maximizing wellbeing because she would be willing to give up more cans of beans to get caviar than the market obliges her to give up. Put differently, the maximum she would be willing to pay exceeds the minimum she is obliged to pay. Consumers call this situation "a deal", which basically means you are paying less than you would be willing to pay to get an extra unit of some product. In this case then you give up beans and buy more caviar.

But when do you stop? Since it is the inequality between the ability to trade-off the two goods and the desire to trade them off that drives the rush to more caviar, something will eventually have to bring these two sides of the equation into line with each other, lest you depopulate the Caspian Sea of sturgeon.

It is pretty clear that the consumer cannot change the rate at which she is able to exchange the two goods for each other. That rate is given by dollar prices and is generally beyond negotiation. But what she can change is the rate at which she is willing to exchange goods, the marginal rate of substitution. That is fairly obvious on an intuitive level. If you ate nothing but caviar you would become sickened to the point at which beans would start looking tasty and you would side with Shakespeare who wrote that "the sweetest honey is loathsome in its deliciousness".

So the trick it would appear is to increase the consumption of caviar until you become so disgusted that the rate at which you would be willing to give up beans for some extra caviar falls down to the market rate at which you are obliged to trade them off. While there is nothing wrong with this view of how consumers adjust their consumption to maximize their well-being, it lacks the precision to clarify just how truly powerful the concept of substitution is. We can do better.

The Substitution Games

LET US GO back to the point where you the consumer are willing to give up fifty cans of beans for one can of caviar but the relative price is twenty-five cans of beans to one of caviar. Suddenly you find yourself the star of an afternoon game-show called *The Substitution Games*. By some artifice of Hollywood the host can measure your happiness or "utility". In your current state you are spending your entire one thousand dollar budget, there is an imbalance between relative price and marginal rate of substitution, and your utility is ten units of happiness. Your challenge is to arrange consumption so that you stay on this fixed level of utility by spending the least amount of money. The game show will pay you the amount by which you manage to reduce spending while still staying at the same level of happiness.

If you think this show is a bit strange then so did many economists, until Eugen Slutsky clarified what was going on here in his celebrated 1915 article, the remarkable story of which is fascinatingly described in the 2002 article by Chipman and Lenfant. They write poignantly that "As is now well known, Slutsky's article is one of the most famous examples of those neglected and ignored works whose originality and importance are recognized only after similar results have been obtained by others." (553). Despite being rediscovered late, Slutsky became acknowledged as the master of this topic.

It is easy to see how to make money in this game. That you are willing to give up fifty units of beans for one unit of caviar means the exchange leaves you at the same level of utility. So go ahead and consume one more unit of caviar and fifty fewer beans. But now your costs of maintaining this utility have fallen because by giving up fifty units of beans the market has allowed you to purchase two units of caviar (remember they cost twenty five beans each). That means you are at the same level of utility as before but with surplus caviar in your disposable budget, which the game show host credits towards the worth of your final prize.

This sounds good, so you keep buying caviar, until that is, you run into the law of diminishing marginal rate of substitution, or the convexity of indifference curves. Yes, all contestants know what that means, but viewers might want a refresher. An assumption running through economics is that the rate at which people are willing to give up of beans to get more of caviar (or any other pairing of goods) while keeping them indifferent to the exchange, is a falling function of the amount of caviar consumed.

It all accords fairly well with intuition. The indifference curve in question is the collection of all caviar-bean combinations that leave you at the same level of happiness. In this case ten units of happiness. Each different level of happiness has its own associated indifference curve.

What all this means for the game is that you are able to save less and less money by increasing your caviar consumption, because the surplus of caviar starts shrinking. It shrinks because the amount of beans you have to give up to keep you on the indifference curves starts rising.

Eventually you reach a point at which no further cost savings is possible. At that point the rates at which you are willing and able to trade off the two commodities is equal. What you have managed in this restricted game setting is to minimize the cost of attaining a certain level of happiness or "utility" given the prices you face and your relative desires for goods.

Economists can actually calculate what this "cost function" of attaining a given level of happiness is provided they have information on prices, income, and the mathematical form of the utility function. As in so many cases of jargon, cost function is a confusing term. It should really be called a "minimum cost of attaining a certain level of utility function". But we will stick with tradition in this case.

Winners of this round of the game get to go to the next stage. In this stage the game show host gives you the caviar you saved by minimizing your costs of attaining ten units of utility, and tells you to spend your winnings as you please. You could go ahead and consume all the extra caviar which would certainly increase your utility. But you could attain the same higher level by now going in the opposite direction from the first round and exchanging some surplus caviar for beans. You would then have extra beans to spare. In the third round you would not spend everything on beans but even things out again, but then, well, you get the message. Eventually you start acting like your own game-show host, parlaying savings from cost minimization at any given level of utility into higher levels of utility. Each time though the savings get smaller and smaller because each time it is only a fraction of the previous surplus that gets kept for the next round. When the extra savings reach zero you have both maximized utility and minimized costs.

If you understand the process of maximizing utility by substituting one good for another then you have roughly half of economics in your pocket. To maximize pleasure, or utility, a person must adjust his or her consumption so as to equate relative willingness to pay with relative price. If relative price changes, then so must consumption in order to bring equality back to both sides of the equation.

The demand curve

EXACTLY HOW CONSUMPTION reacts to changes in price depends on relative pleasure and relative opportunity. Economists call the relation between price and consumption a "demand curve", a concept known to any who have taken a course in this subject. The demand curve is the fraternal twin of the supply curve and equal partner with it in determining something called market equilibrium. It is of vital importance to most of economics so let us examine it a bit more closely.

The demand curve is a "reaction function". It shows how your demand for caviar reacts to a change in the price of caviar, a change in the price of beans, and a change in your income. The demand curve emerges from the rule that you should always be balancing the rate at which you are willing to trade off caviar for beans (the marginal rate of substitution) with the rate at which you are able to trade them off (relative price). This rule is reactive and the reaction is based on optimization of personal happiness. You react to price and income changes so as to best enhance your wellbeing. As such the demand curve tells you how best to change your consumption when these fundamentals that hem us in force us to work within their shifting confines.

The Slutsky equation

MOST PEOPLE CAN accept as self-evident that a rise in price leads to a fall in demand and do not see quite why economists make such a fuss about what they call a demand curve. The fuss however is justified. The demand curve encapsulates two forces that act upon consumption. A substitution and an income effect. Either may work in tandem or in opposition to the other, lending to demand an air of ambiguity and also of depth. This depth is crucial in understanding the effects of certain public policies as well as the meaning of price indices. So let us try to understand the meaning of income and substitution effects.

We have just seen that for any given level of happiness or "utility" there is a minimum cost way of attaining that utility by arranging your levels of consumption of diverse goods. This minimum was attained through a clever substitution of one commodity for the other.

A corollary of this exercise is that substitution is a prophylactic but not complete defence against price increases. Suppose your income is a thousand dollars, you are consuming ten tins of caviar and the price rises to a hundred dollars. If you refuse to change your consumption of caviar your spending on beans must go to zero if you are not to violate your budget. That would present a very unbalanced consumption profile and hence a low level of utility.

By playing the *Substitution Games* scenario in your mind you could buy less caviar and more beans, stay on this low level of utility and have surplus beans to spare, which could then raise you to a higher level of utility, and so forth until the game had converged to the point where no more savings from substitution is possible. This new level of utility would necessarily be lower than the one before the price increase, simply because your fixed dollar budget now goes less far than it did before. But you have protected yourself to some degree.

What would happen if some benevolent soul who knew your budget and utility function calculated how much income it would take to raise you back to your old utility level and gave you the money?

Would you return to the old consumption level of caviar? The answer is no. Recall that maximizing utility is inseparable from minimizing cost. At the new prices, even on the same utility level as before the price increase you would have to shift consumption towards beans. This "substitution effect" would not be quite as large as the raw effect without the gift of the benevolent stranger. Before the gift you had two depressing effects on caviar consumption. One is the fact that even at the same utility as before, consumption would have to fall to satisfy the logic of cost minimization. The second, is that the price rise diminishes what your limited budget can achieve. You have less "real" income when a price rises. This effect on income would lead to an added fall in consumption of caviar and also in the consumption of beans, provided that both are "normal goods". The fall in caviar consumption along the indifference curve is the substitution effect.

The total fall in consumption, less the substitution effect, is the income effect. A normal income effect is one in which consumption rises or falls as income falls. Economists believe that "inferior" goods, possessing the opposite quality are rare to non-existent.

Uses of the Slutsky Equation

Now you understand the Slutsky equation. It decomposes the changes in demand of a consumer reacting to prices in such a way as to maximize utility into two components; an income and a substitution effect. The income effect moves consumers between indifference curves, whereas the substitution effect helps them stay on the same indifference curves. In a celebrated 1915 article Slutsky showed how to get this decomposition mathematically. It is the basis of almost all demand theory.

Take this for example. The distinction between income and substitution effects lurks behind discussions of price increases and is poorly understood by lay people and economists. Yet these concepts must be grasped in order to understand among other things the effects of many different sorts of government policy. To appreciate the importance of income effects suppose that government decided to increase taxes on the consumption of cigarettes in order to discourage smoking. The tax would surely have a substitution effect that reduces what some people smoke. However, because the revenue goes back into government coffers and is spent on behalf of all citizens, including smokers this acts as a countervailing income effect on smoking. For the tax to have its full impact on smoking government would have to burn the tax dollars it earned from its levy on smokers.

Substitution effects are also widely misunderstood and the result shows in the way governments calculate, or rather miscalculate cost-of-living indices. Michael Boskin, author of the famous report to the US president that bears his name, argued that price indices exaggerate the cost of living because they do not take into account peoples' ability to substitute one good for another in order to fight the utility lowering effect of a price increase. The idea came out in our discussion of the cost function but is worth seeing in its most extreme guise.

Suppose caviar makes up half your budget and the price doubles. If you insist on eating the same amount of caviar as before the price increase then your cost of attaining the level of utility you had before the price increase would go up by a half. But if you could find a perfect substitute for caviar, perhaps salmon roe, which cost as much as caviar before its price increase, then you could shift all your consumption to roe and attain the same level of utility as before the price increase in caviar. A cost-of-living index would find that life had become harder, but your ability to find a substitute would mean your cost of attaining a given level of happiness had not changed. The same principle applies to a lesser degree even when perfect substitutes are not available. People can generally adapt to prices by changing what they consume. Utility can rarely be as large as it was before the price increase, but it need not be as small as it would be if they passively stuck to their initial levels of consumption before price increases.

In practical terms this means that if a government wishes to use simple cost-of-living indices as a guide for allowing the poor to continue buying the same, but now costlier basket of products, then the compensation will likely turn out to be greater than that which would be needed to return these people to the same level of utility as before the price increases.

A better strategy is to try to figure out the cost function, that is the minimum cost at which a person can attain a particular level of well-being (rather that a particular basket) by adjusting relative wants to relative opportunities for substitution. This function will tell you how much money need be given to a person to return him or her to the same level of happiness as before the price increase. Because of the prophylactic effect of substitution against price increases, the rebate will be lower than the cost-of-living increase had no substitution been carried out. This rebate will correspond to the income effect component of the Slutsky equation.

We can squeeze a final few drops of relevant insight from the Slutsky equation by examining what happens when all prices increase, including the price of labor, namely wages. This is often called "inflation". Economists believe that inflation which is perfectly anticipated will have no effect on the decisions of consumers, firms, and workers.

Inflation is an equal percentage increase in all prices, be they the prices of goods, or the price of workers, their wages, or the price of borrowing money for risky profit ventures. If no relative prices change, there is no need for anyone to change consumption patterns. The substitution effect in consumption is zero. Since incomes rise at the same clip as prices, the income effect is zero. Inflation completely cancels itself out in the Slutsky equation.

Macroeconomists call this the "neutrality of money". Microeconomists call it the "zero degree homogeneity of demand". Only if people mistakenly believe that the rise in their salaries is greater than the rise in the price of goods they consume might we see an income effect on consumption. If people do not make such mistakes then inflation is neutral.

The relative philosophers

As SHOWN ABOVE, substitution is intimately connected to the notion that people do as well for themselves as they can. "Maximizing utility" is the economic term for this goal of attaining peak happiness. Some very simple reasoning shows that the pursuit of such happiness under the constraint of some income level and prices leads to precise predictions about how people will behave. Yet, does attaining the goal of happiness not require economists to have some deep insight into what makes people happy?

The answer is "not too much". Their prescription for bringing relative marginal desired tradeoffs in line with relative prices removes some aspects of explicit considerations of happiness from the analysis. An economist can say a great deal about how people will behave without knowing their absolute desires.

This is initially very difficult for students of the topic to accept but we can make headway by comparing how the depressive and the enthusiast will react to price changes. The depressive may get far less pleasure from caviar, beans, and other products than does the enthusiast. That is a reflection of absolute desires. But it is quite easy to conceive that both get the same relative pleasure from trading a bit more caviar for a few less beans. That is what economists mean when they say that for very broad categories of pleasure or "utility" functions, people are similarly inclined to trade off one good for the other when placed in similar conditions of income and price.

This is not to say that people cannot differ in their desired tradeoffs, but rather that such differences may be less frequent than we imagine. Preference functions with different absolute levels of joy that produce similar desired rates of tradeoff when consuming goods in similar proportions are said to possess "homothetic" indifference curves. Even if their conception of the individual may be questioned by other social sciences, economists are certainly gifted creators of funky sounding jargon.

Gold in the theory

THE RELATIVE REASONING behind utility maximization has a practical side. Businesses do not need a window into the souls of consumers to see how much pleasure they get from different products. Businesses simply need a reflection. Some idea of the ratio of pleasures and how easily that ratio can be made to change as consumption patterns change are all you need. This means figuring out whether shifting relative prices a little will bring you lots of consumers, which economists call somewhat bizarrely "the elasticity of substitution". This elasticity came to the fore in the early 2000s when a few companies realized that most people would gladly give up sound quality in their music for ease of use. In economic jargon, they perceived that the indifference curve between sound quality and ease of use was quite flat. In more normal terms, a few businesses figured out that people could easily be convinced to give up one feature for another. This realization gave rise to the iPod and its imitators, which used new technology to pack the equivalent of a thousand cassette tapes into a music player the size of a credit card.

People gladly emancipated themselves from incarceration in sacrosanct hi-fidelity basement dens lined with hundreds of reel-to-reel tapes and CDs in exchange for the freedom to roam wherever they pleased, even if it meant listening to tunes through ear-stretching plastic plugs. The insight behind this revolution in consumption lay in recognizing that people could be easily coaxed by a change in prices to trade off sound quality for the heightened convenience of portable access to a vast library of tunes, and to accelerate this shift with new technologies that brought down the price of convenience relative to quality. Businesses did not need to know anything about how much absolute pleasure consumers were getting. All they needed to clue into was relative pleasure.

Substitution as the road to riches

SUBSTITUTION IS NOT only the basis of the theoretical analysis of how people spend their money, but also a practical guide to what needs to be done to create riches. The rule for maximizing utility, or getting the most happiness, was that you had to consume a product up to the point where what you had to give up for another product was equal to what you were willing to give up. The exercise was predicated on being able to measure consumption in fine portions the way a coffee bean dispenser at the supermarket does.

Happiness would be difficult to attain if you could only buy coffee in the 37,500 pound blocks traded on the New York Intercontinental Exchange. Your choices would be stark. Either mortgage your house and turn your garage into a warehouse, or drink no coffee. With the exception of food, clothing, perfume, and medications, many of the goods we buy are of the all-or-nothing sort. One can only buy a whole car, not a part of one, or a whole house, or a whole refrigerator. The indivisible nature of these big consumer items makes it a challenge for a person to finesse his or her consumption to the point where preferences are in line with possibilities and often leave him or her with poorly satisfied demand.

The challenge and opportunities that indivisibilies pose for creating riches goes back to the time of primitive humans. Slaughtering a woolly mammoth required *Cro-Magnon* tribes to hold giant barbecues on the spot. They had no storage technology, other than perhaps smoke-curing, which would allow them to space consumption over a few weeks of meat shortages. They certainly had no freezers. *Cro-Magnon* man was a rough-hewn sample of humanity, living at the limits of his physical capacities, who had to be strong in order to cope with the ups and downs of the food supply. This hearty specimen faded from history once people discovered how to tend sheep and other flocks of small animals that could be moved from pasture to valley according to the season. Animal husbandry was in essence a storage "technology" for spacing consumption evenly across the seasons. A flock of sheep equal in mass to a mammoth could be consumed at leisure in manageable quantities and did not call for the skills and power of a rodeo rider coupled with the courage of a beast master.

By substituting consumption today for consumption tomorrow, humans may at this stage not have grown rich, but they certainly enhanced their chances of survival. Taming beasts and breeding them down to handy sizes did not only allow our ancestors to substitute consumption across time and in manageable packets. It also facilitated substitution across space. This is called spot trade: I give you something now in return for you giving me something now. Trade is beneficial to all because even though nature endows all of us with different abilities and sources of wealth, rarely do these endowments conform to our desires. Early farmers were good at growing barley, but found that a diet of grains was more palatable with meats. They traded their surplus grain for tasty lamb chops with mountain peoples who lived in an environment suitable to animal husbandry. The "parcelization" of food helped in this trade.

Hand-in-hand with advances in parcelization came advances in measurement. For finely graded exchanges to take place you needed a precise idea of how much mutton you were giving away in exchange for how much barley. From this need to trade was born metrology, the study of weights and measures; likely the oldest science. Without metrology, trade would have remained limited by fears of receiving too little or giving away too much. Metrology allowed people who did not know each other to "trust but verify" and gave the incentive to Egyptians, Mesopotamians, and Chinese to discover and develop complex techniques of mass cultivation. Governments from these eras carved in stone and pressed into clay the punishments for those who tampered with balances and weights. Many of the measurement standards from five thousand years ago remain with us, including the inch and the grain. Governments paid close attention to weights because healthy markets that produced private wealth were the source of government wealth through taxation.

Today, attempts to enhance substitutability continue to follow the same path in search of physical divisibility and enhanced measurement. We push technology forward to allow a finer physical division of products so that we may exchange them in ever closer conformity with our needs.

The market for gems exploded in the 1980s when technology advanced to allow miniscule diamonds to be cut. No longer did you have to trade off your motor-home for a three carat diamond ring. Now quarter carat diamonds could be cut in solitaire or emerald styles at costs that required nothing more than the sacrifice of your scooter. Of course, smaller diamonds are not as desirable as larger ones, but their appearance on the retail market relieved people of average wealth from the difficult bulk trade-offs they had been forced to make in an earlier period when technology restricted cut diamonds to being big and expensive. Enhanced techniques of measuring and certifying the carat content and clarity of the product gave buyers the confidence needed to plunk down their hard earned dollars.

The story of the revival of the diamond industry illustrates why substitution is perhaps the most important concept in economics. Most of what people consume is not really new products, but old products made available in more convenient and reliable formats. Today we think nothing of buying one less cup of coffee so that we can purchase a single tune or other type of sound recording through an online retailer. Yet, up until the late 1990s, to own a single song you liked you had to buy an entire album of tunes, most of which you did not fancy. The album would cost you more than a cup of coffee and the bulk nature of the purchase left you frustrated. As digital technology and the savvy to market it matured the sale of individual tunes through the internet and their storage on USB devices became possible and affordable. The results were enormous profits for internet digital music retailers and unprecedented convenience for consumers.

These ubiquitous benefits had to do with creating new products, and they also had to do with making an old product available in a more divisible, that is, substitutable format than before. The increased substitutability that resulted allowed consumers to bring into closer line their willingness to exchange goods with their ability to exchange them.

The example of the digitization of songs shows how transforming the physical nature of a product by reducing it to smaller parts can enhance our ability to substitute one good for another in closer conformity to our needs. But breaking down consumables into smaller physical parts has limits, and in certain cases makes no sense at all. You cannot break a car down into something smaller without destroying its function. You cannot cut a song in two and sell the first half as a meaningful expression of the artist's idea. What you can do is think about what a car does for the consumer.

Renting substitution

UNLIKE A SLICE of salami, you do not "consume" a car at one sitting. Instead, you enjoy a stream of services from the car over its driveable life. While the physical entity we call a car may not be divisible into smaller parts, this stream of services is divisible and can be sold in packets of as small as several hours. This is called rental.

Rental is the sale of a durable object's services for a period agreed upon by the owner and the buyer. By renting a house for a month or a year, you escape the constraint of having to make an all-or-nothing decision about its purchase. Imagine the paralysis in airport travel if to fly one had to buy the plane. What would happen to the tourist industry if instead of being able to rent a car, the out-of-towner had to buy it?

The benefits of parcelling out streams of services from durable objects is so huge that the search for new ways of renting old products is a path to riches for the innovator clever enough to discover a new rental "technology". It may seem like a strange way of using the word, but technology is what is at play in the evolution of the rental market.

Of course, some form of rental has been possible since at least Roman times when five storey *insulae* housed the urban proletariat. Rental was simple because apartment buildings were always fixed to the ground. In contrast, renting horses or clothes or furniture was always problematic because these were not fixed and could be stolen. Today you can rent just about anything that moves. What makes this possible are multi-billion dollar tracking systems, armies of repossession agents, legal institutions, and computer encryption techniques that allow an electronic book to be borrowed for two weeks and then removed from your computer. In all these cases the technology enables the enforcement of the contract to return the rented object to its owner. This is a very different technology from the one used to split a product into smaller physical parts for sale, but it is of similar importance in multiplying the consumer's opportunities for substitution.

Peering into the deeper meaning of rental helps us appreciate that consumers like it when they are offered the opportunity to substitute a little bit more of one product for a little bit less of another. Substitution allows them to arrange the variety of things they consume until the marginal relative worth they place on any two items is the same as their relative cost in the market. These are important manifestations of substitution, but we have not really taken the thought to its limit. Thus far, our line of reasoning has assumed that consumers take prices as given. They then adjust their consumption in line with these prices. Imagine what would happen if consumers could adjust prices.

Prices are in your hands

ADJUSTING PRICES TO our wishes seems like a daydream until we realize that what we buy is not always what we consume. No one eats a frozen turkey just bought from the supermarket. You need to defrost the turkey, perhaps in the microwave. Then you need to season it, stuff it, and cook it, possibly in a computerized convection oven. Seen in this light, the frozen turkey is just one of several "inputs" into a production process that requires your time and the use of fairly sophisticated modern kitchen equipment. The "output" is a processed food product that generates satisfaction. The cost of all the inputs needed to produce one plate of cooked turkey is the real price the consumer faces.

This is where a consumer's empowerment begins. There is nothing that the consumer can do to change the supermarket price of the frozen turkey. But he or she could invest in an appliance that cooks efficiently and delivers a tender, tasty product. Instead of tending to the turkey herself, a busy executive could instead enlist the help of her children on the weekend to baste the beast while she pores over excess work from her office. This substitution of the executive's time for the children's time also lowers the cost of obtaining the final product.

The home is a factory in which the allocation of labor and the use of productivity-enhancing technology such as ovens, power tools, cleaning equipment, garden tractors, and pesticides allow a family to lower the cost of consuming a final product. This is why families that live on farms may have little money, but are sometimes well-off. The household production technology of farmers may be sophisticated enough to allow them to be cash poor, but product wealthy.

A family should invest in household technology according to a calculation. It should consider how much of other goods they must give up to buy the technology compared with the extra product it receives at home from the enhanced productivity flowing from the technology. It is a complicated equation that need not concern us here. What matters for our purposes is to understand that improvements in domestic production technologies give people more scope to decide how best to shuffle their resources.

From consumers to capitalists

So far we have only looked at how consumers can best arrange their expenses. That logic leads to an understanding of the demand curve. The logic shows how people react to prices. The bonus from learning about substitution in the context of what economists call "consumer theory" is that you also get producer theory. With producer theory comes an understanding of the supply curve. This is why some higher-level economics courses prefer to start with consumer theory. Once it is mastered, producer theory can be instantly accessed.

The link between the way firms and consumers behave can be understood by noting that the solution to arranging purchases so as to maximize utility given a certain income and facing certain prices, can be arrived at by the logic of cost minimization. As we saw in the discussion of the Slutsky equation, maximizing utility and minimizing the cost of attaining any given level of utility are inseparable companions. Businesses face similar problems to those of the consumer. In fact, businesses are remarkably similar to consumers. They have an objective: to maximize profits. And they have a constraint, but one which is a bit different from that of consumers. Consumers have a fixed budget which they must divide between goods of fixed price.

Businesses have no fixed budget constraint. They want to sell as much as they can, and will spend any amount on workers and machines if the demand is there. The constraint on businesses is one of technology. A business wants to combine its workers and machines in such a way as to minimize the cost of producing any given level of output. But what do machines and workers combine into? Economists call it a production function. It summarizes the relationship between inputs of workers and machines and outputs of goods. That is what economists mean when they speak of technology. It is a constraint on the business because it limits how much it can produce given a certain quantity of raw inputs.

What do businesses do with this production function? Just as the consumer sought to minimize the cost of attaining any level of utility, the business seeks to minimize the cost of producing any given level of output. The rule for doing so is identical to that used by the consumer. The business must combine workers and machines in such a way that the output produced by an extra unit of labor relative to that produced by an extra unit of machines is equal to the ratio of wages to the cost of machines. If at a given level of production an extra unit of labor contributed twice the output as an extra machine but cost three times as much, then the same level of output could be produced at lower cost by reducing labor and increasing machines. So the business must adjust its mix of inputs until it is indifferent as to whether it increases output by using more of one and less of another.

Such is the logic of cost minimization. From this logic we can discover how businesses will change their use of inputs as their prices change. More interestingly, the logic of cost minimization reveals the business' cost function to be the basis of its supply function. A business' cost function arises from its attempts to arrange inputs in such as way as to minimize the cost of producing a certain level of output. In this sense it should really be called a minimum cost function, as it shows the minimum cost of producing any given level of output. You can also use the cost function indirectly to calculate the minimum cost at which the business could increase output by one unit. This is called the marginal cost at a given level of output. If you do this calculation for each subsequent increase in output you can string together the marginal cost function. If marginal cost increases as you produce more this means that it is becoming harder to combine inputs in as efficient a way as when you produce less.

Economists call increasing marginal cost "diminishing returns" and believe it characterizes almost all production processes. While the logic of cost minimization guides the firm in combining inputs efficiently for any given level of output, the logic of profit maximization goes a step further. Firms use their marginal cost function to determine what their level of output should be given the market price for the product. If a product sells for $5 a unit and it costs only $3 to produce an extra unit (marginal cost) then you are producing too little. You can increase your profits by increasing output to the point where diminished returns raise your marginal cost to the level of the price. Using this reasoning, if price increases then once again your marginal costs are below price and you should increase output. It is in this sense that the marginal cost curve shows how a business will change output in reaction to price. Economists call this reaction function a supply curve. It is an amalgam of the price of labor and machines, and the "parameters" or basic elements of your production function.

Economist, economist

THIS FEARFUL SYMMETRY of consumption and production burns bright in the minds of economists. It suggests a link between seemingly diverse elements in society. As optimizing consumers we must think as producers, and as producers we must understand that we too have an ultimate goal as do consumers. That goal is to maximize profits. Our search for efficiency is expressed in a similar manner no matter whether we are consuming or producing. In some way, substitution unites us and gives the term "democracy of markets" a Madisonian ring.

Economists found these parallels between consumers and producers important because they simplified and clarified what are the deep forces or "fundamentals" behind economic change. For consumers these fundamentals are their incomes, the price of goods, and the weight they put on each good in their preference "functions". For businesses the fundamentals are the prices of labor and machines and the production function that combines these two into outputs. Almost all of economics is about understanding how changes in these fundamentals change our behavior and our well-being. At the bottom of it all is the principle of substitution.

As well, an additional part of economics is about understanding the meaning of prices. Of course a price is what you have to pay to get something. But it can have a deeper, systemic meaning. For suppose that all consumers adjust the rate at which they are willing to trade off two goods until the rate at which they are willing to trade off an additional or "marginal" unit of the good equals the relative price. By "equilibrating" relative preferences at the margin with price all consumers attain a state where they all equally value an additional unit of the good in question. Their preferences may be different, but their behavior drives them to a sort of psychological meeting place where consensus reigns on the relative desired rates of tradeoff.

On the production side, firms generate output until their extra costs of producing equal the extra benefit, which is the price. Price is the point of convergence between consumers' willing rate of tradeoff and producers' ability to make more of one good while making less of another. So what happens in the market is that everyone adjusts his or her consumption and production until all consumers and producers agree implicitly on the value of an extra unit of output of the good in question. Markets do not change preferences or costs. They change behavior to the point at which marginal preferences and costs converge in the sense that desired relative desired rates of tradeoff between two goods equal the actual possibilities for tradeoff.

These possibilities are determined by the cost functions of firms. If everyone is taking prices as given then firms and consumers adjust their consumption and output to the point where the desire of all in society to give up an extra unit of one good to get more of another good is equal to the technical feasibility of producing less of one good and using the labor and capital freed up to produce more of the other good. In market equilibrium every producer and consumer values an extra unit of output equally. The meaning of this convergence of marginal preferences and production possibilities is that prices tell the economist what the social consensus about the value of a change in resource allocation is.

People sometimes talk about prices "conveying information". The traditional model of supply and demand makes no mention of information. Prices emerge spontaneously from the equilibrium process. But information is there. A government that wishes to evaluate the benefits of building a football stadium would like to know what people would be willing to pay for an added possibility of attending the games. Provided that there are no negative non-market consequences of holding football games, such as added noise to the neighborhood where the stadium is to be built, the price of tickets in the market is a guide to the consensus view on the added benefit of the circus component of *panem et circenses*.

Conclusion

WHILE ECONOMISTS SEE substitution as the backbone of their science, not everyone in the real world is as thrilled with the principle as they are. Unions have been engaged for a long time in a battle against the right of businesses to substitute labor for machines. The word "sabotage" comes from an early union movement in France to destroy machines by throwing wooden clogs known as "sabots" into their workings. Big business may also cast a worried eye on substitution. The internet and the possibilities it presents for costless telephony is a constant source of worry to telecommunications giants. Substitution is not simply a principle consumers engage in to maximize their well-being, or which businesses follow to combine inputs so as to minimize the costs of production. Substitution is the engine of market competition.

However, consumers and businesses that are quick on their feet are grateful for the possibilities presented by substitution. People's preferences are finely divided, while the possibilities they are provided with are coarsely presented. People want to minutely adjust their purchases to squeeze the most out of every dollar. They can only perform these desired substitutions if in the real world such substitutions are technically or legally feasible. There are fortunes waiting for firms that come up with the technical and legal means to refine the opportunities for substitution. The example of the iPod encompasses both these dimensions. The iPod was a technological breakthrough allowing users to purchase tunes individually. It was also made possible by legal innovations that protected the sale of individual songs from pirates who would have offered these songs free of charge on peer-to-peer networks such as the Napster network of the late 1990s.

Attention must be drawn to the conflict that substitution can cause between established organizations and beneficiaries of the discovery of new opportunities. Substitution is a means by which people free themselves from the grasp of the economic "powers that be". We learn that a seemingly dry economic concept is in fact helpful in understanding social upheaval and human progress. Which is why substitution is the first and most important concept to master in economics.

References

Chipman, John S. and Sébastien Lenfant. 2002. "Slutsky's 1915 Article: How it Came to be Found and Interpreted." *History of Political Economy*, volume 34:553-597.

Cournot, Augustin. 1897. *Researches into the mathematical theory of the wealth*. Originally published in French in 1838. Published in English in 1897 by the MacMillan Company.

TIME 3

BEFORE ECONOMISTS HAD BEGUN TO think clearly about supply and demand they were busy writing about time. The topic arose forcefully in the 19th century. The industrial revolution was bringing attention to the critical importance of long-term investments in large-scale projects. There could be a ten, or even twenty year lag between the money invested in a tunnel passing beneath the Thames and the toll revenues to be collected from it. Before the industrial revolution the existence of lags between outlays and outputs was difficult to notice. Long-term investments by private industry were few. Farmers might "invest" in livestock or planting a crop, but these seasonal, repetitive activities held little interest for economists. As factories and railroads were built, scholars started asking who in society should get the wealth from these novel investments.

Marxists argued that workers were the source of all wealth but were getting a bad deal from capitalists. Others believed that patience bred profits. To Eugen Böhm von Bawerk, a "political economist" and proto-economist of the budding Austrian school of economics, the time that money or "capital" spent in gestation contributed to the value of final output. It deserved remuneration. Today we barely understand what these squabbles were about but we should not denigrate them. They raised a flag above an important issue: how did time fit into economics?

Neither Marx nor Böhm von Bawerk were able to convincingly fit time into economic analysis because they lacked the intellectual tools. Economists of the 19th century had barely even begun to understand and model how consumers should divide their spending between goods in the here and now. A logically consistent model of consumption over time, a so-called dynamic model, would only start to make a very tentative and simple appearance in the 20th century. The model that gradually emerged was little more than a ramped-up version of the static model of consumption. Instead of choosing only between different goods, consumers also had to choose between consuming more of a certain good now and less of it later.

The names of Milton Friedman and Franco Modigliani are associated with this early attempt to integrate time into economics. They are responsible for discovering the circumstances under which the ups and down in the stream of income a person anticipates to receive during his or her life time are uncoupled in a very particular sense from the ups and downs in consumption that person should plan in order to maximize wellbeing. They argued that in bad economic times a pleasure, or "utility", maximizing consumer would seek to borrow against future income to keep consumption near some desired lifetime average. In good times the consumer would save surplus income in the bank to go back down to that average.

Their analysis was based on the restrictive assumption that even though you might save and earn interest in the future, in a "present value sense" such savings did not really change the sum of incomes you received over your lifetime. This allowed them to view the consumer as being motivated by a single datum called "permanent income". By wrapping lifetime income into the only number the consumer needed to use in deciding how much to consume in any given year, Friedman and Modigliani banished time from the intertemporal analysis of wellbeing in the sense that the timing of income no longer played a role in the timing of consumption.

A more complicated integration of time into economics only started to develop in the latter part of the 20th century when economists realized that time periods might be interconnected in a much more convoluted manner than they had realized. In particular they considered what might happen if the choice to consume less today and invest in some productive technology actually increased lifetime income in a present discounted value sense. By introducing what might seem an innocuous wrinkle into the Friedman-Modigliani analysis these researchers stumbled into a frighteningly complex field of dynamic optimization known as the "calculus of variations", and "optimal control theory". If consuming less and saving more in any period really did increase your lifetime income, then the timing of consumption and the timing of income would have to be bound together. Recognizing this possibility gave birth to the field of real-business cycle macroeconomics. It also shaped our understanding of the constraints that the expectations of individuals may place on well-meaning social planners wishing to optimally guide the economy over time.

Time's simple face

THESE MAY SEEM like obscure propositions so to understand the role of time in economics we need to first look at its simple interpretation as just another sort of good or service. Then we can move to the analysis of time as a distinct aspect of economics rather than just as a reinterpretation of goods in the static model of consumer behavior. A mastery of time may be the greatest challenge to someone seeking a mastery of economics, but one that can be surmounted by understanding that time in economics has but two faces.

To economists trained in the middle of the 20th century, time connoted "the permanent income hypothesis of consumption", a term coined by Milton Friedman in the 1950s. A near copy of the Friedman model is "the life-cycle earnings theory" formulated by Franco Modigliani and developed at the same time as Friedman's theory.

Neither title properly conveys the essence of the theory behind how people choose to space their consumption out over the years. Friedman and Modigliani both considered the economy from the perspective of consumers who had to decide when to spend the income they anticipated they would earn over their lifetimes. When Friedman and Modigliani came out with their theories many economists found the ideas hard to grasp. Then economists began to see that what Friedman and Modigliani had done was to add little more than a twist to the traditional model of how consumers chose between goods.

The twist was to treat the same good, such as a bag of potato chips, as being a slightly different good when consumed next year, and a very different good when eaten in ten years. The difference arose not out of any physical change in the good but from the assumption that people prefer to consume things now rather than to delay their pleasure by consuming them in the future. The only way to entice them to put off consumption would be to offer them some interest payment on the money they put aside today. The interest earned would allow them to buy slightly more of the same good in the future. By "slightly more" they meant that the added interest on savings did not contribute a penny to the present discounted value of lifetime income. So, the only new insight economists needed to fully understand the trade-offs involved between consumption now and in the future was that of present value and the associated concept of discounting. Let us see what these concepts mean.

Present value

THE PERMANENT INCOME hypothesis is based on the idea of an unvarying lifetime "budget constraint" that remains in balance (which accords with Errol Flynn's view that any man who dies with more than $5,000 in his bank account has miscalculated). The sum of the value of spending over a lifetime must equal the sum of income earned over that lifetime, what is referred to here as "lifetime income". Borrowing and lending allow us to make lifetime plans rather than only living in the moment. It is lifetime income, and not income in any given year, that should guide a person's decisions on how much to spend in that year. The conclusion may at first glance seem jejune, but in fact it is of central importance to understanding the effect of government efforts to "stimulate" the economy.

To understand hypotheses about lifetime consumption, we first need to see how we can sum the value of income over a lifetime into one number that the consumer takes into account when planning how much to spend this year. The concept that allows us to sum incomes over time is that of present value and the related principle of income discounting. To those who have taken a business math class, discounting is a concept no sooner painfully learned than eagerly forgotten. To economists it is important to the point of obsession and forms the basis of all analyses of how people choose between doing something now and doing it later. Despite these qualifications, discounting is really not so difficult to understand, and in fact should be a part of every educated person's bag of mental tricks.

To see this, suppose you can give up two years of salary and $100,000 of tuition to earn a Harvard *MBA*. If the *MBA* raises your salary by $100,000 a year over then next 30 years, by how much will your wealth increase? You might answer that it will increase by $3 million, but that is wrong. Even business magazines make the same error. The answer fails because it adds quantities that cannot be compared. No one who has $1,000 US and €1,000 would say that his or her wealth was $2,000 unless the two currencies were at par. Similarly, $100,000 today cannot be simply added to the $100,000 you anticipate to get in twenty or thirty years. How would you choose if someone offered you $100,000 today, or the same amount decades from now? If you are like most people, you would say, "Now!"

People value money now more than later because they want to satisfy their cravings for immediate consumption. Money in your hand now is also an opportunity to invest and get a return over the years. To add up the value of all those future $100,000 salary increases due to the *MBA* we need to be able to convert future dollars to present dollars.

The formula for this conversion can be put in words. How much money would you have to put in the bank today for it to grow to $1 by next year? That is the key phrase in all discussions of discounting. If the interest rate is five percent then with a few strokes on a calculator you find that 95.2 cents in the bank today will grow to $1 next year. In a sense, you can think of this as being able to exchange 95.2 cents today for $1 next year. Put differently, you can "buy" a future dollar for 95.2 present cents. To stretch a point, a future dollar has a present value of 95.2 cents. This is how bonds are traded. No one ever talks about the interest rate in bond markets because what gets traded are future dollars for present dollars. So a bond promising a payment of $1,000 in ten years may sell for $700 today.

One may infer that the present value of $1 in ten years is 70 cents now. So that string of $100,000 revenue increases over 30 years that comes from a Harvard *MBA* is not $3 million. It is the sum of what you would have to save in the bank today to earn $100,000 in thirty years, along with the sum of what you would have to save in the bank today to earn $100,000 in twenty-nine years, and so on all the way back to the present. Not surprisingly, this sum is called the "present value" of the income increase over thirty years. It is also called lifetime income in economic models.

Perhaps the most difficult thing to accept initially about present value is that when a person saves more money now to increase his or her income in the future this has no influence on the present value of his or her lifetime income stream. The proof is simple. If you save a dollar at five percent interest, you get $1.05 next year. From today's perspective the present discounted value of that $1.05 is just $1. This is not just a curiosity arising from accounting mathematics. It is of crucial relevance to the Friedman-Modigliani analysis. It means that savings do not increase the discounted sum of lifetime income. At best savings can help you space consumption between periods. Savings cannot help you to increase consumption in a present value sense across your lifespan.

Permanent income, life-cycle hypothesis

THE CONSTANCY OF discounted lifetime income also explains why people can uncouple the timing of income over the lifetime and the timing of their consumption. The sum of income in every year adds to a single number. That number and not the incidence of income in the series that makes up the sum is what the consumer bases his or her consumption decisions in any period upon. Grasp this and you have the essence of the permanent income hypothesis in your hands. Let us examine these concepts in a bit more detail.

The permanent income, life-cycle model seeks to understand how a person who can either save or borrow against future earnings will decide to allocate consumption between the present and the future. The question of why it even matters to a person how to allocate consumption over time arises for two reasons. First, people are impatient. They value a dollar of consumption today more than the same dollar a year from now. Despite their impatience they are also opportunistic. The reason they do not consume everything in one giant feast today is that the interest to be earned by putting some money in the bank could more than compensate the individual for delaying his or her consumption for a year. Then why not just put everything in the bank and commit to a complete delay of gratification?

The reason lies in the economist's assumption that each increment to your consumption in a given period brings less happiness than did the previous increment. Consumption in any one period brings diminishing returns. To maximize the pleasure from consumption you would want as a first principle to spread your consumption out evenly over all periods. If you bunch consumption too tightly in one period each additional unit in that period is giving you less and less pleasure. It is better to transfer that unit of consumption to another time period where you can consume it with renewed enthusiasm. If you have a table set for a banquet but no guests show up you would prefer not to gorge yourself on all the food at one sitting but to divide your dining into small *Tupperware* containers, to be enjoyed in more pleasurably dispersed dining episodes. That is the crux of the life-cycle model. Because of diminishing returns to consuming in any given period, people have an innate urge to spread out their consumption evenly over time. This basic urge can be somewhat altered if interest rates are high, thereby suggesting an advantage to skewing consumption to the future. On the contrary, if impatience is high then there is a tendency to skew consumption to the present. If the effects of impatience and interest rates cancel each other out then the basic need to consume equally in all periods fully asserts itself and consumers choose to spend the same present-value amount of income in each period.

The sum of the present value of all future income streams is implicit in this discussion. In a world of perfect certainty, the consumer has access to all of his or her future income through a banking system that allows him or her to borrow against these anticipated revenues. In principle you could blow the present value of your entire lifetime income in the immediate present. This extreme example illustrates that to make the most of your possibilities you must take into account the fact that your ability to consume in any given period is not restricted to the income you earn in that period, but to the sum of income through your life. The decision to equalize spending in all periods arises from your consideration of how to allocate the sum of these revenues. This is why the theory refers to the life-cycle.

Economists refer to this methodical manner of deploying one's resources rather neutrally as "consumption smoothing", yet the consequences are anything but neutral. Suppose you win $10,000 in a quiz show. Friends might advise you to throw a party and go on a shopping spree, but you would first look at the returns from putting that sum in the bank and allowing it to grow for several years. The balance you need to strike is between how much it strains you to delay gratification and how much extra gratification you would get in the future from the interest gained on your delayed consumption, that is, your savings. Consumption smoothing means that you would consume your windfall in dribbles, spread out over time. This is what led Milton Friedman to distinguish between permanent and transitory components of income. If the consumer considered the $10,000 to represent a permanent rise in annual revenue then he or she would consider it "permanent income", and spending in each year would rise by as much as $10,000. If the consumer considered it a one-shot event then it would be considered "transitory income" to be consumed in packets spread over the remaining years. Though he called it the "permanent income hypothesis", Friedman could with equivalent logic have called it the "transitory income hypothesis".

We must keep in mind that these are theories about how people following a rational plan should behave. Sometimes people do not stick to plan and blow a lottery windfall in a massive spending spree. These deviations can be worked into the theory, and while they are spectacular, theorists hope that they are rare enough to qualify as aberrations.

We must also keep in mind that I have pulled a slight pedagogical fast-one in explaining the logic behind consumption smoothing as being the diminishing utility from increased consumption in any period. While there is nothing wrong with this explanation, it gets up the dander of purist economists who quite rightly would point out that the assumption of diminishing absolute returns to utility is not strictly necessary. The tendency towards consumption smoothing over time can more generally be obtained from the assumption that the relative rate at which people are willing to trade off consumption between now and later falls as people consume more now and less later. To get such a relatively diminishing effect you do not need to assume diminishing marginal utility but simply diminishing relative marginal utilities. The point of this somewhat tedious exposition is to show that the permanent income, life-cycle hypothesis is consistent with a broad category of preferences. What these preferences have in common is that people tend to prefer averages to extremes. You don't strictly need to assume diminishing extra, or "marginal" utility to get this result. You just need to assume that relative valuations diminish as more is consumed in a certain period. The advantage of keeping preferences structures general is that one can search more broadly in the data for patterns that confirm the theory.

Life-cycle theory and government

AN IMPORTANT IMPLICATION of the life-cycle model is that because people can shift consumption to the future, governments that borrow and spend today may have a limited ability to "stimulate" people into bouts of economy-boosting consumption. People realize that sooner or later government spending will have to be paid for by increased taxes. Looking at their inter-temporal budget constraint they realize that increased government largesse today will be largely cancelled in their lifetime incomes by increased taxes in the future. In reaction they reduce their consumption, thus thwarting the government's attempt at stimulus.

Robert Barro called this "Ricardian equivalence" in his 1974 paper on the topic. He argued that if the life-cycle income theory of consumption is correct, then people should "internalize" government's ability to borrow, spend, and later tax, the so-called government budget constraint, into their calculations, thereby rendering the timing of government taxes and spending irrelevant. More prosaically, a government that decides to boost spending today by borrowing is not going to have any different effect on the economy than a government that boosts spending today by increasing taxes. Most people understand quite easily that tax-and-spend is not a good way to stimulate the economy. On the one hand, government spending stimulates, and on the other hand, taxation depresses. Deficit-financed spending seems to get around this problem. Yet according to Barro and his followers, consumers view deficits with a jaundiced eye. Deficits are harbingers of taxes and as such are conceptually and operationally no different to a consumer than direct current taxation.

The Ricardian Equivalence theorem is an example of an application of the life-cycle, permanent income theory that provoked controversy among academics. If taken seriously, permanent income thinking meant that government had to reconsider its role as an engine of economic growth. The idea that government could stimulate the economy did not really emerge until the depression of the 1930s when Keynes argued that government could "fine tune" and "jump start" economic growth by "stimulating" pent-up consumer demand. Before then economic growth had been thought to be the work of private entrepreneurs rising and sinking through the success of their ideas on how to please consumers. *World War I* trained government to regulate and control the economy in a way that was both modern and unprecedentedly broad. Keynes' views on government's role may or may not have helped government grow. We cannot be certain. Perhaps government did intervene simply because it could.

What we do know is that starting in the 1950s, the appearance of the life-cycle, permanent income model challenged Keynesian apologists for government intervention. The model postulated a forward-looking individual taking full advantage of modern borrowing and lending technology. This individual connected with the future in a way that could thwart government attempts at economic stimulation.

What do the numbers say? In a fascinating book published in 2000 on how economists can use theory to bolster their political views, Robert Leeson describes how neither Keynes, nor his nemesis Friedman, were very convinced that the proof for their theories would ever be found in the numbers. Both were polemicists who used economics as a language by which they communicated in a coherent manner accessible to large numbers of the economically literate their unshakable inner convictions about the proper role of government intervention in markets.

Later generations of researchers were not as pessimistic as Keynes and Friedman. They developed new ways of looking at the numbers to support or refute their theories. For example, Robert Hall (1978) suggested that economists stop trying to identify cause-and-effect relationships. Instead he suggested that the permanent-income, life-cycle hypothesis did not need to be tested by looking at the numbers to see if the level of consumption was related to permanent income in the strict sense dictated by the theory. Rather, you could, if not test, then get a feel for the validity of the theory by seeing if the change in consumption over time as dictated by the equations of motion of the model conformed to actual changes observed in the real world. Change is a far less exacting criterion by which to validate a theory than is some measure of absolutes.

Hall mixed uncertainty about future income into his model to suggest that consumers optimizing their happiness should smooth consumption in such a way that both consumption and wealth followed what statistician's call a "random walk". Namely, consumption should remain steady with year-by-year corrections for unanticipated changes to income and by so doing would also induce a random walk in wealth regardless of whether background changes in salary followed such a random walk or were "serially correlated", meaning they followed an uncertain but nonetheless trending path. Hall's work ushered in a new era into the analysis of time in economics, whereby "equations of motion" rather than cause-and-effect relations would become the dominant theme in the dynamic macroeconomist's research agenda. We we now turn to this important idea.

The complex face of time

SO FAR WE have focused exclusively on how consumers behave in reaction to an anticipated stream of future income, but from where does income derive? The life-cycle hypothesis does not answer this question. It simply assumes that consumers can expect a stream of income in the future that can be discounted and summed into a single number. This data point is then all a person needs to know for him or her to decide how to divide consumption between present and future. Permanent, or life-time income, or whatever you choose to call it is a given. It is the fundamental constraint on life-time consumption patterns and it does not change, no matter what action the consumer takes.

In a way, the strength of this model is that it takes permanent income to be a given. Nothing that consumers do today can influence permanent income. Of course you can save and expect to earn more money in the future, but as shown earlier, in present value terms, those extra earnings from interest represent no accretion to the present discounted value of your lifetime wealth. Borrowing and lending merely serve to displace consumption through time, but not to increase its discounted value. This guarantees the constancy of the budget constraint and vastly simplifies the problem of how the consumer should adjust consumption over the life-time. If consumption decisions do not affect the budget constraint then the optimization problem boils down to a simple spreading of income evenly over time, moderated in part by interest rates, and in part by impatience.

The weakness of the model is that clearly the world does not work that way. People do not simply look to interest rates in order to accrue income. They seek ways of becoming more productive through education or by discovering natural resources or by coming up with some great technical invention, and of course, later they may multiply these enhanced earnings by saving them and earning interest. Lifetime income is not a given but rather a malleable quantity under our control. A decision on how much to consume today is also a decision on how much to invest, because what you do not consume today is saved and then invested. When you invest in some production technology such as machines, or more generally "capital", you add to the stock of capital in every subsequent period. And this stock influences your ability to make money in any subsequent period in a manner that changes the present discounted value of your income.

More technically, by saving today, you influence the entire future path income will take in the future, and once set on this path, if that is the one you wish to commit to, then you must decide upon an optimal degree of consumption smoothing. But each future decision to consume further alters the path to follow which requires further considerations of optimal consumption smoothing "trajectories" and so on. As you might surmise, what we have here are the makings of a devilish problem. In this context any consumption decision you make now, changes the whole profile of future income, which calls for a calculation of future optimal consumptions which change the income profile, calling for a recalculation and so on. Each consumption decision in effect creates a new path of future income which itself has implications for the optimal stream of consumption along that path, with each point on the stream altering the remaining stream. Basically, with every consumption choice you make you are remaking your budget constraint, which in turn forces you to reconsider your consumption choices, which changes your budget constraint and lifetime discounted income, and so on.

This cumulative and reverberative effect of investment decisions would be of lesser importance to intertemporal choice if consumption always had a constant, or linear effect on wellbeing. In that case you really would not care how consumption is spaced, tradeoffs between periods would become irrelevant, and the best path would simply be the one that maximized lifetime present discounted income. The complexity arises when people don't like to gorge themselves or go very short of consumption in any given period and when investment decisions have cumulative effects. Such a situation creates many paths from which to choose. One can see that the problem is in a league beyond that which the permanent income hypothesis could compete.

Friedman and Modigliani avoided assumptions about investment and its cumulative effect on future income and hence its ability to change the budget constraint perhaps out of fear that it might lead them into an appallingly difficult field of mathematics known as the "calculus of variations". As Richard Bellman, one of the great mathematicians of the 20th century wrote of the field, "A course in the subject in college had given me simultaneously a rather low opinion of its intrinsic interest and a healthy respect for its intricacies. It appeared to be filled with complicated existence and uniqueness theorems with self-imposed restrictions, none pointing in any particular direction" (Dreyfuss, 2002, 50).

The calculus of variations of which Bellman voiced his misgivings is a tool for making a sequence of choices that will optimize some target quantity you care about when each preceding choice changes the constraint you are facing for the rest of the life of the problem. As Bellman wrote "An interesting fact that emerged from this detailed scrutiny was that the way one utilized resources depended critically upon the level of these resources, and the time remaining in the process. Naturally this was surprising only to someone unversed in economics such as myself."(Dreyfuss 2002, 49). It is called calculus of variations because its objective is not to find an optimal point that maximizes a function of a variable, as is the case in the simple differential calculus invented by Newton, but rather to find an optimal, and varying path that maximizes the value of a function of that path, or a "functional". This functional associates each path with some value of interest (lifetime wellbeing from a certain path of consumption is an example), as opposed to a simple function which associates a point, such as permanent income, with a target value.

As you can imagine, finding an optimum path is usually a harder problem than finding an optimum point. A modern twist on the calculus of variations is called optimal control theory. We need not worry too much about these distinctions. The main thing we need to understand is that unlike in simple economic optimization problems where the budget constraint is fixed, optimal control allows you to vary the budget constraint. The tradeoff that makes the problem difficult is that enhancing the budget constraint in the future may impose unpleasant costs upon you now. Each moment is a balancing act between enhanced possibilities now and the benefit that brings, and enhanced possibilities later.

To return to the lifetime consumption problem, the trick with investment is to choose between millions of potential income paths over which we must calculate the optimal consumption trajectory. It is like solving millions of permanent income hypothesis problems given that you can vary your circumstances and then trying to figure out which path is best. Few then will be surprised that finding optimal trajectories for whatever control variable you have at hand is a challenge that might be difficult to be met head on. The head-on approach is to derive a so-called analytical or "closed-form" solution that tells you at any precise time how much capital you have accumulated, and how much you should be consuming and investing to maximize lifetime utility.

Finding a closed-form solution to the optimum path of consumption and investment, sometimes called Ramsey's Problem, is daunting and usually forces economists into making highly restrictive assumptions about some of the quantities involved. As Olivier Blanchard and Stanley Fischer expounded on in their classic 1989 textbook on macroeconomics (283), "Can we go from these first-order conditions [equations of motion] to derive an explicit solution for consumption and saving? In general, we cannot, but for specific utility functions and assumptions about asset returns and labor income, we can."

Any time you restrict something that can move in a dynamic system, you greatly simplify the analysis, though at the cost of diminished realism. Not wishing to give up realism, economists had to make an intellectual trade and give something else up in return. Instead of giving us the precise levels of consumption and investment that an economy will follow, many of the more sophisticated models of inter-temporal optimization are satisfied to tell you, through a formula known variously as a differential equation or an equation of motion, how crucial variables of interest such as consumption and investment should change at any given moment. You don't know where the horse will be at any time in the future, but at any given instant you can tell in what direction it is headed.

This form of reasoning shows economists whether consumption and investment will converge to some steady point which is optimal for the economy. Such concepts were implicit in the work of the 1920s Cambridge mathematician, Frank Ramsey. He derived equations of motion for an economy following the best path for maximizing well-being in the face of having to make the decision to sacrifice consumption today to invest and augment consumption later. His work in turn was extended in the 1960s by American economist David Cass. They showed how a free market economy could produce a "Pareto efficient" consumption path. Along such a path consumption and investment cannot be rearranged so as to make at least one person better off without hurting anyone else, the standard definition of efficiency in economics.

The fall and rise of growth theory

THOUGH THIS EFFICIENCY result was important to the first wave of researchers in the field, to subsequent students of economics the insights into human behavior and markets derived with such effort from integrating consumption and investment seemed limited, and perhaps even irrelevant. As a result, academic interest in this field largely stalled in the 1970s. Who, after all, really cared more than fleetingly if a theoretical consumption and investment path extending to infinity was Pareto optimal? Was not the problem of business cycles more important? How could optimal consumption and growth theory, with all its limiting analytical complications, tell us anything worthwhile about these cycles? And who wanted in any case to learn the maths needed to understand what was going on when a much simpler and more elegant approach to consumption was at hand in the permanent income, life-cycle models of Friedman and Modigliani, limited as they might be by the absence of a growth component?

Interest was only revived during the 1970s and 1980s with the work of a wave of researchers who used newly developed mathematical techniques and computer technology to get a more realistic feel for what was going on when people engaged in complex intertemporal optimization decisions.

The key mathematical technique was a revolutionary simplification of the calculus of variations known as "dynamic programming". Under certain conditions it allowed the researcher to find an analytical solution, or at least a very good approximation to one, that illuminated the optimal path that consumption, investment and other control variables took.

Dynamic programming was a new way of solving problems that the calculus of variations had trouble with and one which was ideally suited to computers because it considered time in discrete periods such as this year and next year, rather than as a continuous flow (though Bellman also figured out how to apply his concepts to continuous time to solve similar problems of "optimal control"). Whereas the calculus of variations tried to pick the best path for some "control" variable, such as investment, over the whole planning horizon, dynamic programming broke the problem down into a series of decisions you made on the spot based only on how the decision influenced your wellbeing, or profits, or whatever else you were trying to optimize, in the present period versus what you could get by way of benefits in all subsequent periods by diverting resources to a future in which you had already devised an optimal plan.

In dynamic programming you did not choose one path out of many but rather a "policy" on how to act in any given and subsequent periods which could be cut off from what happened in all previous periods. Of course the old methods from the calculus of variations could still be applied, but getting the solution would be much more laborious. Provided that your value function, or objective, such as total lifetime happiness or utility, was "separable" in the sense that your anticipated utility from a later age did not affect your utility at an earlier age, then the vast inter-temporal optimization problem could be broken up into small, forward looking packets. You started solving the problem for the last two periods of your planning horizon to get an optimal response to whatever resources previous decisions had left you. Then you stepped back a period and decided how to invest given that you already knew what your optimal response to current choices would be, and so forth. Thus you could chain a series of already solved mini-problems into a larger sequence of choices reaching all the way back to the first period of your problem. This produced breathtaking increases in the speed of solving problems of intertemporal optimization. The approach also meshed with Soren Kierkegaard's view that "Life can only be understood backwards; but it must be lived forwards."

The dynamic programming approach did not work well if you tried to apply it to situations where the anticipated benefits of future choices had some influence on your present wellbeing. Then you would end up getting "inconsistent" solutions. You would have arrived at a series of policies you would want to change in the future because in deriving them you had not taken into account what was to have happened in the earlier parts of the problem. You would have to keep "re-opening" your dynamic programming procedure until your solution had converged to what you would have discovered had you just adopted the more complex calculus of variations approach in the first place.

I am grossly simplifying the condition needed for application of Bellman's approach, but roughly speaking it was what Bellman called the "principle of optimality". If the principle held then dynamic programming problems could each be solved as an interlocking sequence of backwardly deduced problems.

Alpha Chang (1992, 22) explained that "if you chop off the first arc from an optimal sequence of arcs, the remaining abridged sequence must still be optimal in its own right." In economic terms, what this meant was that if government was trying to devise some optimal long-term policy of subsidies to industry, then the policy in mid-course would not change from what it had been planned to be at the start. Namely, if you "chopped off" the first half of the policy period, Chang's "initial arc", then the plan stayed the same, or Chang's words, "the remaining abridged sequence" would still be optimal.

Nobellist Thomas Sargent produced the most comprehensive summary when he wrote (1997, 19), "Thus as time advances there is no incentive to depart from the original plan. This self-enforcing character of optimal policies is known as 'Bellman's principle of optimality'". If you used dynamic programming and the principle of optimality did not hold then your policy at any given moment would be "inconsistent", meaning that if you drew up a lifetime plan, at every moment you would be tempted to reconsider your plans.

While this may seem to be mathematical navel-gazing of the most self-indulgent sort, understanding the conditions under which the principle of optimality would hold became a key ingredient in the debate about the role of government in the economy. To appreciate the force of these ideas we need first to understand the intellectual debates that preceded them.

Statistics and the social engineer

METHODS OF INTER-TEMPORAL optimization are peppered with evocative terms. "Dynamic programming", "policy function", and "optimal control" conjure images of engineers guiding society with the help of mathematical equations. The imagery is apt. The inter-temporal analysis of economic phenomena has drawn engineers and physicists into the study of economic phenomena. But beyond the technical talents required, dynamic mathematics attracts a particular sort of individual with a zest for control and order.

Those who used these tools in economics focused at first on the best way for people to arrange their consumption over time. They then shifted their attention to the best means by which governments could intervene to redirect consumption and investment should these have stalled or gone astray, at least according to the best minds in government planning offices. These minds conceived of an economy guided in large part by the use of methods of dynamic optimization. As in most stories of good intentions, this one ends, if not on the road to hell, then at least in frustration at a paradox in the theory of government intervention.

This paradox, called time-inconsistency, has its roots in the 1930s when Jan Tinbergen was inspired by Keynes to map out the structure of the economy. With such a map in hand, it seemed that government could wage campaigns against whatever injustice or inefficiency threatened the integrity of society. More specifically, Tinbergen wanted to know if there was some way to make a statistical link between government interventions such as a tax increase or a spending increase, and unemployment, inflation, and national wealth. With an understanding of these links you could start to build optimal plans for the economy.

In the West, the notion that government could fine-tune an economy was prevalent at the time. Ideas for government intervention were being energized by the greatest experiment in social planning ever conceived. Russia was thought to be using central government control to engineer an ideal society. But western governments could not suit up commissars in leather trench coats and give them the discretion to put the fear of the gulag into the workforce. They needed a more subtle approach based on an understanding of the relationships between an economy's inputs and outputs.

Social engineers such as Tinbergen and his students in "econometrics" were to guide the process. Tinbergen's notion was that if you could work out the basic structure of the economy, such as the manner in which income influences consumption, or money growth influences inflation, and how that influences unemployment, then government could change the money supply, or its own consumption, to stimulate private economic activity. The way in which you worked out the structure was by looking at how these quantities moved together, or "co-varied", over time.

Surprisingly, Keynes opposed this intellectual crusade. In a caustic 1939 critique of Tinbergen he argued that there were far too many forces influencing economic aggregates for econometricians ever to be able to disentangle and identify them.

Keynes wrote mockingly (1939, 560), "Am I right in thinking that the method of multiple correlation analysis essentially depends on the economist having furnished, not merely a list of the significant causes, which is correct so far as it goes, but a complete list?" Nor might the effects of independent forces on, say national income growth be constant.

Perhaps more tellingly Keynes raised the question of how to calculate the effect of profit on investment when investment may itself influence profit. He noted that when profits double, a doubling of investments does not necessarily mean increases in profits will increase investments. Perhaps it is rising investment that increases profits. Or perhaps each have a positive influence on the other, so that the causality is difficult to sift out by simply looking at how the two variables move together. As Keynes wrote (1939, 561), "What happens if the phenomenon under investigation itself reacts on the factors by which we are explaining it? For example, when he investigates the fluctuations of investment, Prof. Tinbergen makes them depend on the fluctuations of profit. But what happens if the fluctuations of profit partly depend (as, indeed, they clearly do) on the fluctuations of investment? Prof. Tinbergen mentions the difficulty in a general way in a footnote to p. 17, where he says, without further discussion, that 'one has to be careful.' But is he?" Had the master turned on his apprentice? Perhaps.

Keynes' critique of Tinbergen is remarkable not simply because it outlined the statistical and conceptual problems that eventually shook the Tinbergen project, but also because Keynes was taking pot-shots at one of his most fervent and talented disciples. Perhaps this intellectual honesty is one of the reasons that Milton Friedman held Keynes in such high regard that in his television series *Free to Choose*, he considered Keynes' early death a disaster. Only Keynes had the intellect and force of character to make his disciples aware of the need for some skepticism of his theories.

Milton Friedman shared with Keynes a distrust of the analysis of economic time series. There were tricks you could use to make almost any two series appear correlated. In this spirit, econometrician David Hendry's 1980 paper on nonsense correlation showed how you could easily play with time-series data to get an almost perfect correlation between monthly precipitation and economic growth (394-395). What few people realize was how closely Keynes and Friedman were allied intellectually in their critique of the Tinbergen project. Robert Leeson has brought this into public consciousness in his 2000 book where he writes on page 6, "Keynes and Friedman were equally perceptive about the dubious nature of mechanical econometrics and equally doubtful that such practices could resolve economic disagreements. Later, contrary to common perceptions, Tinbergen came to accept much of Keynes' Critique and Keynes did not revise his objections to econometrics."

Despite these misgivings, the Tinbergen project of large-scale econometric modeling of the economy barreled ahead until the 1960s. Then, Edmund Phelps and Milton Friedman started noticing that these models were doing a questionable job of predicting the effect of government-induced inflation on unemployment. Inflation could cheapen the cost of labor if wages were written into long-term contracts. An hourly wage of $20 falls to $10 in real terms if inflation doubles, because the real purchasing power of a dollar halves. This would be a boon to employers who would hire more labor and produce more output. But if workers understood government's game, then they could build inflation clauses into their contracts and thwart the intervention. Just because econometric research had uncovered that inflation in the past might have seemed to be associated with a reduction in unemployment, this did not mean that a government could blithely manipulate inflation to decrease unemployment. The story can be told differently to implicate inflation in the deception of firms instead of workers, but the results are the same.

Econometric models that did not take into account the manner in which people anticipated government action and its consequences were questionable as guides for the fine-tuning of the economy. A metaphor for this problem might be that of the donkey and the carrot. The "donkeymetrician" who has extensively studied the barnyard and its menagerie has noted a statistical relationship between the presence of carrots in a trough and the movement of donkeys towards that trough. Thinking he knows the association between carrots and donkey displacement, he harnesses a donkey to a plough and attaches a device to the donkey that dangles before it a carrot. At first the donkey is intrigued and plods forward dragging his load, but noticing the effort of pulling the plough and failing to gain recompense for his march towards the carrot, he reverts to his initial stubbornly passive state. By his mulish reactivity the donkey has thwarted the prescriptions of the barnyard statistician.

Robert E. Lucas Jr. sharpened these insights in a 1976 paper on econometric policy evaluation. As mentioned earlier, if you wanted to predict the results of a government intervention on the economy, you not only had to know the basic relations between such macroeconomic variables as income and consumption, but you also had to know what people thought about those interventions.

If a government was spending more today, then you had to know whether people thought the increase was temporary or permanent to judge how they would react. Econometric policy evaluation had to take into account not just how the basic relations between macroeconomic variables would react to government interventions, but also the manner in which people would react to government interventions. Because the parameters, or guideposts, of relations between macroeconomic variables were sensitive not just to economic fundamentals but also to economic policy, these parameters would change whenever the way of doing government business changed. That meant government had to go reformulate its policies in light of these new relations between economic variables, which in turn meant that expectations changed again and government would be forced back to the drawing board.

Eine kleine time paradox

PERHAPS THIS APPROACH might converge to a stable equilibrium where the predictive models were consistent with expectations, but by then policy could have been modified to the point where it was far from the original vision. Policy conclusions built on mechanistic Tinbergen models that did not account for people's reactions to policy, could be misleading and if taken to their logical limit could produce policies greatly mutated from their original form.

The precise formulation of this view came in 1977 with the publication of a paper by Finn Kydland and Edward Prescott on rules versus discretion. A dynamic programming approach to economic policy epitomized the rational planner using some clever optimizing strategy as a means of fine-tuning the economy. Kydland and Prescott argued this hands-on or "discretionary" approach to policy could be a prescription for economic instability.

The problem that arises when applying a dynamic programming logic to the formulation of government policy is that dynamic programming was really invented to deal with entities guided by inertia, such as rocket ships. When the entities are sentient, as are humans, a government that sets policies using dynamic programming is acting as if policy at any future stage does not influence the function to be optimized at much earlier stages. Rocket ships satisfy this requirement but people seldom do. People might anticipate future government actions. If this is the case then the benefits the social planner imagines society receives at some future date through the optimal plan also influences the benefits from earlier policies. In such a case people's expectations about future government policies wind the future and the present too tightly into each other for Bellman's principle of optimality to hold. If government does not understand this and acts as a naive dynamic programmer it can see its policies blunted.

For example, suppose a federal government wants to guide economic development in one of its provinces. Government determines that at any given moment it will compensate for shortcomings in provincial investment, due perhaps to a limited access to capital markets for local investors by providing a subsidy. Here is a clear dynamic optimization problem if current investments determine future income growth in a cumulative manner and if utility is a declining function of consumption. The trade-off government must consider is between spending money now on social programs and investing it in regional development which will yield higher wealth in the future. The stated policy is that if firms are unable to invest the amount in machines that they wish government will make up the difference. Suppose government assumes that businesses will not react to its policy but passively allow it to bridge their investment gaps. Then the principle of optimality will hold. The government's anticipated yield (the benefits to society) from its policy of subsidies at a future date does not influence its yield at an earlier date because future subsidies do not change private investment behavior today. If they did, then the total stock of capital today would go down.

Only without such forward looking subjects can the government act as a dynamic programmer who starts his or her plans at the end and works backward, not worrying about earlier steps in planning. Government cannot divide its planning problem into simple portions like this if what it is anticipated to do at the end influences the yields at the start of the planning horizon. For if government acts in this manner a surprise is in stock for it. If investors know the government strategy, they will hold back their investments in the expectation of obtaining future government largesse. Using simple dynamic programming to determine subsidies, the optimal strategy will require government to re-open its planning calculations at each period.

This is quite a conundrum. If you approach the problem purely as a dynamic programmer then the shortfall of investment provoked by your policy actually looks like a great opportunity to reopen the dynamic program and offer up more subsidy. But if investors also anticipate this intervention this will lead to a further retirement of private investment, calling for a further increase in subsidy, and so on. At each iteration in the response cycle of government, greater taxes have to be levied, and these present an exponential drag on the economy. So to achieve what was initially a simple and rational objective of economic growth now becomes a fool's game of doubling down for linear gains versus exponential costs. Kydland and Prescott called this need to trim one's policy sails at every turn the "inconsistency of optimal plans" or simply "time inconsistency".

The problem government encounters when it acts as a clever dynamic programmer is that it must react to people's reactions. If, instead, government could stick to a rule, then it would short-circuit these reactions. But then rather than being a dynamic programmer who acts with discretion according to circumstances it would be a passive enforcer of rules. If government declared it would send a fixed level of subsidy to a province regardless of what private businesses were investing there, then businesses would not reduce their investments in response to government aid.

What staggered economists and continues to bewilder students of the Kydland-Prescott article is that the "dumb" strategy of simply declaring an immutable policy dominates the "clever" dynamic programming strategy of adapting the equation of motion to feedback it is receiving from changes in the economic environment. How can this be so? There is a technical and then an intuitive explanation.

Technically, when people react to a government policy by anticipating it, they wind the future and the past into the government's planning in such a way that makes it difficult if not impossible to chop up the maximizing problem into chunks manageable by dynamic programming. This just means that no consistent policy is initially possible, but it does not mean that dynamic programming is useless. As government adjusts its policy at any given moment to peoples' reactions, eventually policies and reactions might converge to some stable point at which no further readjustments are necessary. At this point, the repeated application of the dynamic programming technique would have converged to the optimal policies. By then it would have achieved consistency but at a cost. The problem with adopting dynamic programming methods that need to be continually reopened to converge is that government accepts more general restrictions on its ability to maximize society's well-being than had it simply opted for rigid rules. It immediately restricts the "space" of available optimal policies.

More intuitively, comparing the sub-optimality of discretionary government policy to following a fixed dumb policy is not an indictment of dynamic programming theory, or more general methods of dynamic optimization. Given its decision to intervene according to an optimal program, the best government can do at any given moment is to react to people's reactions. This is actually the optimal thing to do in the environment government has itself created by deciding to follow a discretionary plan based on the repeated application of an inconsistent dynamic optimization approach to policy. The problem is that the optimum attainable in this government-created environment is inferior to the optimum possible in a different environment where government decides to act mulishly and never deviate from a fixed rule. Therein lies the answer to the paradox of the time-inconsistency of optimal plans.

The failure that Kydland and Prescott identified is not uniquely one of dynamic programming, but rather is a failure of government to integrate the reactions of private individuals into its plans. Once that is done, the problem of optimal government intervention becomes one of political will. Ultimately what Kydland and Prescott were saying is similar to what Lucas and Friedman had warned of earlier. The expectations of private individuals are a constraint on the effectiveness of government intervention. Governments break this constraint by submitting to rules that effectively cut the cycle of reaction. If government does not commit to rules it activates these constraints and thereby limits the range of best possible outcomes. That was really all the debate was about. Simple, no?

Quite apart from yielding unexpected insights into the challenges to the efficacy of government intervention, dynamic programming gave birth to the field of business cycle simulation based on intertemporal models of optimization by consumers and firms. Simulation had long existed in macroeconomics. Keynesian econometric models were all about simulation. But what had earlier been lacking, as strange as it may sound, was a model explicitly based on the assumption that people maximized profits and wellbeing.

Other applications of inter-temporal analysis

EARLIER KEYNESIAN MODELS were so-called *ad hoc* creations built up from loosely connected assumptions. Real business cycle models were built up from a mathematically coherent view of interactions between firms and consumers explicitly seeking the best for themselves over the long-term. Dynamic programming allowed such models to be solved, or very closely approximated and thus allowed economists to explore the consequences of random shocks to the economy and also of diverse forms of government intervention.

Among the first to build such a model were, you guessed it, Finn Kydland and Edward Prescott in their 1982 article "Time to Build". This bravura display of technical economics explained how to exploit the happy union of intertemporal optimizing techniques with the modern computer and economic reasoning. Their work allowed economists to see in clear pictures how an economy in which individuals maximizing their well-being by the choice of an optimal investment plan would evolve. Using dynamic programming techniques they built a dynamic model of the economy that was consistent with the past real evolution of consumption, investment, employment, and other variables. They achieved consistency by fiddling with, or "calibrating" the model's fundamental constants or "parameters" until the model could reproduce the past. They also showed how to make chance variations in the productivity of industry, due to technological change, a factor that people took rational account of in at first making, and then updating their plans. Friedman had given this a shot by developing the concept of "transitory income" but his attempts had the tacked-on feel of an afterthought. The Kydland-Prescott model left nothing to surmise. It was a fully-cranked view of an economy evolving under the rational actions of optimizing agents.

The model that resulted could simulate what would happen to economic growth under different types of government policy such as permanent decreases in taxation versus temporary decreases. Kydland and Prescott's conclusions about government policy mirrored those of the simpler permanent income, life-cycle model of consumption. Government's attempts to stimulate the economy could be thwarted by forward-looking people who understood that any act of government generosity today had to be paid for later.

The Kydland-Prescott model went much further, though, than the Friedman-Modigliani model because it tied the productive side of the economy to the consumption side in a forward-looking manner. This enhancement allowed Kydland and Prescott to show how people's decisions today could reverberate through time. The Friedman-Modigliani permanent income model has no arrow of time because it compresses time into the single datum of permanent income. The Kydland-Prescott model, moreover, allowed one to address the question of how random shocks to the economy, due perhaps to storms, or wars, or unexpected inventions, could also create cycles of ups and downs in national income. These cycles were not the product of irrational investors, as Keynes had bruited, but were the consequences of rational plans built in an uncertain environment. Thus was born real business cycle simulation.

There was a downside. Even if you were confident the numbers backed up your equations of motion you could not be certain whether it was your view of the world, your model, that was responsible for this time-path, or some other model. All you could say is that the numbers were consistent with your model. This is the enduring *Achilles* heel of the Kydland-Prescott approach to dynamic economic simulation. What calibration means more simply is what Sherlock Holmes does when he deduces from a man's hat that he is married but in bad standing with his wife, that he cannot pay the gas bill, that he is of genteel but impoverished background, and that he has recently bought a Christmas goose. Those are facts that "fit" with or are in effect "calibrated" to the image of the world implicit in the hat. The problem of course is that there are many other interpretations consistent with the state of the hat. The interpretations you make now will then influence deductions you make about changes that may befall the owner of the hat.

Time in the general economic view

THE APPLICATIONS OF time in economics go beyond macro-economics. I chose life-cycle income and some aspects growth theory because developments in this field make a nice story for illustrating the salient issues that arise when people try to best adjust their affairs over time. The presence of cumulative effects of past consumption behavior on investments clearly illustrates how an arrow of time can be established in economics.

This arrow of time can be seen in other fields as well. For example, there is branch of economic dynamics that does not focus on the consumer's effect on his or her budget constraint, as growth theory does. Instead it focuses on the effect our choices have on the formation of our tastes. This is a much more intimate topic. Gary Becker and Kevin Murphy were among the first to apply the tools of dynamic growth theory to a question that touches deeply on the values that make us who we are. They believed that the consumption of certain products led to the formation of habits in consumption. These habits grow because past consumption may have a cumulative effect on our preferences for present and future consumption. One can imagine a person accumulating a stock of "consumption capital" that influences the ability to enjoy certain goods or activities. The consumption capital cannot be expressed in a constraint, as physical capital was in the problem of optimal investment over the lifetime, but rather appears directly in the individual's utility. Nonetheless this raises the same issues as in optimal investment because the consumption decision now determines a path of pleasure in the future, just as consumption decisions in the investment model determined a path of future income. The past sets you on a firm course to the future and in this sense considerations of before and after are of prime importance in understanding how people behave.

A brief time of history

QUITE APART FROM training us to appreciate the subtleties of economic modeling, studying the economic approach to time heightens our perceptions of the past in a manner historians might not be able at first to appreciate. For what is a theory but a prescription for recognizing patterns in real life which we might have missed but for a bit of inspired and systematic guesswork?

A case in point is that until recently there was little we could do but live by the vagaries of the seasons. The *Bible* speaks of the difficulties of living through seven years of famine and the dubious pleasure of an ensuing seven years of feast. Famine and feast cycled through human lives for two reasons. Until about 200 years ago there was really no reliable means for storing food except the short-term expedients of curing meat and preserving vegetables in root cellars. Grain silos and refrigeration technology for meat did not exist in viable forms until the mid-19th century. Subsequently canned products were invented, but their reliability was poor until the 20th century. Until recent times, food was difficult to store, with the exception of alcohol.

Alcoholic beverages are a high-yield method of preserving a potable liquid with large caloric content against contamination by microorganisms. The long-term storage potential of alcohol is an example of the quest by humans to displace current consumption towards the future. The invention and refinement of spirits was the greatest advance in this quest. Spirits really only became widely consumed in Europe during the early 18th century. To produce the high alcoholic content of hard liquor, a great deal of heat is needed. Access to heat was not widely available until the industrial revolution of the late 1700s. This revolution produced the steam engine and iron rolling-techniques that allowed railed vehicles to transport coal in bulk to far-off places. The price of producing heat plummeted. The low price of heat allowed people to distill spirits and transmute the caloric content of coal into the caloric content of drinkable, storable alcoholic beverages. Today, alcohol is not seen as an essential nutrient and is even frowned upon by growing segments of society. Two hundred years ago, distilled alcohol was a caloric godsend that lowered the cost of contamination-free nutrition. To borrow a passage from Sophocles' *Oedipus*, written during the caloric boom made possible by the exploitation of the olive 2,500 years ago, "There grows the grey-leaved olive whose rich oil breeds up our sturdy youth, so that no brash young general or arrogant commander can ever uproot, pillage, or plunder the quiet of these silvery grey groves."

Technological improvement in storage increasingly protected individuals from cycles of boom and bust, but just as important in creating stability were advances in the ways of commerce and the law. Before the 1800s, people thought hard about whether to put their money in the bank or leave it under a mattress at home. Thieves could rob your home, but banks might equally go bust or embezzle your funds. Out of the industrial revolution arose a reserve of wealth that allowed banks to insure each other against failure. This was the start of a banking "system" in which each member conformed to norms of probity and sound management and in return benefitted from help given by other members should a crisis beset it. This newfound stability encouraged people to deposit their savings in banks rather than stuff the funds in their mattresses. By investing the money, banks became an institutional "storage technology" that not only gave their depositors a degree of assurance that their funds would be available to them in the future, but also that a sum of interest would be earned on the deposit.

The key in applying economic concepts to history is to understand the cumulative link which the past has to the present. Storage technology enables the creation of stocks that connect past and present in complex ways never imagined possible by the ancients. They lived season-to-season, and even day to day. Such bucolic simplicity is no longer a realistic component of our lives. We have left Walden Pond so that we might gain the power to shape our futures. This quest has forced us to think in a new manner about what happiness means in a world of change. The economic analysis of this quest for happiness in new and turbulent settings is mundanely labelled as "intertemporal optimization". As we have seen, the challenges this analysis poses are anything but mundane.

Conclusion

TIME IN ECONOMICS has two faces. The first face, glanced upon by Milton Friedman and Franco Modigliani was that if you expected a fixed stream of income over your life then you could reduce all your decisions about how much to consume in any give year to one variable: the present discounted value of the sum of your income stream. The Friedman-Modigliani synthesis produced some insights on the effect of government stimulus packages. But it ignored that people's income streams are not fixed in a present value sense. That was the second face of time.

By investing in new technology or education you can raise the present value of your lifetime income. The effects of investment may be cumulative. This cumulative feature of investment presents people with a dilemma. You can save heavily today and massively increase your future income but this reduces your present enjoyment. How should you choose the best from an infinite number of investment paths to maximize the happiness derived from consumption over your lifetime? This turns out to be a very difficult problem with no pat answer. Economists applying the techniques of dynamic optimization to the consumer problem had some success but also got it into their heads to see if government could not apply similar techniques to guide the economy. The problem with government's use of these techniques was that individuals could anticipate what government was doing and subvert the optimal program. The result was a government policy that was "time-inconsistent".

There are many applications of the theory of time in economics I have not talked about, such as the Swan-Solow model of economic growth, and the Lucas-Romer approach to economic development. Surveying the field of dynamic macroeconomics was not my goal. I have discussed the essentials of time with an eye to understanding the manner in which people decide to consume and produce. With these insights in your pocket you can easily move to a mastery of the entire field of time in economics.

References

Barro, Robert J. 1974. "Are Government Bonds Net Wealth?" *Journal of Political Economy*, volume 82: 1095-1117.

Becker, Gary, and Kevin M. Murphy. 1988. "A Theory of Rational Addiction." *The Journal of Political Economy*, volume 96: 675-700.

Blanchard, Olivier Jean and Stanley Fischer. 1989. *Lectures on Macroeconomics*. The MIT Press.

Chang, Alfa. 1992. *Dynamic Optimization*. McGraw-Hill.

Dreyfuss, Stuart. 2002. "Richard Bellman on the Birth of Dynamic Programming." *Operations Research*, volume 50: 48-51.

Hall, Robert E. 1978. "Stochastic Implications of the Life Cycle-Permanent Income Hypothesis: Theory and Evidence." *Journal of Political Economy*, volume 86: 971-987.

Hendry, David F. 1980. "Econometrics—Alchemy or Science?" *Economica*, volume 47: 387-406.

Keynes, John Maynard. 1939. "Reviewed Works." *The Economic Journal*, volume 49: 558-577.

Kydland, Finn, and Edward C. Prescott. 1977. "Rules Rather than Discretion: The Inconsistency of Optimal Plans." *The Journal of Political Economy*, volume 85: 473-492.

Kydland, Finn, and Edward C. Prescott. 1982. "Time to Build and Aggregate Fluctuations." *Econometrica*, volume 50: 1345-1370.

Leeson, Robert. 2000. *The Eclipse of Keynesianism: The Political Economy of the Chicago Counter-Revolution.* Palgrave.

Lucas, Robert E., Jr. 1976. "Econometric Policy Evaluation: A Critique." Carnegie-*Rochester Conference Series on Public Policy*, volume 1: 19-46.

Sargent, Thomas J. 1987. *Dynamic Macroeconomic Theory.* Harvard University Press.

CHANCE   4

C HANCE OFTEN STRIKES PEOPLE AS the sole domain of
statistics. Is it not the statistician's first duty to calculate
how likely some uncertain event is, such as a coin flip
coming up heads? The "probability calculus" that statisticians
developed to aid them in this pursuit can be quite daunting
to learn but life as we know it in the modern world could not
proceed without it. The entire life insurance business depends
on the mathematics developed by statisticians to predict life
expectancy. Yet knowing how likely an event is does not tell
you how to react in the face of uncertainty. If you know that
your life will end with a certain probability at a certain age
and someone tries to sell you life insurance, you have to ask if,
given the probabilities, the price of the insurance is reasonable.
Thus probability by itself is no guide to action. People must
weigh the probabilities they observe along with other factors
to decide how to face an uncertain future. Understanding how
they decide has become largely the domain of economists.

People of course had been shielding themselves from the
vagaries of chance long before the economist came on the
scene to explain to them how they are thinking. The extreme
conservatism of most cultures throughout history shows how
daunting a force chance has been in limiting human endeavors.
Hamlet summarized this attitude to risk in extreme form when
he ruminated "that the dread of something after death, the
undiscovered country, from whose bourn no traveller returns,

puzzles the will, and makes us rather bear those ills we have, than fly to others that we know not of." Economists only really started having something to say when risk became a marketable commodity in the 19th century. This happened with the development of insurance markets. They had even more to say with the development of stock markets in the 20th century.

The study of choice under uncertainty is not just a meaningful way of understanding how insurance and stock markets work, but may also cast light on seemingly unrelated social changes. By allowing people to shield themselves from risks, modern financial innovations have liberated the individual from the terrors of uncertainty. Without these terrors, human creativity and self-expression have increased exponentially. We become acutely aware of this liberation when we compare developed economies to economies where insurance and stock markets are poorly developed. The extremely conservative social attitudes that prevail there may reflect an economic necessity to tone down individualism and the concomitant risky exploration of possibilities this entails. Without insurance markets such risks may be deemed excessive. The message for those wishing to foster economic development is that understanding the relation between insurance markets and social attitudes may be the key to helping some societies break out of excessively conservative, and possibly limiting outlooks.

Thus we see that in the case of chance, as in so many other economic fields, the seemingly dry topic of optimization in the face of some constraint is actually a key to understanding profound changes in society. However, before we can understand these social consequences, we need to understand what exactly is being optimized in an uncertain world and what the relevant constraint is. Let us start with the perhaps simpler notion of a constraint, then move on to analyzing objectives under uncertainty.

The constraint

A CONSTRAINT IN economic markets shows consumers the possibilities for purchase that they face. What the consumer garners from his or her budget constraint is how much income is available for him or her to spend and the price of various goods on which it can be spent. This may seem quite straight-forward when we are considering how many apples and oranges we can buy. If an orange costs twice as much as an apple then your budget constraint enables to you to trade-off two apples in exchange for one orange. But how does any of this translate to an uncertain world?

Economists ask us to think of uncertainty as splitting the world into a variety of possible future states. Apples and oranges will still taste the same in all states and our preferences will be constant. The only factor that distinguishes states is how likely they are to be realized. There may be an extremely unlikely state of the world in which you lose all your money and a likely state in which your money is intact and ready to be spent on apples and oranges. The issue of trade now becomes one not of how many oranges and apples to consume, but of how much income to give up in the good state in exchange for income in the bad state. Did you catch that? Few people do the first hundred-or-so times around, but the idea is really quite familiar to us in our everyday lives.

Suppose you have $100,000 in a bank that might or might not go bankrupt next year. This fear has robbed the ordinary person of sleep since banks for the masses came into promi-nence in the 18th century. In a way, you are looking at a store shelf upon which sit two possible products. In the "state of the world" in which the bank goes under you come out of the "store" with your shopping cart empty. If the bank survives you leave with $100,000 in your cart. Those are quite extreme alternatives. It would be nice if you could trade off money in the good state (no bankruptcy) to "buy" extra money in the bad state (bankruptcy) just as in a normal store you can give up a few apples to buy more oranges.

This sort of trade-off exists in the real world. It is called insurance. Suppose that if you pay $1000 now for full insurance, then in the bad state of the world you get $100,000 of insurance claim less your $1000 premium. And in the good state you just keep your $100,000 but are out of pocket for the $1000 premium. You have "bought" $100,000 of income in the bad state with $1000 from the good and bad states. So you end up with $99,000 of net income no matter what state occurs through the purchase of full insurance. Insurance here helps you "span" future uncertain states of the world so that you find yourself at the average of states rather than at their extremes. Surprisingly the price of trading income between states is not the premium, though it is related to the premium. The price is how much of one dollar in one state must be given up to get a dollar in another state. In this example you have traded off income in the good state for income in the bad state at a rate of one dollar for ninety-nine. That is the relative price of trading income between states. You give up a thousand dollars in the good state and get a hundred thousand in the bad state, less the thousand you paid as a premium, for a payoff of ninety-nine thousand. Hence the cost is one cent in the good state to buy ninety-nine cents in the bad state.

Let us store this piece of information and go see now how much a firm will charge you in a competitive insurance market.

Bear with me because the result is quite surprising and of crucial importance to understanding what happens not just in insurance markets but also in stock markets.

The odds ratio

I DO NOT really like to keep people in suspense so allow me to blurt out what the price will be. Competitive insurance markets bring the price of a dollar in the bad state (in terms of money in the good state) down to the ratio of the probability of the bad state divided by the probability of the good state, the "odds ratio".

Economists arrive at this result by conceiving perfect competition as a condition of the market in which the expected profits of insurance firms are zero or close to it. Firms are held to be effectively neutral with respect to risk not because their owners are fearless in the face of the vagaries of chance but because, in a very precise manner, chance poses no risk for firms. Firms attain this condition by pooling thousands of individuals into their clientele. While one individual's fate may be highly uncertain, the fates of the many assume a near certain character.

To grasp the absence of risk to firms managing risk, think of playing a slot machine where in one game out of ten you will double your dollar. You might play ten times and win nothing. But if you played ten thousand times your winnings would come close to being a thousand dollars. Repeated play is similar to the law of large numbers by which extreme runs of good and bad luck cancel each other out, and all that is left are the average or "central" tendencies of the game.

Insurance companies, especially those selling life insurance, employ statisticians to calculate these probabilities for the human "slot machine". The statistics tell them that people of a certain age share a common chance of dying. What this means, strangely enough, is that the best price an insurance firm can offer you depends not on your own personal risk of dying, but on the group of people, or "pool" into which the company puts you. There are two types of risk in this pool. One is called idiosyncratic, and the other is called systemic or "aggregate" risk.

Idiosyncratic risk is the particular deviation from the norm an individual brings with him into the insurance pool. It should have nothing to do with what the insurance company charges him or her. Pooling large numbers of people together and adding in the positive elements of idiosyncratic chance cancels the negative elements. An efficient insurance firm "diversifies away" all idiosyncratic risks to offer its clients cheaper insurance than the competitor. The competitor must follow suit. The result is that no one charges you for any genetic quirks you bring to the pool.

After diversifying away idiosyncratic risk, what an insurance company is left with is that an almost certain fraction of an age cohort, representing the common element of chance, will die in some future year. These fractions determine the price of insurance, due to the economic condition that perfect competition drives expected profits to zero. If the chance of death is one percent and the payout is one hundred thousand dollars, then what premium needs to be charged to assure zero expected profits? The answer is one thousand dollars. The firm pockets a thousand with certainty, but has an expected payout to make of a hundred thousand dollars times one percent, which is one thousand. From the point of view of the insurance consumer he or she has to give up a certain dollar in both states to get a hundred dollars in the bad state and zero dollars in the good state. Meaning that the tradeoff rate between money in the good and bad state is one in ninety-nine. But one in ninety-nine is exactly the odds ratio of the bad and good states happening. In a perfectly competitive insurance market the rate of tradeoff between good and bad states is the odds ratio. That is the relative price of spanning income states.

The first thing that strikes one about the relative price of spreading income between possible future states of the world is that here is the quest of an actuary pumped high on amphetamines. What did Caesar know about possible states when he crossed the Rubicon and exclaimed "let the dice fly high"? We have come a long way since the civil wars of the Roman Republic. We now know how to calculate the risks of letting the dice fly in most of the important situations that concern ordinary people, such as life, fire, and deposit insurance. This knowledge helps drive down insurance to its lowest possible price, as companies use this knowledge to outcompete each other. The perfect competition result of pricing insurance according to odds ratios leads to the highest possible level of wellbeing for people concerned about risk.

The third thing that strikes one is that demand and supply do not have much to do with the price. Most people think that supply and demand should interact so that high demand leads to high price. Not so in the insurance world. Only the supply side seems to matter. The implications of this weird aspect of the insurance market will rebound on our analysis of the stock market, where a similar insight holds.

Happiness in an uncertain world

WHAT HE HAVE achieved so far in our analysis of choice in uncertain circumstances is to establish that perfect competition creates insurance markets where the cost of shifting income between possible states is equal to the odds ratio of these states. How much income should the consumer buy in the bad state? The answer depends on his or her fear of the bad state coupled with the likelihood of this state. Economists believe that the individual comes up with a likely number for his or her satisfaction (or "expected utility") if insured, and compares it to his or her utility if not insured. If the first number is greater, then you buy insurance.

Now here comes the tricky part. What "happiness number" do you attach to your choice of not buying insurance? You don't know which of two possible ways the world will go. In the good state you would have much disposable income, in the bad state little. How do you attach one number then to happiness, or "utility", arising from a situation in which two possible outcomes are possible? Put differently, since income in different states cannot be consumed simultaneously the way goods in the here and now can be consumed, we have to ask in what sense income levels in each state can be added up to produce a single number that tells you on average how well off you will be in the future. Economists call that number "expected utility". It is the centerpiece of choice under uncertainty because it enables an individual to compare his or her level of satisfaction with and without insurance. This, however, is not a simple average where you add the utility of riches in the good state and deprivation in the bad state and divide by two. Rather, it is a weighted average where you give a higher score to states that are more probable. Then you multiply each state by its score and add the two. The scores in question are the probabilities that one or the other state will be realized.

If your bank has only a one in a hundred chance of going under you would attach a score of only one in a hundred to the utility of the destitute state, and a score of ninety-nine out of a hundred to the utility of the prosperous state. Economists call the sum of these two weighted scores "expected utility". You would make the same sort of calculation if you bought partial insurance, applying the one in a hundred chance to your level of compensation in case of accident, less the premium you pay, and the ninety-nine in a hundred chance in case of no accident, to your full wealth less the insurance premium. If expected utility is greater in the insured than in the uninsured state, then you buy insurance.

Risk aversion

So far, all we have done is identify the factors that are important in the individual's choices and which frame his or her decision-making process in terms of these factors. This does not tell us whether he or she will buy insurance or not. Nor does it even begin to show why chance occupies such an important place in economics.

In a certain world a person will want to buy more apples if the value of apples (as measured by what he or she would be willing to give up in oranges) is lesser than the actual amount of apples he or she must give up to get an orange. In other words, substitute more apples if your relative valuation is greater than the relative price. To see how this applies to an uncertain world, imagine you are presently uninsured and are once again facing the bankruptcy scenario. Now ask yourself how much your expected utility would change if things were a bit different and you received a dollar less in the good state but a dollar more in the bad state. If you are like most people, then having a dollar less when you are already doing well will not cause much disutility.

But having an extra dollar when you find yourself in a destitute situation could mean a great deal to you. Economists believe this comes about because of diminishing returns to the pleasure we get from spending money. Every dollar spent gives more pleasure but in decreasing amounts. By implication every dollar lost to spending inflicts pain in increasing amounts. If you feel you live in a risky world where the gain of a dollar brings you less pleasure than the pain from losing a dollar then you might want to buy insurance. Economists call you risk-averse. In such a case you might want to trade income from the good state and shift it to the bad state.

Your fear of risk is just one factor determining how eager you are to buy insurance. What also matters is how likely it is that something bad will happen, and the cost of the insurance. Insurance allows you through the premium to shift income from the good state to the bad state.

Because of risk-aversion, that is, diminishing returns to the pleasure from income in any given state, as you buy insurance and shift income to the bad state, the expected value of an extra dollar in that state falls while the expected value of an extra dollar in the good state rises. The ratio of the two represents the extra money you are willing to give up in the good state for money in the bad state. Economists are always considering extras or "margins" because that is where people push things to decide whether to go a little further in their consumption of one good and less of the other. A little less expected utility in any state is called expected "marginal utility".

The ratio of expected marginal utility from increasing income in the bad state to income in the good state might be five. This means you are willing to give up five dollars in the good state to get one dollar in the bad state, or inversely you are willing to give up a dollar in the good state to get twenty cents in the bad state. This ratio falls as you get more in the bad state and less in the good state. You stop buying insurance when the expected value of extra money to you in both states is equal to how much money you have to give up in the good state to buy a dollar of coverage in the bad state. In more general terms, you keep buying insurance until the rate at which you are willing to trade off income in both states is equal to the rate at which you are able to trade off that income. Once you have attained this equation you can do no better.

Now that is a quite a bit of reasoning to process but we should not be daunted. All we are saying is that people seek a sort of balance in their consumption between possible states that is commensurate with the price of dispersing income between these states and the value they attach to income in these states.

Remember that the price of trading off income in the good and bad states is the odds ratio in a competitive insurance market. Applying the logic of trading off marginal expected utility in different states so that they equal the odds ratio gives a surprisingly clear result. In perfect competition people would choose to be fully insured so as to assure themselves the same level of income in both states.

The mathematical proof can be found on page 161 of Hal Varian's 1984 textbook but we can see quite easily why it is so. The rate at which you are willing to trade off income in the good state for the bad state is the probability of the bad state multiplied by the added pleasure of extra income in that state, divided by the probability of the good state multiplied by the added pleasure of extra income there (yes, all is meant as you read it). This expresses the relative valuation of an extra dollar in the bad versus the good states. Now suppose income in both states were the same. That means that extra, or "marginal" utility in both states would be the same. So in the ratio these two quantities drop out. All you have left in the ratio of willingness to exchange income in one state for another are the probabilities. And these represent the odds ratio. And there is your result. Consuming equally in both states converts your willingness to trade income in both states into the odds ratio. But the odds ratio is also the market price of shifting income from one state to the other. This proves that under perfectly competitive insurance markets and utility with diminishing returns to income in any given state, the desired policy is full insurance.

The troublesome question of separable utility

THE EMERGENCE OF the odds ratio as the price of insurance under perfect competition and the desire for full insurance under diminishing returns to income in any given state produce the clear and powerful result that people will seek to equalize income across states by purchasing full insurance.

The more precise a theory the more it is open to question. The theory of choice under uncertainty relies critically on the assumption that utility is separable between states. This is what allows us to speak of expected utility. We can separate the utility from income in any given state, weigh it by the probability of that state and add it to all other weighted utilities to arrive at the sum which is called "expected utility".

The even stronger result of full insurance as the desired objective depends on the assumption of diminishing returns to income. In a way this assumption is the child of the separability of the utility function. In consumer theory, under certainty you can get the result that consumers prefer to evenly balance their consumption of goods, without falling back on the assumption of diminishing marginal utility. You just need to know that the relative desired rates of tradeoff between one good and another will diminish as you consume more of that good. Separable utility forces you to assume diminishing marginal absolute utility to arrive at a scenario where people seek to balance income between states.

Why does any of this matter? Because expected utility is an average this means its mathematical form must be a sum. This means that the income you get in one state should not influence the utility you get from income in another state. Formally, economists call this the separability of utility across states. Being so specific about the form of the utility function troubles economists because it forces them to take a specific stand on the sorts of preferences people have. That opens them to the critique that people do not react to chance in so particular a manner.

To justify their assumptions economists have tried to show that, in a way, they are not assumptions at all but rather features of maximizing utility under uncertainty that emerge from rock-solid "axioms". The axiomatic approach to expected utility does not start with a specific utility function or any discussion of probabilities. It only makes some very general and reasonable assumptions about peoples' attitudes to risk. What pops out of these assumptions is a utility function that must be separable across states and that utility in each state must be weighted by some fractional factor that can be interpreted as the probability of that state.

The axiomatic approach may suggest that expected utility maximization is a reasonable pursuit for most people but does not prove it. At worst it may simply prove how far very clever researchers will go to convince themselves that what they are doing makes sense. Most economists do not lose sleep over this issue, but it is a potential weakness of expected utility theory we should keep in tucked in the band of our thinking caps.

The main point to note is that we have shown how to conceive of consumption and the constraints upon it in an uncertain environment. While insurance markets are important and interesting, this analysis also has vast implications for many different forms of choice in uncertain settings. Before getting to the really meaty topic of stock markets, which are an extension of insurance markets, I want us to take a breather and go on a mental safari into an economic bushland where notions or risk are seldom, but fruitfully applied.

Crime

AN IMPORTANT AND somewhat surprising consequence of studying decisions made in uncertain circumstances arises in the study of crime. A seemingly endless debate rages between those who say that greater punishments deter crime, and those who claim that, instead, greater funding is needed to increase the chance of catching criminals. The economic analysis of uncertainty judges that both sides in the debate have a point. A government that wants to have the most impact on crime needs to find the optimal "mix" of punishment and enforcement. This optimum turns on how people react to the mix.

Consider the white collar crime of tax evasion. The evader faces two possible states of the world: one in which no one detects the evasion and he or she profits; and one in which government discovers the crime, takes back the money owed, and imposes a fine. Every increase in the fine hurts progressively more with every additional dollar of penalty. This is the flip-side of the diminishing returns to getting rich. Fines are increasingly effective.

However, raising the probability of being caught only diminishes a person's expected utility in constant steps. Going from a 5% to a 6% increase reduces expected utility by one per cent. Going from a 6% to 7% increase reduces expected utility by one per cent, and so on. On the cost side, raising fines is relatively cheap but increasing enforcement is increasingly costly.

The linear effect on crime of the probability of apprehension may be no match for the non-linear power of penalties as deterrents. Being caught is not so dreadful a prospect as being punished. Perhaps this explains why tax authorities can manage to collect vast sums without ever imposing fines on more than a small percentage of the population.

This logic has its limits in modern society. Pushed to the extreme it would prescribe lynching people for parking violations. We are not ready to accept such extreme penalties, perhaps because we fear that we may be mistakenly convicted. Several hundred years ago, punishments for crime were savage, probably because the enforcement "technology" did not exist to make the likelihood of apprehension sufficiently high to act as a deterrent.

While such examples may seem eccentric, they illustrate the principles that underlie a vast subfield of economics that analyzes crime, the underground economy, tax evasion, and criminal law. All are children of the basic economic analysis of choice under uncertainty.

CAPM

A SECOND AND far more widespread application of chance in economics lies in the pricing of stocks. The celebrated Capital Asset Pricing Model or CAPM is the one of the most successful applications of economic concepts to the real world. It tries to do what everyone wants, namely to show you if the market is under or overpricing certain stocks. At best you can use this model to make money. At very least you can use it to manage risk intelligently in your portfolio of investments. Yet despite its origins in the field of economics, the CAPM divides economists and finance academics into mutually disdainful camps.

Economists think of researchers in the finance field as specialized drones looking for patterns in financial data with the aid of models whose conceptual content is slim, and which show little sign of evolution nor scope for the application of economic imagination. Milton Friedman once chided the young Harry Markowitz, a founder of portfolio theory, for being a mathematician rather than an economist. Finance experts think of economists as flabby-thinking generalists who cannot be bothered to probe the details of their asset pricing models. Their lack of intellectual focus prevents economists from really grasping what is going on in finance. Economists simply don't "get it". A Linnaeus surveying these squabbles would suggest that finance specialists had broken from the trunk of economics to form a new species, *jocus fiscus*, or in English "finance jock". Both camps have a point, but taking sides tends to obscure what asset pricing models are and what they can achieve.

We need to look past the squabbles of either camp and grasp three essential notions. We need to know what is meant by "asset pricing model", we need an idea of what is important to people in their choice of financial assets, and we need to know how equilibrium comes about in the asset market. I am going to suggest to you a model of asset pricing so ridiculously simple you will wonder what all the fuss is about. Yet as we will see, it contains the major elements of the far more complicated but fundamentally no different models that now dominate finance.

Imagine a company that will close down tomorrow and split between its shareholders a guaranteed payoff. The price a share in this company should sell for is a subject for asset pricing theory. It is pretty clear in this case that a share should sell for exactly the value of the payoff coming to it. If one share is entitled to a hundred dollar payoff then no one would sell it to you for less than that. You could buy it of course, but then your return on the investment would be zero. Return is the net increase in the value of your share relative to what you paid for it, or more simply the percentage increase in share value. There is no net increase over the period of your ownership if you buy it the day before the payout.

In fact it is pretty clear that no matter what stocks you are talking about, an asset with a certain payout tomorrow or some short time thereafter will have zero return for investors. If an asset with certain payout had a positive return this would be an opportunity for massive profit-making by potential investors. If I offer you a share with a guaranteed payout tomorrow of a hundred dollars for the price of fifty you will think I am delusional but will be quite happy to buy as much of this share with whatever money you have in the bank. You will also run to loan-sharks to borrow as much money as you can, even at usurious rates as high as forty-nine percent overnight interest to buy the share, because every dollar you invest will give you a guaranteed rate of return of fifty percent in just one day. Buying low and selling high with a guaranteed return is called "arbitrage". If others see the opportunity they will bid up the prices of these shares until the return comes back to zero.

Notice what we have just accomplished. We have built an equilibrium model of stock prices based on investor preferences. It may not seem like much of a model but it has some key elements. Preferences are simply that people prefer more to less. The price of the share is equal to its proportional payout. The price adjusts through a process of arbitrage to make the rate of return zero. People care only about share price insofar as it determines the rate of return on a dollar. Put differently, rate of return is the object of focus. Share prices adjust in the background to equilibrate rates of return. This feature of asset pricing models leads to enormous confusion as to why they are called "pricing" models. The only thing that this model of arbitrage determines conclusively is the rate of return. But rate of return by itself is not a sufficient datum for share price. Price is a function as well of the final payout.

Asset pricing models take this payout as given and have nothing to say on how it arises. Payouts are determined by "market fundamentals" such as demand and supply for the firm's product. Thus a division of labor arose in asset pricing models. Finance jocks would focus on how arbitrage determined rates of return and content themselves with an intellectually narrow activity which could bring in a great deal of money. Economists could be left to go deeper and worry about fundamentals such as what determined the price of a firm's product, and be original while sewing leather patches over the threadbare fabric of their jacket elbows. So while it makes sense in a remote way to speak of asset pricing models, in reality they are asset return models. The distinction will perhaps become clearer as we spice the pot by making final payouts uncertain.

Suppose a firm's final payout could be higher than what you paid for the share with a certain probability and lower with another probability. In the first case your return is positive, in the second it is negative. If you are not worried about risk, that is, the pleasure you get from an additional dollar is equal to the loss of pleasure you get from having one dollar less, then all you really care about is the average, or more precisely, the expected return. This is pretty much the same scenario as in the certainty case. Prices have to adjust so that expected return goes to zero.

Things start to become interesting if your preferences exhibit diminishing returns to income. Put differently you get less pleasure from an upswing in your revenues than you feel pain from an equivalent loss. In such a case you are said to be shy of risk, or risk averse. The maximum amount a risk averse person would be willing to pay in certain dollars for a share of the stock, and by extension the minimum acceptable return, is not so simple to calculate.

As a utility maximizer you would take certain dollars out of your pocket to pay for a stock with uncertain returns until the loss of utility from a certain dollar just equals the gain in utility from that dollar placed in the risky stock. Put in these terms the arbitrage condition becomes obscured because expected return is no longer the quantity of interest. What matters to people in these circumstances is how returns are dispersed among the different possible states of the world.

A stock which gives the possibility of a very high and a very low return is less desirable than one which gives the possibility of the same average return, but with spreads only half as high and half as low. Both stocks have the same expected return but what matters is how these returns are dispersed. The stock with high dispersion gives you the possibility of lots of money which you value in decreasing increments, and the possibility of very low, negative returns which make you suffer in increasing increments. Thus when we bring expected utility into the picture the individual levels of return in different states take on importance. That was not the case in the certainty and risk-neutral cases where only the average of returns mattered.

The goal of all sciences is to simplify. When you start giving importance to individual events separately from others, you vastly complicate the problem of solving for the outcome of the system. In this case the outcome is equilibrium leading to a stock price and return. Equilibrium would come about and a stock price settled upon when people had adjusted their purchases of stock, and stock prices had changed such that everyone was just indifferent between giving up a certain dollar of income for the utility gain (not the expected money gain) to be expected from investing in the stock.

Yet this approach is bad, or at least awkward science because it is really not a very practical characterization of the problem. The main item of disappointment is that expected return disappears from the calculation, to be replaced by the expected utility of income in the different states of the world corresponding to different possible levels of stock return. Return still figures in the problem, but in a highly fragmented manner. We are no longer able to speak simply of expected return, which is the sum of all possible returns weighted by their probabilities. Now we have to consider each possible return to a stock individually. Discovering what the equilibrium stock return should be is a nightmare.

One way to get out of the mess of figuring out asset prices using a model of maximizing the expected utility of investing in stocks is to make assumptions about either preferences or the probabilities of the different possible states of the world. Nobellist James Tobin (1958) took this line and discovered that in some cases you do not need to worry about the utility of income in thousands of states, and the attached probabilities, to solve the consumer's choice on how to spread income among states. When preferences contain only a linear and a squared term (a case of diminishing returns) or the probabilities of different stock returns follow a normal distribution (an equation that contains a linear and squared terms as parameters), a simple formulation of a person's investment choices becomes possible. Under Tobin's assumptions we can reformulate the person's decision problem as being one of trading off risk and expected return. Risk, or more precisely the variance of your investment portfolio creates spread in the returns you expect. People are willing to assume more risk only if compensated by a higher level of expected return. One can thus think of a tradeoff people are willing to make between risk and expected return. They invest in risky assets to the point at which their willingness to trade off risk and return is equal to the rate at which they able to trade them off. It is difficult to exaggerate how brilliant is the simplification of the investment problem that flows from these assumptions. Instead of worrying about the investor's optimization problem in potentially millions of possible states of the world, one need only worry about how the investor can trade off risk and return in the stock market.

The risk-return frontier

OF COURSE NO stock market sells you risk and return directly, just as no supermarket sells you nutrition and flavor directly. In stock markets investors combine stocks into portfolios that produce different levels of risk and return, just as grocery shoppers combine purchased ingredients into a final culinary product. Is there some analogue in the uncertain world of the arbitrage condition that in a certain world gave such clarity to the equilibrium return of stocks? In fact there is, and as you might guess, this arbitrage condition is the only factor determining expected stock returns in a partial equilibrium sense. Recall that as yet we have no way of predicting how the final payout to stocks come about. That is a datum arising from full equilibrium in product markets that have nothing to do with finance models. This separation of equilibria, as it were, is the reason why finance models focus on returns rather than stock prices. Expected returns are creatures uniquely of arbitrage once we take as given the final payout.

So what is the arbitrage condition in question? In a certain world the arbitrage condition for equilibrium is that all stock prices should adjust so that all stocks have zero return. In an uncertain world people are willing to accept risk to get greater return. Now a whole range of positive returns is possible, accompanied in a consistent manner by varying levels of risk. If there is a stock or portfolio of stocks that offer more return at a given level of risk than others at that level of risk, people will rush to buy stocks in that portfolio until their prices rise to lower the expected return back to that in the herd of stocks in other portfolios grazing at the level of risk in question. Or the prices of the stocks in these portfolios could fall. All that matters is that no stock or portfolio offering a higher level of return than others should have an equivalent or lower level of risk. That is the arbitrage condition in question.

The risk-return arbitrage condition is believed to be a powerful force driving stocks to their equilibrium levels of expected return because if the condition is violated a savvy investor can make a great deal of money. All you need do is short-sell, that is, "borrow" the portfolio with similar risk but inferior returns, sell it, and buy up the portfolio with similar risk but higher return. You then sell this portfolio at a higher price to investors wishing to efficiently manage risks in their portfolios and pay back the person who "lent" you the inferior portfolio.

The arbitrage condition is more complicated to describe than in the case of certainty but is no more complicated in principle. The complicated part is in seeing how investors go about building the so-called "efficient frontier" of tradeoffs between portfolio risks and returns, and equilibrium comes about.

After Tobin's signal contributions to the field, economists had no answers. The task fell to finance jocks, the first and foremost being Harry Markowitz. He showed how an individual investor could build an efficient frontier for substituting risk and return. His student William Sharpe then showed how this led to stock market equilibrium. Let us see how these two thinkers founded the modern field of financial economics.

The Markowitz algorithm

THE MATHEMATICAL METHOD for combining available stocks to give a risk-return frontier was discovered by future Nobellist Harry Markowitz in the 1950s. His insight was that, given some group of stocks, you could combine them in different proportions (with different "weights") to produce a level of variance of the return and given expected return. His "algorithm" for finding the efficient frontier was to postulate a level of risk and ask what weights on some or all the stocks created the greatest expected return for this level of risk. You gave the problem to a computer and let it solve the highest possible return for every risk level and that gave you the efficient frontier. In following such an algorithm the investor could choose the portfolio that best satisfied her desire for tradeoff between risk and return while assuring herself that she was squeezing the most return out of her chosen portfolio given the risks involved.

Despite its simplicity, Markowitz's efficient frontier is often misunderstood to be a tool which tells people how to invest. This is as mistaken an idea of its meaning as it is to think that a consumer's budget constraint tells him what to buy in the supermarket. The confusion is understandable. It arises because the efficient frontier is derived in relation to preferences; the wish to minimize risk and maximize return. Ordinary consumer budget constraints have nothing to do with preferences, but only with the prices and incomes given to people. Markowitz's efficient frontier is a strange creature in the menagerie of economic ideas because it is a hybrid of peoples' risk-return preferences and the possibilities of combining stocks to attain different levels of risk and return. The frontier seems to filter out the worst risks, but then it is still up to the investor to decide situation himself thereupon by choosing the appropriate portfolio.

Markowitz's formula is also misunderstood to be by itself a description of how stock markets work. It is in fact Markowitz's view of how an individual investor should eliminate inefficient portfolios from his or her set of feasible choices. As such it is a purely personal prescription for how to conceive of what the most efficient portfolios might be. It thus fell one step short of helping to understand how stock markets determined asset returns.

We saw in the insurance example that the zero-profit assumption led to an asset price, in this case insurance being the asset, which was proportional to the odds-ratio for the two states in question. But what was the analogue of the zero-profit condition in the multi-state portfolio model? More generally, what was the "equilibrium condition" that would achieve consistency between the formula investors should follow and the actual price of assets in the stock market? Markowitz opened the door to the answer but did not step through.

The answer was provided by Markowitz's student William Sharpe in 1964, and independently by John Lintner in 1965, and Jan Mossin a year later. They were the most prominent expositors of Markowitz, but not the only ones. Other academics worked toward a solution, and pretty much came to the same conclusions, though in different contexts and by expressing themselves in different terms. The purveyors of great ideas sometimes arrive, whips cracking, like jockeys at a photo finish. In this race, Sharpe nosed out the others. He won the Nobel Prize in 1990 along with his teacher Markowitz.

Stock market equilibrium

As MARKOWITZ WROTE in his Nobel Prize lecture, "My work on portfolio theory considers how an optimizing investor would behave, whereas the work by Sharpe and Lintner on the Capital Asset Pricing Model (CAPM for short) is concerned with economic equilibrium assuming all investors optimize in the particular manner I proposed" (1991, 469). The wording of this sentence is important.

The equilibrium Sharpe and Lintner proposed works like this: suppose you have a group of people looking at anticipated stock returns, that is, how much you can expect to gain by investing. If one portfolio with an expected rise in price is dominated by a portfolio with the same rise in price (the return) but lesser variability, then the stocks in this first portfolio need to fall in price so that the rate of anticipated price rise increases. The prices of all stocks must adjust so that they can justify their presence in portfolios lying on Markowitz's efficient risk, expected-return frontier. Sharpe showed how millions of investors following the Markowitz algorithm of weeding out inefficient portfolios would drive stock prices and hence returns to conform to a market-wide efficient risk-return frontier. Sharpe also showed that in the presence of a risk free asset there is only one efficient combination of stocks. The risk-return frontier narrows to a straight line joining the expected returns of this efficient "market portfolio" with the returns on the risk-free asset. All that is left to individuals is to choose the combination of the risk-free asset and the unique efficient portfolio, called the market portfolio that most closely suit their aversion to risk and desire for return. The one efficient portfolio is what determines the unique returns to stocks. Because there is only one relevant portfolio all individuals should hold, variations in individual preferences do not figure in returns. This makes good sense. The efficient frontier is derived from everyone's quest to exploit arbitrage opportunities. Since everyone has the same quest to very simplistically make money from arbitrage, variations in complex individual desires do not figure in the determination of stock returns.

Once again we see a similarity to insurance where in equilibrium the parameters of demand were absent. In the stock market these parameters are only felt indirectly through the efficient portfolio which is based on the very simple assumption that less risk for the same return is good but does not involve preferences in any more explicit manner. In the insurance market what made demand irrelevant to insurance price was the zero-profit condition. In the stock market, demand has no influence on stock returns because nature imitates art. The artist in question is Harry Markowitz. If only one person were to follow his algorithm for holding a mean-variance efficient portfolio he would become rich, and attract attention from other investors who would imitate him until there was no longer any opportunity to "beat the market". Stock prices and hence returns would have shifted to the mean-variance efficient frontier by the efforts of investor's following the Markowitz method.

All of which makes me wonder sometimes whether Markowitz might not have done better by keeping his mouth shut. He had the perfect recipe for beating the market but by revealing it he allowed everyone to catch up and wipe out the possibility of extraordinary profits. Instead, people following the Markowitz algorithm are picking up crumbs. It also makes me wonder whether someone just as bright, but less attracted to the spotlight than Markowitz might have already come up with a better way of managing risk and returns and is quietly amassing a fortune. If I were her I too would keep mum.

Diversification, efficiency

THERE ARE TWO aspects of the Capital Asset Pricing Model I have not elaborated upon because a full discussion would lead us deeper into the field of finance that we need go to understand its place in the economics of chance. But the two aspects do deserve brief mention, one because of its utter weirdness, the other because of its connection to the notion of an "efficient market".

The first aspect of the CAPM that many find difficult to grasp is that the return to a stock depends on the portfolio in which it is held. To see this note that a single stock suffers from two sorts of risk. One risk is that inherent to the company, the so-called idiosyncratic risk. Another risk is shared, perhaps unequally, with other stocks and arises from economic upheavals that touch all enterprises. Suppose you combine one stock with another that to some extent countervails the risk in the first, just by pure luck. Sometimes when the first share is up, the second share by chance is down. This share is like the new member of an insurance pool whose idiosyncratic risk cancels out the idiosyncratic risk of another member. It is possible to reduce to negligible proportions the idiosyncratic risk when you pool roughly fifty randomly chosen stocks. But these are details. The point then is that the rate of return of a stock should not depend on its individual risk.

People have trouble swallowing the notion that idiosyncratic risk should be absent from expected stock returns. If ACME Corporation has an emotionally labile CEO this should not have any influence on its expected rate of return. If the market thought the idiosyncrasies of the CEO were a negative feature, then a clever investor could buy up shares of the ACME and pool them into a portfolio where other companies have CEOs with equally up-and-down character traits. The effects of these character traits would cancel each other out on average in a portfolio. The investor then beats the market because he has neutralized the risk by including the stock in a diversified portfolio. If other investors think this way they will bid up the price of ACME and subsequently drive down the expected return of the stock. The stock market neutralizes idiosyncratic risk just as well as does the insurance market. As William Sharpe explained in parsimonious terms, "Through diversification, some of the risk inherent in an asset can be avoided so that its total risk is obviously not the relevant influence on its price" (1964, 426).

Allied to the concept of idiosyncratic risk is the notion of system-wide or "undiversifiable risk". After diversifying away idiosyncratic risk you are still left with some risk all stocks share, but unequally and in a tied manner. One way of characterizing the common risk is to think of how the expected return on a stock varies with the expected return on the entire portfolio. In finance it is called the "beta". If it varies by more than the portfolio then it is adding risk "pollution". This pollution has to be compensated for by a lower price, hence higher return, at which you are willing to include the stock in your portfolio.

The point about both idiosyncratic risk and commonly felt risks is that the returns to a stock in equilibrium should depend on the portfolio in which that stock is situated. It is one of the weirder aspects of finance and arises because of statistical laws and arbitrage relations.

The second aspect of the CAPM worth noting is its role in testing whether stock markets are "efficient". The CAPM provokes ire by claiming that stock markets are efficient. It should not. The notion of efficiency in the CAPM is circumscribed to relative stock prices and returns. The CAPM does not pretend to be able to predict the price of stocks. It can only tell you if a stock's expected return is too low relative to other similar stocks.

In 2013 when arbitrage specialists won the Nobel Memorial Prize in economics the media reported they had done so for predicting stock prices. Not quite so. Their work was focused on whether the prices of some stocks were out of line with others according to the arbitrage criterion embedded in the Capital Asset Pricing Model. Prediction is not the goal of these models. Sniffing out opportunities for arbitrage is the goal. Investors in the stock market may be savvy when it comes to ensuring the efficiency of relative pricing but they may be dimwitted when it comes to divining the absolute value of stocks. A market crash can happen in the context of a market that is a blazon of efficiency in the CAPM sense. A crash can take place because almost no one was able to predict what would happen to markets in an absolute sense.

Here we return to the anticipated payoffs to a stock. Profits determine crashes and booms. The CAPM implicitly includes anticipations of such events into its formulation. But what explicitly determines the expected profits of a firm? Going deeper, what determines the expected demand and price for their product? The CAPM is not equipped to answer these questions. It can only frame the question. For a sense of how people form expectations of the prices of the goods and services upon which the value of firms ultimately must be based, we must turn to the field of rational expectations economics.

Rational Expectations

WE JUST SAW that asset returns depend on an undiversifiable risk factor encapsulated in the market beta of a stock. Asset prices are a trickier quantity. Yes, once you have determined asset return and once you know the anticipated payouts of stocks, then calculating the anticipated stock price is a trivial exercise. But where does the anticipated payout come from? How do you predict it? The CAPM is mute on this topic. The CAPM is not a model that is sufficient to determine stock price. It is a model based on an arbitrage principle that is highly specialized into predicting asset returns.

How then do investors determine the payout of a company? Or more generally, how do they form expectations about the equivalent concept of future company revenues? This may seem like a respectable but anodyne question of interest only to horn-rimmed academics, yet it has become a triumph of the analysis of uncertainty in economics and shapes government policy as perhaps no other idea does.

An early attempt to understand the formation of expectations is due to Alfred Marshall, better known as the 19th century popularizer of the demand and supply diagram. In Book V, Chapter V of his celebrated *Principles of Economics*, he considered the case of a cloth manufacturer who must anticipate the price of wool in order to know how much to invest today in the machinery needed to provide future cloth. Marshall spoke somewhat vaguely of something he called the "normal price" of wool. What he may have meant was what today we would call the anticipated, or expected price. He argued (1895, 443-444) that, "in estimating the normal supply price of wool, he [the cloth manufacturer] would probably take the average of past years, making an allowance however for any probable change in the causes likely to affect the supply in the immediate future".

Marshall was saying that to form expectations, you need to know something about how prices have evolved in the past, but you cannot simply be backward looking. The cloth manufacturer would also try to understand how supply conditions in the future would influence price (that is, how the market works) and would try to form some notion about how random events would change supply. Marshall went on to suggest that market players do not need to delve into the psychology of workers or others involved in production. All they need to do is understand whether some regular pattern is at work. Here were the seeds, which were to lay long dormant, of a school of economics that came to be known as Rational Expectations, or simply, RE. Marshall's thinking was ahead of its time by about sixty years. Economists in those years took little notice of this aspect of Marshall's research and did not attempt to integrate people's expectations of the future into the economic view of how people should behave.

It was only in the late 1950s that Marc Nerlove tried to redress this omission in economic thinking by arguing that people formed expectations about the future by looking to the past. His thinking was the foundation for oscillatory models of supply and demand that came to be known as cobweb models.

Suppose you are a student thinking of investing in education and you see everyone who graduated in the last few years making good money. You then invest in education. But so do many others, thinking as you do. When you all arrive on the job market there is a glut of skilled workers and wages fall. The low wages then discourage people from investing in education and in a few years there is a shortage of skilled workers. This cycle may repeat itself over many years and may even increase in amplitude. The oscillations are due to mistaken anticipations. When people overestimate the need for educated labor in the future they will over-invest in education. This means that the needs of the labor market and the abilities of workers are being mismatched, which is a waste of resources.

While Nerlove's work rekindled interest in expectations, some economists started to question his view that people formed expectations just by looking back. Nerlove's heart was in the right place but his approach seemed misdirected. The protracted waste of resources arising from oscillatory market conditions predicted by adaptive expectations raised the question of whether there was a more "rational" way of dealing with uncertainty. One such way was for buyers and sellers to form some idea of how markets worked, rather than to act as retrospective simpletons. If you know something about markets, the way Marshall described in his passage on cloth producers, then you look to the past only to form an impression of how chance irrupts into the regular affairs of business. These affairs are normally regulated by the laws of supply and demand. They are upset by what economists call "random shocks", or by what Shakespeare called the "slings and arrows of outrageous fortune". So, basically, it helps to know how the world works normally, but also to take into account upsets to the regular course of things. This regular course is determined by forces that conform to economic models of supply and demand.

In the early 1960s, economist Richard Muth provided a simple but seminal view of how economic equilibrium could arise if people acted as if they were making forecasts of the future based on the best statistical techniques and some idea of underlying economic structures. As original as Muth's work was, the response to it in academic circles was muted.

Then came Milton Friedman's address to the American Economic Association in 1968 in which he challenged the Keynesian intellectual justification for government intervention. Friedman's theme was that Keynesian prescriptions for government intervention were based on *ad hoc* (meaning tacked together) assertions that had nothing to do with rigorous economic thinking.

The example he latched onto was the Keynesian belief that increasing inflation could reduce unemployment in a consistent and lasting manner. Friedman argued that economic analysis only allowed such an outcome if government tricked people, and that such tricks ultimately would prove detrimental to societal interests.

So huge were the implications for economic policy of Friedman's thinking that even as listeners left the auditorium some of them set about sharpening the outlines of the argument he had sketched. The challenge was to clarify how expectations based on some knowledge of the economy could be brought into the fold of classical economic thinking about equilibrium between supply and demand. This would rectify decades of lassitude in which otherwise-occupied economists had neglected expectations to the detriment and even shame of their science. Friedman had provided the intuition and a primer. Now it remained for the formalists to hammer out precisely what his vision meant and whether it was logically consistent with fundamental economic thinking.

Money illusion

FRIEDMAN EXPLAINED THAT indeed government could increase employment by increasing the money supply and pumping up inflation. But at the heart of such a mechanism lay trickery. His story was formalized in 1972 by Nobellist Robert E. Lucas Jr., who developed something called the "islands" model of inflationary trickery. The story that emerged is as follows. When the money supply goes up, but nothing else changes in the economy, all prices also tend to go up, in a case of more dollars chasing the same number of goods, a concept embedded in what is called the "quantity theory of money". The problem employers face is that they cannot be quite certain of whether the rising price they immediately observe for their good, well before they have information on the average of all prices, is really just for their good, or whether all prices in the economy have risen. In this sense employers feel they are living on small islands, isolated from other firms, and having to form impressions on what is happening on the entire economic archipelago from local price movements and a knowledge of the past history of the entire system.

If the price rise is unique to the good the employer produces, then he or she has an incentive to produce more because what gets sold will bring in extra revenues capable of buying other goods. In other words, the extra revenues will be "real" in the sense of materially being able to improve the life of the employer. If, however, the rise in price is just part of a larger number of price increases in the economy, then the extra money earned on a unit of good produced will not allow the employer to buy more of other goods, because their prices have also increased. In technical economic language, when all prices increase, no production or consumption should change because of the "zero-degree homogeneity" of demand and supply functions.

Through experience and some knowledge of how the economy works, people quickly learn how to break down visible price increase in to real and inflationary components in a process of "signal extraction". They become inured to rises in the general price level as they hone their anticipations of the government trick and their ability to separate real and inflationary price increases improves. What results is that government monetary policy risks becoming "neutral", that is, impotent. Only by trying to fool the people about what it is doing with the money supply can government stimulate production. In other words, for monetary policy to have real effects it has to be unpredictable.

Rising monetary unpredictability adds "noise" to the signal extraction problem employers seek to solve in order to separate real from general price increases, and thus cater to real needs in the economy. The result is that monetary policy can end up being worse than neutral. It can actually be a fog in which firms blunder, making costly mistakes about how much they should be producing. To avoid these risks propagated by government trickery, people rationally blind themselves to true opportunities signaled by the market. The economy then stalls.

Self-fulfilling equilibria

WHILE LUCAS BLAZED the trail towards an understanding of rational expectations, the clearest exponent of what rational expectations equilibrium meant was Sanford Grossman, a twenty-two year old economic prodigy putting the final touches on his *Ph.D.* dissertation at the University of Chicago in the early 1970s. He helped to clarify how expectations and the classical structure of economic equilibrium meshed.

Grossman's exposition began by putting a new twist on an old story. In any group interaction, economists seek to understand the equilibrium that will result. That is, they look for some steady pattern of exchange between people that will need no further adjustments in prices. In a certain world equilibrium can be characterized by a price such that the quantity producers offer is the quantity demanders request. This may sound fairly mundane, but it has as its basis something called "Nash equilibrium". This is a state in which no participant in some group activity finds profit in changing his or her plan of action given the strategies of all other participants. In market equilibrium people somehow come to a point at which no one feels the need to change his or her consumption or production in the face of what everyone else is consuming and producing. That was the traditional story of economic equilibrium under certainty. But what happened when the world was uncertain?

Grossman suggested that in an uncertain world equilibrium is a state in which the expectations of buyers and sellers about the future price of some product have very specific features. For businesses, their expectations induce no further present adjustments in preparations to produce in the future. For consumers, expectations induce no extra savings in anticipation of getting "deals" from future buying possibilities. Expectations and reality converge because economic actors have some idea of the structure of the economy in which they are working and act upon these ideas in such a way that, in an average sense, the future is the result of a self-fulfilling prophecy.

Take the case of farming where the seeding decisions taken today influence the crop to be harvested, but in an uncertain manner. Some general idea, or "central tendency", or expectation of a crop can be arrived at, but due to quirks of the weather and the varied depredations of weeds and other parasites no certain number can ever be attached to the future crop. Only some idea of the expected crop and a spread of possibilities around that expectation are possible. A farmer deciding today how much to plant does not simply look at the past price, as in Nerlove's adaptive expectations model. The farmer has some idea of the structure of supply and demand. By taking into account how others who have a similar knowledge will behave he plants a crop in unison with similarly minded farmers such that the future possible spread of prices currently anticipated induces no further change in seeding activity.

Here again Nash equilibrium pops up, but in an unexpected, challenging manner. The future anticipated statistical distribution of prices is consistent with present production and consumption decisions in the sense that people, knowing the effect mass action today will have on the future range of possibilities, feel no further need to react to these future anticipations. What is truly mind-bending about this analysis is that by anticipating these distributions, they realize them. It means that, in a certain sense, our expectations about the future make us prepare for that future in such a way that these expectations become self-fulfilling prophecies. This self-fulfillment is based upon people's anticipations of how they should react to other people's anticipations about the future.

If we think the price of gasoline will rise, then we had better stock up now. Producers anticipating my anticipation will raise the present price and curb our stocking up. We start converging to an equilibrium today based on our views of the future.

At the equilibrium, the consumer's expectations are such that when plugged into the data sheets of companies, they see no reason to expand or contract their anticipated production.

Grossman thus explained that rational expectations is an equilibrium concept, not a concept based on the predictive power of those involved. Peoples' forecasts were based on a notion of how the world works, reinforced by memories of mistakes and successes in past forecasts. These forecasts do not stand alone but rather shape equilibrium price, which in turn shapes the forecasts, and so on. The predictive power of these forecasts could be quite weak. What is important is that people interact in such a manner that no matter what their predictive abilities, some stable consensus on the future emerges, and over the years the way the future turns out tends to validate the way people make their decisions. In an understated way Markowitz and Sharpe had anticipated such a process in the portfolio allocation model.

Despite the self-assured modelizing of high-flying economic intellects, the self-fulfilling aspect of rational expectations is an intellectual lump hard to digest. Yet, as weird and disembodied from intuition as this concept may seem it is at present the best means by which economists may make sense of the interplay of mutually reinforcing expectations that arrive at some stable economic outcome. It is unbelievable, weird, and probably right on the money. Only time will tell.

Chance and the individual

OUR EXCURSION INTO the economic analysis of chance has taken us in a straight line from the basic principles of choice under uncertainty, to pricing insurance, then pricing stock market shares, and finally understanding how expectations of the future are formed. Yet in our haste to cover this modern ground we may have forgotten that chance and the human response to it have always been with us. And that we have always struggled to tame risks for most of history through repressive social norms, and then, with the development of "risk management technology", through insurance and stock markets. These modern developments have not only protected us from risk but have liberated us from age old cultural constraints.

For most of history, tradition, unchanging custom, and even taboo and superstition governed our investments, be these the sowing of a new field, the humble purchase of a plough, or the acquisition of a deed to an alehouse in Elizabethan England. Superstition and custom are mechanisms for either consciously or subconsciously restricting behavior so as to avoid unseen dangers. The dangers were unseen because information on prices was unavailable, or sparse. It is upon such information that today's purveyors of financial products can tout a combination of stocks as a portfolio that removes needless risk from the anticipated returns of investors. At a simpler level, it is upon information about individual lifespan that life insurance can be sold. These modern techniques of taming risk have liberated people from having to obey cultural bonds that had a purpose but were extremely restrictive. The person living in a modern society need not conform to the expectations of the community nor of his or her ancestors.

The contrast with existing primitive societies is stark. In a primitive society, or one which is "otherwise-civilized", the individual is a secondary concept. Its members possess a herd mentality—with good reason. Otherwise-civilized people live at the margin of survival and any deviation of the individual from his or her time-tested roles imposes risks that might weaken the whole community. The modern concept of the individual, which is widely taken for granted in developed countries, has its origins in the development of humanism during the Italian *Renaissance*. The Italians of that period generated the wealth that allowed some of them the luxury of indulging individual deviation.

Opening gates up to the individual allowed human stars to shine. Giotto and Fibonacci are but of few the famous names we now associate with this period. The experiment in Italian humanism was short-lived, but was taken up again, haltingly at first by Montaigne, and then with vigor at the start of the industrial revolution with the philosophical writings of Hume, Smith, and Kant. Though history labels them as philosophers, they were really psychologists, delving into the meaning of individuality, that is, the things that matter to, and motivate, the individual. Their insights might have remained unexpressed in an earlier age where people were tuned out of the notion of individualism. As Mircea Eliade explains in his essay, "The Myth of the Eternal Return", society has lived in a timeless state since its beginnings. So entrenched was the conservative mind-set that people were caught, or perhaps it is better to say they sought refuge, in a loop of production, procreation, and fixed social hierarchies.

Though it would be difficult to prove, one might trace the rise of individual consciousness to developments in economic techniques, and possibly even to economic thoughts, that have helped to shield people from risk. It is under such a shield that individuals have learned to stop living in perpetual fear of rebuke by the community and have begun to explore the possibilities inherent in each one of them. Such is the meaning of civilization. The concept of the individual facing an unlimited vista of possibilities which are his or hers to explore and perhaps even to create, is what distinguishes modern, developed peoples from the otherwise-civilized where a herd mentality prevails and where deviation from social norms are subject to swift and savage repression.

These are weighty matters so let us end on a mischievous note. If the history of the past can be illuminated by the economics of chance, is there anything to be said about the history of the future? To answer this question we should pose another one. Can manifestations of chance in stock market returns tell us if time travel exists? If you can start to formulate an answer then you are well into your apprenticeship as an economist.

References

Eliade, Mircea. 1954. *The Myth of the Eternal Return: Cosmos and History*. Willard R. Trask in the Bollingen Series, number 46.

Friedman, Milton. 1968. "The Role Of Monetary Policy." *The American Economic Review*, volume 58: 1-17.

Grossman, Sanford J. 1975. "Rational Expectations and the Econometric Modelling of Markets Subject to Uncertainty." *Journal of Econometrics*, volume 3: 255-272.

Lucas, Robert E., Jr. (1972), "Expectations and the Neutrality of Money," *Journal of Economic Theory*, volume 4: 103-124.

Marshal, Alfred, 1895. *Principles of Economics*, 3rd Edition. MacMillan and Company.

Markowitz, Harry M. 1952. "Portfolio Selection." *Journal of Finance*, volume 7: 77-91.

Markowitz, Harry M. 1991. "Foundations of Portfolio Theory." *The Journal of Finance*, volume 46: 469-477.

Muth, John R. 1961. "Rational Expectations and the Theory of Price Movements." *Econometrica*, volume 24: 315-335.

Nerlove, Marc. 1958. "Adaptive Expectations and Cobweb Phenomena." *Quarterly Journal of Economics*, volume 72: 227-240.

Sharpe, William F. 1964. "Capital Asset Prices: A Theory of Market Equilibrium under Conditions of Risk." *Journal of Finance*, volume 19: 425-442.

Tobin, James. 1958. "Liquidity Preference as Behavior Towards Risk." *The Review of Economic Studies*, volume 25: 65-86.

Varian, Hal. 1984. *Microeconomic Analysis, 2nd Edition.* W.W. Norton

SPACE

W E BEGIN WITH A STORY about space as most people understand it. In the 1970s letters in the US were delivered by the government mail company. It had an official monopoly that extended only to first class mail and not to packages. The US Postal Service was not worried about competition from package mail because so few people sent anything that way. Then came the *Boeing 727* and other airplanes that made it possible to deliver cargo rapidly and economically by air. A bright young entrepreneur figured out that a private company could deliver packages at reasonable prices, overnight to and from anywhere in the US provided its hub was properly situated. That did not mean putting the hub in the geographic center of the US but rather in the demographic center. To find this center you first had to cut a sheet of plywood in the shape of the US. Then you drew a fine grid on the sheet. Then you calculated what proportion of the population inhabited each grid. Then you took a hundred weight of metal ringers and placed them on the tiles of the grid in proportion to the populations of each tile. Finally you found the demographic center by finding the point upon which the sheet could be balanced on a pole. That center happened to be Memphis, Tennessee.

It did not take an economist to figure out the best place to locate to satisfy customers, but economists had been thinking along these lines for some time. Their goal had not been to find new means of transportation but rather to study how new discoveries lowered the costs of transportation and spurred development. The innovations they studied were varied and fascinating. The invention of multi-modal containers lowered the cost of transporting goods across the world and led to an explosion of trade in the late 20th century. Teleconferencing eliminated distance as a factor in business negotiations. Before the mid-19th century livestock had to be consumed where it was slaughtered because transporting meat over even small distances led to rapid wastage. The invention of refrigeration in the mid-19th century allowed frozen meat to be transported from Chicago to New York and then around the world, leading to a boom in world protein and caloric intake. In each case changes in the cost of overcoming distance led to changes in production and consumption. Cataloguing such costs, looking at how they change, and then seeing how this has influenced market relations became the subject matter a field known as economic geography.

Somehow economic geography became the preserve of geographers. Economists felt there was insufficient challenge in the field. Little room to push economic reasoning further. An economic geographer was an intellectual clock-puncher applying the same thoughts to different situations in a productive but mundane manner. Then came successive insights that made space a topic worthy of being studied by the best minds in the field of economics.

The first insight was to notice that space was not just a barrier to moving goods around, but rather a field upon which competitors jostled to be nearest to their customers. Harald Hotelling, perhaps one of the top five economists of all time, came up with the idea and showed how it transformed the theory of competition.

The second insight lay in realizing that space was not just a span in the physical world, but also a span in abstract dimensions that mattered to consumers, workers, and voters among others. Kelvin Lancaster, one of the best economists never to be anointed with a Nobel Prize, showed that a good such as a house was made up of many different characteristics, such as proximity to parks and amenities, age, and size. Each of these characteristics could be visualized along an axis. Each could be measured in "characteristics space". Different goods containing many characteristics could be combined with the other to "span characteristics space", meaning to reach combinations of characteristics not possible by consuming single goods alone. His realization launched the field of home economics and sensitized economists to the reality beneath the appearance of products. A computer looks much the same as it did 30 years ago but its deeper characteristics have changed. This insight has had crucial ramifications for how we should measure economic progress and calculate price indices.

The third insight came with Sherwin Rosen. He warned that people can become trapped in characteristics space because of who they are. Before Rosen the standard view was that people weigh alternatives in the face of material constraints. The fallout is a shower of prices that equilibrate what people want with what others supply to them. All that matters is price. The identity of the buyer and seller do not matter to this outcome. The used-car dealer does not care whether a buyer is of noble ancestry or a vagrant. All that matters is what the buyer is willing to pay for his "pre-owned" vehicle. Similarly, the buyer does not care if the dealer walks to work, or rides a Bactrian camel. All he or she wants is a good deal.

Rosen showed that in some cases considerations of who the seller and buyer are become pivotal to whether a trade takes place and to the price. The importance of identity arises from the "tied" nature of exchanges in characteristics space. A tied exchange is one that implicates each party as a seller and a buyer at the same time. The young worker seeking a first job is not just selling his labor but also receiving on-the-job training from this employer. The sale of his labor is "tied" to his simultaneous receipt of training. The wage adjusts to compensate the employer for providing this service and by means of this "equalizing difference" the market clears. A government policy such as the minimum wage may not allow the worker to sufficiently compensate his employer through a lower wage. The result could be that either the employer seeks out people with previous experience or, if possible she simply reduces the level of on-the-job training she provides to the employee. Such an insight is not possible in the standard analysis of labor markets.

Another example of a tied sale is marriage. Both parties each desire a list of features in the other. Each feature is measured on a subjective scale and the set of such features situates the candidate as a "point" in characteristics space. If the points of the man and woman are too far apart (in traditional marriage), a money transfer such as a dowry or bride price may be the equalizing factor that closes the deal and leads to marriage.

The language may appear contrived, but the concept applies to disparate situations. Employers and employees also seek the right fit with each other; in that case, salary acts as a monetary equalizer that leads to an employment contract. Identity assumes importance in transactions because of the inability of the parties involved to "unbundle" the features that are important in the exchange. Cash then may overcome the distance and a deal is made. Sometimes though the list of tied characteristics is so long that no financial compensation can clear the market. Rosen's insight has surprising implications for government policies such as the minimum wage and anti-discrimination law, as well as for certain laws governing divorce.

I would be less than frank with you if I tried to pretend that all economists have enthusiastically made space an essential tool of their craft. They have not. The role of space in economics is recent. Despite some early enthusiasm, it has struggled to find a large following, though like an underground Pennsylvania coal fire it continues to smolder and threaten to erupt. Space, especially in the case of tied-sales, adds a complexity to models that many economists would rather not have to be bothered with. Yet in some cases it is the best way we have of understanding why people behave as they do and what the consequences of government intervention may be. For these reasons an understanding of space is necessary for anyone seeking to attain a mastery of economics. Let us examine how Hotelling, Lancaster, and Rosen essentially created the field.

Hotelling and the competitive continuum

IN HIS 1929 essay, "On the Stability of Competition", which is easy to read and as full of relevant insights today as it was nearly a hundred years ago, Harald Hotelling sought to understand why markets were far more stable than economists thought they should be.

According to accepted thinking the ability of consumers to switch brands posed a problem to the theory of collusion between small numbers of firms. If firms fixed prices then such price fixing could not be stable. Even the smallest price reduction by one firm cheating on the collusive agreement would instantly attract all consumers to the thrifty product. Other firms would lower the price until prices finally collapsed back to their free market level. Then collusion would raise them up again and price instability would plunge them down again, and so on. You see this sort of thing happening every day at rival gas pumps.

Hotelling wanted to understand why markets showed more stability in reality than in theory. His answer lay in the money it costs to travel to a market. Suppose you live in a one-street town where *Grandpa's Grocery* is located half-way between the center and the east side of the town, and *Farmgirl's Grocery* is half-way between the center and the west side. If you buy from either grocery then your time-cost of traveling has to be added to the market price of what you buy to come up with the full price. Some consumers live closer to *Grandpa's* than do others, so that their total costs are lower than those who live further away. *Grandpa's* has to be careful not to set prices too high. If *Grandpa's* price is greater than what it would cost his nearest consumer on the side of *Farmgirl's* to travel to *Farmgirl's* and bring back the rival product then *Grandpa's* would lose all its customers to the west of it. *Grandpa's* could gradually regain customers by lowering price and attracting those within a span where produce price plus travel cost to *Grandpa's* is lower than produce price and travel to *Farmgirl's*. The crucial insight here is that gradual changes in prices do not precipitate mass movements of consumers, but rather gradual movements. Hotelling saw in this inertia of consumer allegiance a source of stability in competition between firms. From this simple basis he was able to calculate the different prices that differently situated firms would charge for the same product.

These were not exactly earth-shaking discoveries. But Hotelling was just warming up. What if instead of being fixed in one place and varying price, firms could change their location? He showed that for a wide variety of scenarios, firms selling similar products would tend to cluster close to each other in order to protect themselves from "spatial competition" by other firms. If *Grandpa's* moves west to the center of the one-street town not only will it get all the business back eastward to its original destination, but also will attract half the customers who lie between *Grandpa's* new location and *Farmgirl's* location. To regain these businesses *Farmgirl's* must also set up shop in the center.

Here was a more interesting discovery, not only because it predicted how businesses would behave but also because it pointed to an inefficient aspect of competition. Consumers would save on travel costs if businesses selling the same product were uniformly spread out over the city. But if this were the case, any company, no matter where it was located, could always snatch away business by moving to the center. Hotelling proved mathematically, but it is not hard to intuit, that forcing all consumers to travel to the center makes the sum of travel costs exceed what it would be if businesses were uniformly distributed along the street. Perhaps this is why property developers do more than build houses. They also lobby municipalities for zoning laws that prevent businesses from excessive clustering.

Yet Hotelling's idea ran deeper than this. He conceived of space not simply in geographic terms but also as encompassing the features of a product. As he explained, "distance, as we have used it for illustration, is only a figurative term for a great congeries of qualities. Instead of sellers of an identical commodity separated geographically we might have considered two competing cider merchants side by side, one selling a sweeter liquid than the other" (1929, 54). He used his model to infer that competition in "sweetness space" would force both sellers to offer ciders of a sweetness situated such that half the number of consumers preferred a more sour product and half a sweeter product. This "median" sweet product might be to few people's liking, especially if tastes were evenly bunched up at extremes where many people enjoyed very sweet ciders and many enjoyed very sour ciders, with a sprinkling of people in between. The bulk of consumers would be best served by a sweet cider producer and a sour producer, but to capture the sprinkling of consumers between these extremes both producers would converge towards providing a product situated at the median of consumer tastes.

Hotelling lamented (1929, 54) that, "The tremendous standardization of our furniture, our houses, our clothing, our automobiles and our education are due in part to the economies of large-scale production, in part to fashion and imitation. But over and above these forces is the effect we have been discussing, the tendency to make only slight deviations in order to have for the new commodity as many buyers of the old as possible, to get, so to speak, between one's competitors and a mass of customers."

Had he been less busy railing against markets Hotelling might have extended his model just a little bit further to consider why, if consumers were being left high-and-dry by the inefficiencies of spatial competition, did not some clever businesses come up with a solution? The answer, which was within Hotelling's grasp, was that if the costs permitted, producers would differentiate their products into "lines" which spanned the characteristics space. So instead of choosing a point in characteristics space, the producer would spawn a variety of products to cover that space.

One should not take this as a critique of Hotelling. How much can we ask of a man who in an article of a few pages creates a new field in economics? I mention the example of product differentiation to illustrate how great economic models create insights. Often these models find some failing in the market. Then the model can be extended by asking how markets would react to correct the inefficiency. A good model will confirm what we see happening in the real world, something which Hotelling's model certainly does.

Hotelling's model not only clarified how people would compete in a spatial setting, but also challenged us to be creative in our conception of space. As an example of such creativity Hotelling mentioned in his article, almost as an afterthought, that his model could also be applied to political competition in "policy space". He thus was the first to propose a mathematical model of political equilibrium. Duncan Black (1948) and later Anthony Downs (1957) would elaborate on this insight to create the famous median voter model of politics. It was Hotelling's idea. And it really was just all about space.

Lancaster and characteristics space

THE SECOND EVOLUTION in spatial economics was due to Kelvin Lancaster. His insight was that the basic qualities that consumers seek could be manipulated by combining different products. Hotelling had not considered this possibility. He had been content to accept that one good provided one underlying feature that could be measured in characteristics space. Lancaster saw the matter in greater breadth. Dinner was not just food on a table. It was an attempt to manipulate the basic constituents of flavor and nutrition into a satisfying gastronomic experience. Being a good cook meant knowing that taste had several dimensions including sweet, salty, sour, and savory.

For a meal to be agreeable, it had to combine these elements of flavor and it also had to be easily digested, suggesting that nutritional dimensions such as greasiness, protein content, and temperature had to figure into the cook's understanding. These basic culinary entities could each be thought of as lying on a left-right scale, or space. The ideal meal, then, sought to combine these features by varying each one as precisely as possible. The challenge, though, is that the kitchen is not a laboratory where atoms and molecules can be precisely combined into new structures. In the kitchen you must combine ingredients that may each contain many of the features you are trying to fine tune. The tomatoes that go into pasta sauce give nutrition, but are acidic. Sugar must be added to moderate the sourness that comes with acid. The more ingredients at your disposal, the better able you are to fine-tune the six or seven basic characteristics of a good meal.

The point is actually more difficult to grasp than we first appreciate. Ingredients are an imperfect means to an end. Each ingredient contains different combinations of one or more and perhaps even all of the basic characteristics. By combining ingredients we enhance or blunt the effect of different characteristics in the final meal. The fixed composition of characteristics in the ingredients may never allow us to attain precisely the ideal mix of characteristics we seek. The skill of the cook is in combining the ingredients at his or her disposal in such a manner as to approach as closely as possible this ideal "point" in the multi-dimensional "gastronomic characteristics space".

In 1966, Kelvin Lancaster generalized this concept in a mathematical model that laid the basis for what is now known as home economics. The idea is to try to specify some domestic "production function" that shows how basic inputs, each with different amounts of the end-characteristics sought, can be combined to maximize some objective of the consumer. Production functions of course are not the only consideration.

You have also to consider the prices of the basic inputs. The most practical application of home economics comes in calculating the budget needed to keep a person acceptably fed. You need to tabulate the caloric, protein, fat, and vitamin content of hundreds of foods and find the combinations that yield the best mix of these characteristics for the lowest price. This is how armies have determined their menus, and while military fare may not be the most highly prized, it is at least following Lancaster's algorithm for the cost-minimizing combination of ingredients.

The ideology of constraints vs. preferences

THE NEED FOR Lancaster's approach to consumer theory was in a certain sense ideological, but not in any political sense. The ideology in question was the belief that as little appeal as possible should be made to the consumer's preferences, in trying to model how he or she would choose between goods. Preferences are not directly observable and as such should be invoked as seldom as possible when interpreting differences in consumer behavior. Since the only things we can directly observe are incomes and prices we should focus on these in tests of the validity of our theory of the consumer.

By seeing the ultimate object of consumption as characteristics and not goods Lancaster was introducing a new and, he hoped, measurable source of variation into the consumer model that could resolve some of its seeming weaknesses. Sometimes people seemed to consume more of one good even though neither its price nor their incomes had changed. The easy but untestable explanation was that preferences had changed. Lancaster's approach suggested we first look to see if the characteristics content of that good had changed. Maybe quality had gone up, and this was the explanation for the rise in demand. If you could measure quality you could apply some simple statistical analysis to see if variation in quality "explained" variation in demand.

Looking beneath the surface of goods to see where they were situated in characteristics space also inspired economists to rethink how economic progress should be calculated. If you compared just the price of a *PC* in 1981 to the price thirty years later, you might find that there had been a only slight drop. But a *PC* thirty years later was thousands of times more powerful than the original. Comparing apples and oranges is a weak metaphor to describe the problem. A more apt metaphor is comparing garden sheds and skyscrapers. The characteristics approach allows one to go beyond such metaphors so that comparisons can be made on the basis of numbers. The trick is to identify the characteristics relevant to the performance of a computer and see how their costs have fallen. Millions of operations per second used to be an important benchmark, but others, such as memory, can be imagined. If the price of a *PC* has remained constant over thirty years, but the number of operations has increased by a multiple of a thousand, then the price per calculation, which is the relevant characteristic, has fallen a thousand fold.

A new perspective of the meaning of price

ECONOMIST WILLIAM NORDHAUS explained the problem this way, "If we are to obtain accurate estimates of the growth of real incomes over the last century, we must somehow construct price indexes that account for the vast changes in the quality and range of goods and services that we consume, that somehow compare the services of horse with automobile, of Pony

Express with facsimile machine, of carbon paper with photocopier, of dark and lonely nights with nights spent watching television, and of brain surgery with magnetic resonance imaging" (1997, 30).

Nordhaus followed up on this insight by asking how changes in the quality of lighting had improved our material condition over the ages. Call it a character study of lighting. The relevant quality characteristic of visible light is the lumen. Wood fires are an inefficient means of generating lumens because of the large amount of energy needed to produce a lumen using this "technology". Candles are slightly more efficient and thus have a lower cost per lumen, but not by much.

The cost of generating lumens explains why through much of history people went to sleep at dusk and rose at dawn, and why streets were rarely lit. The invention of gas lighting vastly reduced the cost per lumen. The result was reduced street crime, a boom in the evening entertainment business, and factories and businesses that never ceased operating. Electric lighting led to further falls in the price of lumens to the point where at the end of the 20th century the price of a lumen was thousands of times less than what it would have been two hundred years earlier.

To help appreciate the importance of this insight, Nordhaus asked how much labor it would have taken for the average person to buy lighting in the past, and lighting in the present. He found that " ... one modern one-hundred-watt incandescent bulb burning for three hours each night would produce 1.5 million lumen-hours of light per year. At the beginning of the last century, obtaining this amount of light would have required burning seventeen thousand candles, and the average worker would have had to toil almost one thousand hours to earn the dollars to buy the candles" (1997, 50).

The practical lesson to be drawn from this fascinating study of lighting is that the way we measure the consumer price index is severely flawed. Instead of putting goods and their prices directly into the index we should reduce all goods to their constituent characteristics. Then we should evaluate how these good can best be combined to minimize the cost of consuming these characteristics. Such an approach would allow us to include new goods in the consumer price index without worrying about whether the index of today is comparable to that of ten years ago when the good did not exist. Such an approach would also allow governments to more precisely calculate the rate at which welfare and other forms of aid should be increased. At present such calculations tend to overestimate the cost of living because they do not take into account the manner in which increases in quality reduce the monetary cost of maintaining a certain standard of living.

While these may sound like important applications of Lancaster's approach, their adoption has been slow. Judging what the underlying characteristics of goods are is in part a subjective exercise. People prayed and still pray in front of candles. Few people I know pray in front of 20 watt, self-balasted, compact florescent bulbs. Do you include a spiritual component to lighting quality, and if you do, how should you measure it? Questions such as this one have denied in practice the ample promise that Lancaster's theory showed when he first introduced it.

Rosen and the equalizing difference

IN LANCASTER'S CHARACTERISTICS space, people have room to maneuver. Consumers combine goods representing a "vector of characteristics" while balancing costs to produce an amalgam of characteristics close to their desired point. In this manner they "span" characteristics space. In Lancaster's world, characteristics could be freely varied by combining goods in different proportions.

In his 1974 and 1986 articles Sherwin Rosen asked what would happen if you were limited in how you could move about through characteristics space. He pointed out that sometimes when buying a product with several underlying characteristics you could not just go out and span characteristics space by buying a bit of another product with the same characteristics but in different proportions. The reason was that sometimes when you buy something, you are selling something at the same time and are able to sell uniquely to one purchaser. Recombining goods to balance characteristics to suit your tastes is not possible. Rosen called such exchanges tied-sales.

The oldest kind of tied-sale in the world is marriage. Both parties to a marriage bring a bundle of characteristics to the bargaining table. Within the framework of economics each is selling himself or herself and buying something in the other partner simultaneously. If the characteristics balance each other the match may proceed. If not, then a dowry, or in the inverse case, a bride price may be required. Rosen called this cash emolument an "equalizing difference".

What is special about tied-sales is that who you are can matter as much to the sale as how much you pay. This forces tied-sales markets to work on two levels. First there is a matching problem to be solved, so that people with the most desirable exchange of characteristics find each other. But should these characteristics not balance each other, then on a second level an equalizing difference of cash is required. Rosen showed that tied-sales could lead to the segregation of people by their types. Segregation has a bad name, and justly so. But Rosen also argued that the worst effects of segregation could be palliated by a market that resolved supply and demand of complicated tied sales situations through a monetary payment he called an "equalizing difference".

Cyanide and gold

A SIMPLE BUT relevant example of how tied-sales trap people in characteristics space is that of a dirty job such as gold mining. Some mines use toxic cyanide to extract ore. Others use a simple non-toxic grinding and filtering method. Workers are all equally capable, but all differ in their tolerance for poisonous working conditions. Some mind quite a bit, others a bit less, and some not at all. Companies all differ in their costs of adopting the clean technology. Here is a labor market with a tied-sale. Workers sell their services to the mine, but at the same time the mine implicitly "sells" a certain level of cyanide toxins to the workers while buying their services. To entice workers to these sites, companies that use cyanide must offer a wage premium above that paid to miners working on clean sites. Rosen called this premium an "equalizing difference". Workers are the implicit purchasers of the disamenity, but unlike the market for goods that brings positive value to consumers, when the good in question is a disadvantage or hazard, the worker must be explicitly paid to "consume" it.

Most of those enticed to work at the dirty site will actually be paid more than what they would accept as minimum compensation because their distaste for pollution may be quite mild. Only the workers on the margin of indifference between clean and dirty jobs feel they get a compensation just equal to the disamenity they feel they suffer.

How much a mine is willing to pay workers to consume poison depends on how costly it is for the company to stop using cyanide and invest in clean technology. Some companies may find it too costly to operate a clean mine. Others may have an aptitude and skill for running a clean mine. Those firms for whom the wage premium is above the cost of cleaning will run clean mines and those for whom the wage premium is below cleaning costs will run dirty mines. As a result we have potentially different gold mines and workers. Some gold mines will decide to use cyanide techniques, and some miners will choose to work in the resulting poisoned environment. Other companies will decide to be clean and some workers will join them.

How does this sifting and segregation take place? Assume that workers all have the same skills so competition between them for jobs will ensure they all will get some base salary. At this base salary almost no one wants to work in a dirty job except the few workers for whom dirt is of no account. There is a surplus then of workers seeking clean jobs. To correct this imbalance firms with some dirt will bid up the premium. The premium will adjust until the group of high-tolerance workers are employed by the mines with high cleanup costs, and low-tolerance workers are employed in the clean mines, which end up selling cleanliness by not offering the wage premium. The premium helps to segregate workers according to their taste for pollution.

Technically, the level of segregation is efficient in the sense that it would be impossible to change the wage premium in such a way that any single firm or worker were made better off without making someone else worse off. Economists call this a "Nash equilibrium". On an intuitive level, the segregation is efficient because workers who do not mind toxins are paired off with companies who have a hard time cleaning it up, and people who mind toxins are paired with people who are good at cleaning it up. What in the end balances this sorting is the wage premium, which varies until everyone is matched up. Or you might use the word "segregated". Segregation of tolerant workers with dirty firms and intolerant workers with clean companies through the wage mechanism gets the toxin issue out of the way and allows the underlying labor market to compensate workers for their productive contributions.

Rosen's prime motivation for analyzing situations in which wages act as a balancing monetary component pertinent to a tied sale, was somewhat obscure. He was interested primarily in showing how to interpret impact factors or "regression coefficients" arising from efforts to see the connection between labor market disamenties and wage premiums. In order to correctly interpret the regression coefficient as the wage premium all workers require to be just sufficiently compensated for a little bit more of the disamenity, they basically had to all have the same distaste for it. That seems quite obvious. But Rosen went on to use his model to show how, when workers differ in their preferences, the economist could still draw meaning from the regression coefficient, as either an upper or lower bound on the equalizing difference.

While this might at first glance seem like the musings of an overspecialized economist, Rosen's work was in fact of key importance to the field of cost-benefit analysis. It pointed the way to evaluating the benefits of government interventions that reduced the suffering from industrial pollution. Rosen's method could also be used to evaluate how much people would pay to avoid having to bear a small risk to their lives. This came to be misnamed as the "value of life", but despite the nomenclature is of vital importance in evaluating the benefits from government infrastructure projects such as road improvements, that make roads safer. His method of analysis also had a huge impact on understanding how labor markets, and any other types of markets requiring tied sales worked. These insights can be unusual and provocative and force us to reconsider common perceptions about how government can fruitfully intervene in tied-sales exchanges. Let us examine these situations more closely.

Equalizing differences and segregation

EVEN THOUGH THE labor market tries to cope with the tied-sale through a wage premium it would be better for society if someone invented a costless way of eliminating the toxic by-products of gold mining and allowed the market for labor to proceed unhampered by the tied-sale.

I mean "society" in the following sense. Companies that were previously polluting would not have to pay a wage premium, while those that were clean would not have to pay cleanup costs. Not everyone would be happy with this change. Some "infra-marginal" workers in the polluting industry who had a high tolerance for pollution were earning more than they needed to be compensated to continue in their jobs. In fact, most workers in the toxic mines were better off with pollution than without it because the compensating wage premium rises until it just barely compensates the most reluctant worker to enter a toxic mine.

Anyone who has worked in some northern wasteland on a oil rig knows this. Provided you are hearty, job conditions do not matter much to you and you rejoice at the wage premium. That premium exists to draw in those extra workers the company needs but who have no stomach for the work. The premium the hearty worker receives is a pure bonus or "rent" as economists call it. The example illustrates why economists are so finicky about the distinction between margins and averages. The wage premium in the market adjusts until the last worker drawn into the toxic mines is "at the margin of indifference" between that and a clean job. Those "infra-marginal" workers already drawn to dirty mines have a higher average tolerance for pollution, and thus earn on average "rents" from the wage premium. While these workers would lose out from the disappearance of pollution, their loss would exactly be balanced by the gain of previously polluting companies who no longer have to pay a wage premium.

So far then, the exercise is a financial wash. The net gain to society comes from clean companies who previously were cleaning their mines. If the new technology allows costless elimination of pollution then these companies would save and that would also represent a net savings for society. I keep talking about "society" because economists are interested in how human behavior adds to the pile of real wealth in the world. While the wealth may belong to individuals, it still represents an accretion for the society in which they dwell and as such may be accessed by that society through taxation.

Barring the invention of a costless means of cleaning pollution, a wage premium that matches preferences for cleanliness with abilities to clean up toxic sites is a limited but elegant response to the problem of the tied-sale of work and pollution, for it allows demand and supply to equilibrate. Without the wage premium, firms with low pollution costs and workers with high tolerance would not be able to exploit their abilities to clean and tolerate. Clean and dirty jobs would now look the same to workers and companies. What might equilibrium look like in such a case? Well, if the wage cannot vary with the pollution workers with low tolerance for toxins would keep knocking on doors of businesses they knew to be efficient cleaners. They would lobby for a position because short of that, they would have nothing to distinguish them from an identically skilled worker with a high tolerance for toxic waste. Lobbying is no guarantee of getting a job but the effort invested would be like money spent buying lottery tickets. Similarly, companies with high cleaning costs would solicit high tolerance workers to come work for them. It is possible to prove that an equilibrium, with the same degree of segregation as in the wage premium case would emerge. In other words, "things" would get "sorted out".

The difference from the case where equalizing differences were possible would be that in the sorting, the effort to lobby would chew up or "dissipate" resources through the competitive lottery to find a job or hire a worker. Without the wage differential the simple process of achieving an equilibrium solely through matching would call for a huge and wasteful expenditure of resources on lobbying.

Here is a hint of the wisdom of spatial analysis. In tied-sales, any sort of government attempt to control prices may have unexpected and unpleasant consequences. This is not an indictment of government but rather the reverse. Intelligent intervention requires an appreciation for the subtleties of markets, and in these, spatial analysis abounds.

Racism and the dissipation of wealth

IN THE CASE of the gold mine, workers have preferences for certain employers that go beyond the wages paid. We can also see this play of preferences at work in the case of racial discrimination. When racism is at work the employer prefers a type of worker that has nothing to do with that worker's productivity but rather with the worker's race. What emerges from this toxic brew of hatred is a wage premium for the favored racial group. But racism in the market sort of meets its match at the margin when the wage premium starts making some employers with a lower taste for the favored group consider the attractiveness of hiring equally productive members of the despised group. As in the case of mines, an equalizing difference in wages emerges that sorts favored workers with employers who have a strong taste for them, and despised workers with employers who don't mind them so much.

Here, as with miners toiling in environments contaminated by cyanide, the wage premium allows everyone to find work quite easily but in a segregated setting. Yet racial discrimination is a bad thing, just as is cyanide pollution. What if we pass a law saying that everyone must be paid the same wage? Now companies with a taste for racism cannot use a premium to attract favored workers and firms that previously were not racist have no financial reason to hire members of the despised group. But racism has not disappeared. The racist group may use informal means, such as lobbying favored workers to join their firm. And non-racist companies may now hire members of the favored group because there is no wage discount to entice them to prefer members of the despised group. This may force members of the despised group themselves to actively lobby non-racist companies to hire them.

The result of all this lobbying may result in the depressing outcome that the same old segregation emerges. In addition to which no one will be better off than before. Racist companies will have dissipated in lobbying expenses the premium they once paid favored workers, and despised workers will have expended the windfall from the new equal wage they are earning on efforts to gain employment.

This example shows that space and tied-sales have the makings of a curse. Remedies we apply may work against our best intentions. Hope may lie in education and research that reduce the dimension of these spaces by cleansing hatred from the heart and pollution from the workplace.

The curse of dimensionality

IF YOU THOUGHT space was a curse in one dimension, such as racism or pollution, imagine how bad its effects can be when both employees and employers have a list of demands for the other.

In deciding where to work, a teacher will not just care about salary but also about the quality of the school's students and its amenities. Schools care how well a teacher educates. This may depend not just on his or her abilities as vouched for by testimonials and degrees earned but also on the types of students he or she will be teaching. How well that teacher interacts with a particular school's students will depend on his or her age, ethnicity, sex, and potentially many other factors which may only be of particular interest to that school, such as perhaps a tolerance for lack of discipline.

Rosen explained the problem as follows: "While teachers may have well defined preferences for schools and students of various characteristics, it is also true that schools may well have distinct preference for various types of teachers and their attributes. The matching problem is therefore more complicated ..." (1986, 664). To clear this market, there must be a separate wage premium, or "equalizing difference" for each possible combination of dimensions which matter to teachers and schools. The simplest case is that of predominantly black or white schools in the US and the salaries they pay to black or white teachers. There are four possible wage situations here. White teachers and white schools may have a preference for each other, yet there may be too few white teachers to fill all the posts so black teachers with a preference for black schools may have to be attracted by a wage premium. This drives up wages in black schools which must fill their need for teachers, so some white teachers on the margin of indifference between teaching in black or white schools may be attracted away from white schools. In the end, both black and white schools will have mixes of black and white teachers, and any teacher of one race will have to be paid a different premium to teach in a school of different race. The degree of mixing may be quite limited if teachers interact poorly with students of different race and have strong preferences for teaching students of their own race. Of course the same problem was evident in the case of racism in hiring decisions, but there was "only" the racial preference of the employer to contend with.

When racial considerations by both employers and employees must be considered, the conundrum of clearing the market swells. Wage premiums may have to be large in order to clear the teaching market. These may kill off schools and leave teachers unemployed as the racial factors involved in the tied-sale may be so varied that there is no market clearing price for teachers of one race in schools of another race.

Such is the curse of dimensionality in space. As more features figure in the tied-sale, wages progressively lose their ability to make markets clear. That means personal characteristics become the only features that matter regarding where you work and whom you wish to work for. The price of such indulgence of preferences can be foregone productivity, as people who could be a productive asset in one business are blocked by prejudice. Our preferences balkanize us instead of uniting us.

As we can see, space is an unwelcome relative in the family of economic concepts. It can make nonsense of the most reasonable propositions. It can also lead to surprising conclusions about government policies that show contemporary economic sages in a diminished light.

Curving economic space

ONE SUCH SURPRISING application arises in the labor market. Some jobs are about more than just wages. Workers are not simply selling their labor. They are also buying certain desirable on-the-job amenities such as child-care, comfortable parking, and cafeteria services. They "purchase" these amenities by providing employers with desirable qualifications and perhaps by accepting a wage that is below what they contribute to the company's profits. The sales are "tied" because they are an inseparable part of working in the chosen firm.

One of the most studied aspects of tied labor market transactions is the value of on-the-job training for young, low-wage workers. In pre-industrial times apprentices valued this training so much that they paid their employers for the privilege of working the seven years it took to become certified in a trade. Even the young James Watt, later the inventor of the modern steam engine, trudged all over Scotland and England in a desperate attempt to find someone willing to train him in the trade of scientific tool-making. Today schools have assumed the task of teaching trades. Yet one can still detect an echo of this process in medicine, last of the surviving secretive medieval trade-protection organizations. Interns work like serfs in the expectation of princely salaries to follow.

Apprentices and budding physicians are not the only ones who benefit from on-the-job training. The same can be said of young, low-wage workers. Firms may be willing to take them on and train them up provided that they can be compensated for their efforts. Young workers will compete for jobs that teach general skills by offering their services at a wage sufficiently low to compensate employers for the learning experience. Finnis Welch wrote that "since workers can take the benefits of training with them when they leave for other employment, firms may have little incentive to offer training. But they can offer on-the-job training in exchange for lower wages" (1978, 31-32).

The reason such training is of necessity to a tied-sale is that not everything can be learned in the classroom. Sherwin Rosen explains that "It is a common observation that most specific job skills are learned from work activities themselves. Formal schooling complements these investments, both by setting down a body of general knowledge and principles for students as well as teaching them how to learn. But even in the case of professional training there is no perfect substitute for apprenticeship and for work experience itself" (1986, 677). There is no educational substitute for elbow grease.

Into this discussion, add the minimum wage. Few people, even few economists, associate this seemingly humanitarian government policy with worker training. Yet a bit of reflection clarifies that in the tied-sales environment of the workplace the minimum wage may rob workers of the chance to learn job skills that could raise them out of poverty. As Sherwin Rosen has explained,

> An effective minimum wage puts a distinct ceiling on the worker's ability to pay for on-the-job training, and this constraint is more binding the lower the worker's productivity ... Minimum wage legislation not only denies on-the-job training opportunities for those

who are displaced from employment, but also constrains young workers' access and opportunity to those work environments with intensive training and learning components (1986, 680).

The logic is that when the minimum wage rises it creates among workers an excess demand for on-the-job training. At current levels of training the minimum wage effectively reduces what workers must implicitly pay through an equalizing difference in their remuneration. With this excess demand, firms can to some degree "curve" characteristic space by reducing the amount of training their jobs offer. With sufficient flexibility to curve this space, the supply of workers equilibrates with the demand by businesses. Put less technically, if government mandates that you be paid a great deal to do a job which is basically a form of education and stepping stone for other jobs then you can expect that many outsiders will try to compete for your position. These competitors may be willing to accept less on-the-job training than are you. Companies will oblige them and you will be obliged also to accept less on-the-job training.

This complicated view of labor markets may help to explain a finding that crops up now and then. Minimum wages do not seem to lower employment in some cases. According to *Economics 101* when the price of something rises people demand less of it. If you raise the wage, the price of labor, employers should demand less of it. But some serious examination of real-life data shows that this is not so in some cases. Which is not to say that the minimum wage has no effect on equilibrium in labor markets. What it means, as seen through the lens of Rosen's model, is that we must realize that the employer has a certain degree of control over the job characteristic which is being implicitly purchased, namely training. This control allows firms to clear markets with fixed minimum wages by lowering training. Conventional economic theory argues that such markets will not clear because the minimum wage should create a surplus of workers. The tied-sales view of the labor market suggests that the action lies elsewhere. Minimum wages have unfortunate consequences where they are least expected. They reduce on-the-job training for the young.

Married in space

WHERE YOU FIT as a person in characteristics space is a central determinant of whom you will marry. In a marriage each partner is simultaneously providing the other with positive and negative features while receiving in return positive and negative features from the other. If the features do not balance, the marriage may not take place unless some residual cash payment is made to equalize the remaining differences.

In the distant past in Western countries, and in some countries today, if in addition to housekeeping, a woman had good breeding potential she could command a "bride price". This cash exchange would compensate her family for the genetic bonus of having produced a daughter deemed to be fertile. The letters between Lorenzo de Medici and his mother in the 15th century speak of potential brides as being "comely", having good hair, teeth, posture, and thus being worthy of sharing in the family fortune in exchange for producing heirs. Inversely, women deemed less desirable would have to compensate the groom with a dowry. The equalizing cash difference in these cases helps to clear the "marriage market". This type of market leads to a segregation of highly fertile women with men who have a strong preference for such unions and the ability to pay for them. Less fertile women pair off with older men or men with less economic potential. Just as in the labor market for mines, the equalizing difference allows some accommodation between unequally matched people who nonetheless are not too far off in what they are seeking from each other. The factor of accommodation is the equalizing cash difference.

Looking at marriage in this light may seem antiquated but alerts us to the unexpected consequences of government intervention in this most intimate of markets. Until the 1950s, divorce was difficult to obtain in Western countries. Opponents of divorce believed it would lead to the downfall of the family. The economics of space predicted otherwise. Suppose the liberalization of divorce law tempts the wife to leave the union because over time she has grown dissatisfied with the initial matching and the bride price her parents negotiated for her. Under threat of divorce the wife may insist that the husband change his ways. This means bending his characteristics space by perhaps slimming his belly, or taking anger management classes. If he finds himself too set in his ways to curve space, he may compensate the wife with extra money for her family or for her personal needs and desires. Thus liberal divorce law may not lead to the breakdown of the family, but rather to a redistribution of resources within it. We can only understand this possibility by looking at marriage as a spatial matching problem resolved by the addition of an equalizing cash payment to make up for unequally matched characteristics.

This economic view of marriage is complementary to the romantic view. A tenet of romance is that the characteristics of the person should be of secondary importance. What matters is the person inside. Romance is a meeting of spirits. Seen from an economic perspective the spiritual dimension is supposed to fill the gap left by an awkward matching of beauty and beast. Yet when you take an equalizing cash payment out of the calculation, beauty and beast may remain single. The gap in physical and mental characteristics may be so large that qualities of spirit are not able to bridge the gap between partners. That is the economic view based on the immutability of who we are. Perhaps the staggering sums people invest in transforming their bodies through exercise, steroids, and surgical interventions, and the rise of the cult of mental and spiritual self-improvement are attempts to bend characteristics space in an effort to attain true spiritual union between partners. These expenditures may be seen as a reaction to the collapse of the age-old marriage market in which all such disparities could be overcome through simple cash payments.

The final frontier

I BEGAN WITH a story so kindly allow me to end with one. In 1963 Martin Luther King gave his famous "I have a dream" speech in which he said "The marvelous new militancy which has engulfed the Negro community must not lead us to distrust of all white people, for many of our white brothers, as evidenced by their presence here today, have come to realize that their destiny is tied up with our destiny. They have come to realize that their freedom is inextricably bound to our freedom. We cannot walk alone. And as we walk, we must make the pledge that we shall march ahead. We cannot turn back."

King's speech actually came at a time when African-Americans had improved their lot steadily since *WWII* by moving from southern states, where the spirit of discrimination was strong, to northern states where it was weaker. Many occupations were segregated, but that was changing as migration allowed for a better match of "tied-sales" between minority employees and employers who did not mind hiring minorities. To complete the match, labor markets adjusted salaries in such a way that a wage premium or "equalizing difference" was being paid to whites. Discrimination existed even in Northern states. There was only so much that migration could do to narrow the discriminating wage premium.

King and other social reformers can be seen as wishing to eliminate and thus in a sense "untie" the racial component from labor market exchanges through a campaign of education and persuasion. Their approach to tied-sales may depart from the neutral stance that economists try to adopt concerning people's preferences, but King had the right idea. Changing preferences is one of several ways to overcome the matching problem in markets with tied-sales. King's vision can be seen as a sort of psychological technology which eliminates counterproductive criteria for matching, thereby making exchanges easier to conclude.

A complementary approach is to physically untie criteria from the match. This does not mean altering preferences but rather coming up with some means of physically separating elements in the tied-sale from each other. This is clearly difficult if you have a taste for hiring a particular racial group. But it is feasible in the case of a parent wishing to work at a business that has a daycare. If daycare can be subcontracted to a separate business economically and thus removed from the employment contract it no longer becomes a factor that might thwart a match between employers and employee.

The separation of functions allows firms to concentrate on what they do best and allows for the tightest fit between employee aptitudes and the company's ability to channel those aptitudes to productive ends. A "socially conscious" enterprise that acts as a caterer to the varied life-tastes of its employees is actually doing a disservice to all. For in attempting to be all things to all employees it provides social services at excessive cost by diverting its efforts from its core competencies and mis-directing them towards the administration of diaper change stations and meditation classes. If a company is able to eliminate all tied aspects of the hiring decision then the equalizing difference has no further role to play in equilibrating labor markets. It is a goal towards which all forms of tied exchange should strive.

That is the dream of those working on the economics of space.

References

Black, Duncan. 1948. "On the Rationale of Group Decision." *Journal of Political Economy*, volume 56:23-34.

Downs, Anthony. 1957. *An Economic Theory of Democracy.* New York.

Hotelling, Harold. 1929. "Stability in Competition." *The Economic Journal*, volume 39: 41-57.

Lancaster, Kelvin J. 1966. "A New Approach to Consumer Theory." *The Journal of Political Economy*, volume 74: 132-156.

Nordhaus, William D. 1997. "Do Real Output and Real Wage Measures Capture Reality? The History of Light Suggests Not." *The Economics of New Goods.* Edited by Robert J. Gordon and Timothy F. Bresnahan. University of Chicago Press for the National Bureau of Economic Research. 27-70.

Rosen, Sherwin. 1974. "Hedonic Prices and Implicit Markets: Product Differentiation in Pure Competition." *Journal of Political Economy*, volume 82: 34-55.

Rosen, Sherwin. 1986. "The Theory Of Equalizing Differences." *Handbook of Labor Economics, Volume I.* Edited by Orley Ashenfelter and Richard Layard. Elsevier Science Publishers. 641-692.

Welch, Finnis. 1978. "The Rising Impact of Minimum Wages." *Regulation*, volume 28: 28-37.

EQUILIBRIUM 6

THE CONCEPT OF EQUILIBRIUM MOST likely originated in the sciences. In physics, discussions of equilibrium arose in the 19th century in the subfield of thermodynamics. A thermodynamic equilibrium is attained when a system of atoms has become so randomly dispersed that no further work can be squeezed out of them. The atoms may knock about but not in any manner that can be channeled to some specific use. Equilibrium in this context is generally a description of sterility or "system-death". In the life sciences equilibrium is considered a temporary state in which nature is preparing some burst of creative energy that will carry it to a different state. Such equilibria are considered rare. Biologists prefer to look at nature as a process that rarely settles down to some fixed relationship between organisms. Despite these differences, both sciences see equilibrium as a group phenomenon. In physics the group is made of atoms, planets, and even galaxies attracting and repelling each other, while in biology, groups of one or several life-forms interact.

Economic equilibrium is also a group phenomenon, but it differs from the types found in physics or biology. Humans are not atoms nor rigidly programmed life-forms. They do not drift aimlessly, nor are they ruled by instinctive programs as are animals. They are conscious of the best way to take advantage of the present, and they dwell on the future. What they do with this consciousness is to seek some acceptable balance in their dealings with others. It is this search for balance that pushes groups of people to attain a type of equilibrium distinct from that found in the sciences. In physics equilibrium is a state of dissipation. In economics equilibrium is an optimal state, or at least a state that strives towards an optimum. This optimum engages all individuals and stands or falls on whether a sufficient number of them find the ledger of "social accounts" to be in some acceptable balance.

The quest to define and understand equilibrium in economics is the culmination of a research program begun with a radically different emphasis by Greek philosophers. Plato and his followers sought to define how social accounts should be arranged so that people can live in harmony. I am not sure if he ever used the word equilibrium but it cannot have been far from his thoughts. Starting with Adam Smith in the 18th century economists, or rather proto-economists who called themselves political philosophers, sought not to dictate how society should work but to understand how it does work.

The agenda of economists ever since has been to divine what accounting systems societies use to coordinate the actions of their members so as to attain a degree of stability and perhaps even prosperity. The accounting system now most widely accepted in economics is that of market supply, demand, and the equilibrium between the two brought about by the movement of prices.

Equilibrium may seem like a dry topic to a non-economist but only because economists have not sung their own praises sufficiently. Market equilibrium, and the criterion economists have invented to evaluate its worth, so-called Pareto efficiency, are discoveries that allow us to make sense of and evaluate the actions and interactions of the many. The Greeks would have marveled at this coherent, powerful intellectual device for peering into the workings of society. While market equilibrium is not the only possible accounting system upon which societies may be based, those wishing to propose alternate systems should take note. A thorough understanding of markets and the equilibrium that emerges is basic training to would-be social engineers as well as to those who would oppose them.

Balancing social accounts

BALANCE IN SOCIAL accounts may be the basis of equilibrium, but what do "balance", and "accounts" mean? One view of societies is that they are groups of people bound together by a mixture of agreement, force, convention, and necessity. If the bonds are strong enough to keep the group together then society may be displaying a form of equilibrium.

The individual parts each have a role to play. In every person's mind there is a calculator that tallies what he or she does for others and what others do for her or him. The calculation is personal, and may change as one matures and learns to count one's blessings and forgive transgressions. Forgiveness is an instant means of balancing this mental ledger. Yet at any given moment the balance may be in the red. The world has harmed you. Friends betrayed you. Customers owe you money. If you see no balance ever coming back into your account you may either choose to "make an end with a bare bodkin" as Shakespeare put it, or if you are in a more proactive mindset you "stiffen the sinews, summon up the blood, and lend the eye a terrible aspect." In other words, get mad.

If social accounts then are in people's heads and are subjective, can economists have anything to say about them? It turns out that economists' mathematical models of equilibrium are in fact tools for imagining how social accounts are balanced

under very specific conditions, known today as "market economics". These tools, which we will examine in detail can trace
their lineage back to a time when market relations did exist
but were not widespread. One of the earliest statements of
the need for a balancing formula in relations between people
comes 3000 years ago from Rabbi Hillel. In my book *Pareto's
Republic*, I wrote:

> The Pharisaic rabbi Hillel the Elder had such a formula in mind
> when he stated that "What is hateful to you, do not do to your
> neighbour: that is the whole Torah, the rest is commentary." This
> was a very precise mathematical statement of social obligations.
> It sought perfect balance in every exchange of effort or resources
> between people. Perfect balance meant you did not take advantage
> of someone when he or she was down to buy his or her farm at a
> depressed price. Hillel's balance was a strict and highly specific
> formula for human interaction. Rabbi Hillel's rule for balance in
> social interactions was one of many variants on what has come to
> be known as the Golden Rule. (2011, 7)

Golden Rule societies were small groups of people who were
able to maintain cohesion as long as everyone contributed to
the others in the group by at least as much as she or he got.
There was often no need of a market or money or prices. In
small, tightly knit societies, people helped each other infor-
mally in a self-balancing act of long-term social preservation.
The neighbor, the village gossip, the *paterfamilias*, all were the
agents enforcing due diligence in social accounts. Opprobrium
attached to those who failed to contribute their fair share.

Golden Rule balance or "equilibrium" in social accounts
may have seemed a reasonable way for people to get along but
such accounting had a limitation. It could not be easily scaled

up to large, fast moving, anonymous collections of people. A new system of accounts had to be invented to help large numbers of people who did not know each other intimately to come to some agreement on how to use resources. Without such a mechanism of coordination, societies could not grow.

From central control to markets

WORKING OUT THE details of mass coordination through social accounting took thousands of years and went through false starts. Until a few hundred years ago, in the West the dominant model was to have a ruling military or priestly nobility dictate the terms of the accounts, that is, who should get what in return for what. A scribal bureaucracy helped verify that all was in balance. Egypt was able to subsist along these lines for over 4000 years because of the precise accounting possibilities inherent in a knowledge of the Nile. Knowing the relationship between the height of the river in any given season and the crops that could be expected to grow, Egyptian administrators were able to "tax to the max" and still keep the class of farmers just at the subsistence level needed to avoid rebellion. Similar examples of "hydraulic despotism" based on precise crop yield calculation can be found in ancient Mesopotamia and China.

Despite their longevity, all of these societies were highly unstable. There was a lack of surplus production that could be used to cushion unforeseen imbalances in the social accounts. When invaders attacked from outside the kingdom and overwhelmed the coercive capacities of the ruling class, servile classes often took the opportunity to rebel and go on the rampage. The result would be plunder and chaos by disparate groups who were not bound by social accounts. It could take generations to re-establish an equilibrium along the old lines, usually with different rulers. Ancient Rome seemed free from these problems for a while but the stability had an expiry date built into it. Rome balanced its social accounts on a constant diet of genocidal conquest. Some historians estimate that Caesar killed a million Gauls and enslaved a further million, effectively wiping out the young male population of what we now know as France. Tiberius did much the same to the Pannonians when they troubled Rome along the eastern stretch of the Danube. When Rome could push no further into barbarian lands it cannibalized itself by poaching slaves from among the free populations of its own provinces. Punitive taxes and debasement of the currency were further attempts by the ruling classes to patch up social accounts.

Christianity arose as a parallel to the Roman Empire and eventually evolved into a competing system of social accounting. It touched on most aspects of communal and even personal life. In serving as a model for the types of governments that would come after the Empire collapsed it attempted to moderate the depredations of rulers. In this sense Christianity was similar to Confucianism which arose in China to inculcate in the mandarinate a sense of social conscience.

Despite its novelty, Christianity did little more than breathe new life into the age-old model of central economic control of resources. Markets did exist, but for standard items such as wheat, wine, and wool. The really big decisions calling for imagination, such as property development, irrigation, education, and even what you could do with your labor, came from a small ruling elite. This elite looked with a worried eye on markets. Commerce was generally done outside the structure of social accounts dominated by military aristocracies. Even more troubling was the slow realization that the social accounts being balanced through markets were radically different from those balanced through central control. Markets worked on the principle of private property held by many different individuals. In deciding what to do with this property these individuals were creating a decentralized form of resource allocation.

Decentralized resource allocation through trade in property remained a marginal activity until about the 18th century. Then a series of administrative innovations allowed governments to accord private property the legal protection it needed to become a viable, large-scale tool of social accounting. The social accounting resulting from the trade in property allowed disparate individuals, perhaps even in different countries, to borrow money against their property and invest in large-scale ventures such as building toll roads or canals. You did not need to know who these people were, and you did not need to trust them as you would have to in a Golden Rule society, because property was starting to carry with it the systematic legal protection which today we call the rule of law.

In its ideal form, rule of law is the principle that the law should be knowable, constant, and the same for each person. Constancy means that if your business partner embezzles funds you can expect the court to apply the same punishment as it has applied to other such cases in the past. Similarity means that the judge will weigh your arguments against your partner as it would weigh his or her arguments against you should he have been the one bringing the suit.

What it amounts to in practice is a system of social accounting in the spirit of the Golden Rule that provides certainty and eliminates arbitrary advantage by treating all in the same manner. The importance of this system of accounts is that it is self-equilibrating on a case-by-case basis. If you buy a house that is deficient you can be certain of the redress you can seek, and you can be confident that the seller cannot crush your case by coercing the judge. Equilibration takes place without the need for guidance by a superior power. Rule of law enables imbalances in social accounting to fix themselves.

The shift to rule of law immensely broadens the scope of partners with whom you can engage. No longer must you know someone for years nor live in the same community to carry out balanced exchanges. Under rule of law you can be confident of mutual gain not because a Golden Rule is being followed but because the rule of law protects you against imbalance in social accounts. It is a mechanism for social accounting ideally suited to the needs of fast-growing societies where people are strangers to one another.

Pareto efficiency

ECONOMISTS ONLY STARTED to think conceptually about the manner in which markets equilibrate social accounts towards the end of the 18th century and systematically at the end of the 19th.

Between these intellectual bookends the field belonged mostly to philosophers. They sought utopian methods of social accounting in which the decentralized function of the market and rule of law was eliminated or heavily influenced by a powerful central mind. Amongst them the Utilitarians felt that the best society was one that maximized the sum of well-being.

This sounded nice on the surface but what it really meant was that social accounts achieved their balance by favoring some people who derived greater pleasure from a certain allocation of resources at the expense of others who were judged to suffer less pain. Marxists took a parallel line to Utilitarians and developed a form of social accounting in which it was acceptable to extirpate a group deemed to be outside the accounting structure, such as the bourgeoisie. Marxists tended to favor a group known as the proletariat.

The type of social accounting implicit in the market exchange of private property under the rule of law differed from these utopian systems in that it did not require a central authority to bully disenfranchised classes into compliance. Market exchange was decentralized and voluntary. Each exchange was balanced, as it only took place if both parties saw some benefit to it. Balancing each change in the use of resources at the individual level guarantees balance at the societal level. This realization captivated some thinkers from the late 19th century who saw in markets a basis for the emergence of the harmonious self-organization of society, a completely new way of thinking about human groups.

The first really precise statement of decentralized balance in social accounts is due to Vilfredo Pareto, a 19th century locomotive engineer who in middle-age hung up his railway man's cap to embark upon one of the most unlikely and remarkable careers in the social sciences. An allocation of resources is Pareto-improving if it harms no one and benefits at least one person. This is a bit vague, so in practice economists view a Pareto-improving change in the way resources are used as one which does not damage or violate the property rights of others without their consent and possibly payment of compensation. But such details need not concern us here. All we need to keep in mind is that once all Pareto-improving uses of resources have been discovered and exploited a state of Pareto efficiency is reached. No opportunity has been overlooked that will provide mutual gain without harming some third party.

As a form of social accounting the Pareto criterion seems quite easy for people of any political leaning to accept. After all, who can object to some use of resources that hurts no one and potentially makes some people better off? Perhaps sensing the broad appeal of his concept, Pareto attempted, with partial success, to prove that free markets were efficient, thereby producing a socially balanced and even desirable use of resources. His efforts launched a research agenda which is one of the most remarkable in the social sciences and which was only brought to fruition in the middle of the 20th century. To see how we came to understand the emergence and merits of social accounting through market equilibrium we need to look with a more focused gaze on how economists conceive of equilibrium.

Market equilibrium

MARKET EQUILIBRIUM IS the result of two distinct groups reacting in opposite ways to the shared stimulus of the same prices. Opposites may attract but in equilibrium it is more precise to say that people with opposite reactions can be driven in the same direction depending on where they stand. Suppose buyers of some product find its price to be too high. "Too high" means that at the going price those buyers will not buy and suppliers are stuck with unsold stock. To empty their warehouses suppliers must drop the price of this product. As prices fall some consumers buy more. Meanwhile, at the other end of the market, as prices fall some suppliers become less inclined to offer for sale large quantities of the product. For a few, selling the product even becomes unprofitable. The fall in price drives consumers and producers from the opposite sides of too little demand and too much supply towards a fixed point at which there is no further shortage in demand nor excess of supply.

The fixed point towards which markets gravitate is what economists call market equilibrium. It unites consumers who are most willing to pay for a product in an exchange with the most efficient (meaning lowest-cost) producers. If the situation were otherwise the market would not be in equilibrium. If, at the going price, a high-cost producer is selling while a lower-cost producer sits idle, something is wrong. The lower-cost producer should be able to out-compete and oust from the market the less efficient rival. On the other side of this market divide something is wrong if a consumer willing to pay only a little buys the product while a consumer willing to pay more is kept from making a transaction. Here the consumer with greater willingness to pay should be able to express his or her superior willingness to pay with money and displace the less enthusiastic buyer. As we can see, markets tend toward equilibrium because they are sorting devices; they match up people who have the greatest ability to satisfy each other.

By uniting consumers willing to pay the most cash with producers able to offer the product at the lowest cost, markets move to an equilibrium which is Pareto efficient. A market attains Pareto efficiency if no further shuffling of resources between people would raise the well-being of at least one person without violating the use, right to revenues from, and right to modify features of their own property. At the equilibrium price there is no potential buyer willing to pay sufficiently more to make an actual buyer part with his purchase. Nor is there a firm outside of those presently producing with sufficiently low costs to entice new buyers at the equilibrium price.

Pareto efficiency does not mean markets produce the greatest good for the greatest number of people. It does not conform to utopian notions of who should get the spoils of life. Pareto efficiency in market exchange is simply the result of people being allowed to buy, sell, or barter their property under the rule of law. It is efficient in the sense that each person seeks to sell or buy in a way that brings him or her the most benefit without violating anyone else's right to property and people continue buying and selling until there are no further possible mutual gains from exchange. There are no "big bills" left on the pavement.

The efficiency of equilibrium

THE ASSERTION THAT market equilibrium is Pareto efficient initially relied on verbal explanations. Pareto was among the first of a long line of economists who were not satisfied with describing the situation in words. Proof had to come from mathematics. Market relations were amenable to mathematics because they could be summarized neatly in equations generally described as "reaction functions". These functions are more popularly known as supply and demand equations.

Demand shows the quantity consumers will want of something at a given price. Supply shows the quantity of something that producers will make. By using the high-school technique of solving two linear equations in two unknowns (demand and supply, quantity and price), economists can find the price at which demand and supply equal each other. Even for non-linear curves the exercise is not usually more complicated.

The simplicity of finding the theoretical price that equilibrates the supply and demand equations hides how broad yet compact this form of social accounting is. Thousands of people, each with varying means and desires and abilities, make up an economy. Yet demand and supply equations completely compress or "encapsulate", to use the expression coined by Makowski and Ostroy (1992), all this human variety into a few equations. Using encapsulation, economists are able to prove the two "welfare theorems". We have already worked our way through the first theorem in our discussion of the efficiency of competitive equilibrium. In this first theorem encapsulation gives economists the precise tools for determining how much output will be produced at what cost and also the value people will place on consuming this output. By comparing the equilibrium pattern of production and consumption with other possible non-equilibrium patterns they can produce an elegant mathematical proof that only competitive equilibrium is Pareto efficient. Other patterns of production and consumption are not efficient because they leave some demand unsatisfied and do not fully exploit the mutually beneficial gains people can realize through market exchange.

The conditions under which the first welfare theorem would hold were not clarified until the works of future Nobellists Kenneth Arrow and Gerald Debreu in the 1950s. Their articles are largely impenetrable to most economists due to their mathematical sophistication, but a simplified proof is available in Hal Varian's 1984 textbook *Microeconomic Analysis*, (200-203).

Arrow and Debreu discovered the crucial conditions for competitive equilibrium to be efficient: that no exchange should violate the property rights of a third party. Among the "violations" Arrow and Debreu had in mind were pollution and monopoly. Buying paper for your laser printer is not a Pareto-improving exchange if the pulp company pollutes a river to which downstream anglers and farmers have no established riparian rights. In such a case, the market gets the social calculation wrong because the absence of property rights allows costs to be piled on farmers and anglers without any compensation by the pulp company. The mistake may be so profound that the damage from the pollution destroys more value than that generated by making paper. Monopolies violate Pareto efficiency by forbidding potential producers with a better product from offering it to consumers. By thwarting mutually beneficial exchanges monopoly turns the market into a desert with limited possibilities for mutually enhancing trade.

Economists as far back as Adam Smith had long felt confident in the existence of something like the first fundamental theorem and were aware of the threats to it, but the solid mathematical proofs that came out in the 1950s were reassuring.

The second welfare theorem

ARROW AND DEBREU also proved the second welfare theorem, which in some ways is even more remarkable than the first. A very broad statement of the theorem is that it does not matter how resources are distributed in society, eventually the economy will work its way to an efficient equilibrium. The theorem is remarkable in part because it appeals to both socialist and free-market thinkers.

If you believe the distribution of wealth in society is unfair you need just ask government to come up with a new distribution. With their new endowments people will trade their way back to a Pareto efficient state. As Nobellist Joseph Stiglitz explained in a lecture at Glasgow University, "Of course, the distribution of income which emerged from the competitive market may not be to a society's liking. And this is where the second Welfare Theorem enters. It says that every Pareto efficient allocation of resources can be attained by means of the market. All the government needs to do is to engage in some initial redistributions, and then leave the rest to the market process" (1991, 4).

If you are a fan of free markets, then you might like the theorem for what it says about privatization. When *East Bloc* countries abandoned Communism there was some confusion about what to do with the vast government holdings of wealth. Free-market believers in the second theorem advised the post-communist governments to carry out "voucher privatization" in which each citizen received a share of government assets. Many had no use for shares in factories or lands and sold theirs to people who felt they could better manage those resources. The idea was that an initially inefficient distribution of share ownership would eventually evolve to an efficient competitive equilibrium as ownership moved from the indifferent to those feeling themselves more competent.

Ronald Coase pushed this idea to its limit in his analysis of pollution. In his 1960 article, "On the Problem of Social Cost" he argued it did not matter for efficiency whether a railroad owned the wheat fields which its locomotives set ablaze from time to time by casting sparks, or whether the field belonged to farmers. If farmers owned their fields they could take the railroads to court and be reimbursed for the cost of losing crops to fire. Railroads would have to count this as a cost of using this route to deliver people or goods and might decide that by reducing the number of trips the cost saved would be greater than the revenues lost from foregone passengers and freight.

If instead, the railroad owned the fields, it could set fires without fear of being fined, but in the end, the costs to it would be the same, because the fires it set would end up burning railroad crops grown on railroad land. If it decided not to grow crops and instead rent the land, farmers would reduce their offers by the anticipated cost of crops lost to railway fires. So for the calculations people made who owned the land was a matter of no consequence.

Here then was the celebrated *Coase Theorem*. The railroads would be faced either with visible fines for scorching someone else's land, or with less visible but equally tangible "opportunity costs" from putting their own land to the torch. In the end, transport and crop growth would end up being efficient in the sense that farmers and railway operators would produce up to a point where the benefits they received from the last "marginal" unit of production just equalled the cost. There were no lost opportunities for trade because all costs were taken into account, or "internalized". If farmers owned their land and you imposed a regulation stating that railroads must not set fire to crops, you drove the market away from Pareto efficiency because the sacrifice of a few crops might allow transport that was far more valuable to the railroads than the crops saved. In such a case, farmers would have allowed—and even encouraged—railroads to burn their crops up to the point where the payments just marginally exceeded the value of the lost crops.

Coase's initial reasons for writing his article may not be known. He never mentioned a theorem in his paper. That moniker was bestowed by a later generation of economists (intellectuals love to label). But what he ended up providing was an intuitive explanation of the second welfare theorem's claim that ownership patterns are irrelevant for efficiency. Coase argued that efficiency was attained by making people face the full costs of their actions and realize the full benefits. Most critically, efficiency did not depend on how much money you started out with in life with, whether you got a surprise share in a privatized government firm, or whether a sinkhole swallowed your house. Efficiency was always functional and this is what led people back to a Pareto efficient equilibrium.

The deep waters of equilibrium

WHATEVER THEIR POLITICAL beliefs, the second welfare theorem was warmly embraced by economists. It relieved them of needing to worry about criticisms that their profession heart-lessly ignored the unequal distribution of wealth in society. In Stiglitz's words, the second theorem "says that we can sepa-rate out issues of economic efficiency from issues of equity. Economists need not concern themselves with value judg-ments; whatever the government's distributive objectives, it implements these through initial lump sum taxes and subsi-dies, and then leaves the market to work for itself" (1991, 4-5).

Stiglitz's qualification that redistribution must be "lump-sum" is often overlooked by enthusiastic fans of the second theorem, but it is a key factor in both its limitations and its strengths. A lump-sum redistribution is simply a handout with no strings attached. It is also a tax that has nothing to do with how much you work, or consume, or invest. The redistribu-tion is not influenced by any action you might make. A busi-ness subsidy tied to how many homeless people you employ is not lump-sum because it can be influenced by, and in turn influence, your behavior.

Non lump-sum, or so-called "tied" transfers, can be the ene-mies of Pareto efficiency because they can warp people's behav-ior away from profitable exchanges based on the true condi-tions of the economy, such as wants and capabilities. Various real estate bubbles have been attributed to the effect of govern-ment aid intended to help prospective homeowners purchase their first dwelling. Housing bubbles grow because banks lend to high risk borrowers, knowing that government will come to their rescue should the market collapse. Without a government safety net, lenders would look before leaping into the high risk mortgage market. A rational calculation balancing future risks against current gains would contain to some extent the degree of any crisis, should it arise. With a government safety net in place people may blithely ignore real market conditions and strike deals that destroy wealth. The second theorem says that provided we do not warp people's perspective on true wealth with non lump-sum transfers, government transfers can lead to a Pareto efficient market equilibrium. Government mortgage guarantees subvert the second theorem because as anticipated transfers in the case of crisis these entice us to embark upon excessively risky real estate ventures.

Stiglitz saw the lump-sum condition as a fatal flaw of the second theorem. He did not believe that government was able to redistribute money in a lump-sum manner, mainly because people would cheat on their taxes in a manner systematically related to production.

Consider that tax evasion is a form of transfer from the government to the evader. Those businesses best able to cheat would gain a competitive advantage over their rivals and drive them out of the market. You could end up with a market of inept producers who were adept at cheating on their taxes, thereby driving out people who were efficient but honest. The trick to seeing the weakness of the second theorem lies in recognizing that tax evasion is a form of transfer that might be tied to some feature of the person evading.

Stiglitz also believed people would lie about their needs to get government subsidies. On the surface the lump-sum subsidy should not be related to any feature of your environment you can change. But if you can fake being sick you can get subsidies. The inefficiency that arises is that a class of shirkers forms to exploit subsidies. Previously they could have been gainfully employed. The difficulty of implementing lump-sum subsidies was really the story of the disappointing results in the war on poverty and inequality and the collapse of the Soviet empire, where shirking took on such massive proportions that a special term for it was invented: "economic wrecker".

Yet was this a fatal flaw of the theorem or of the conditions under which it was made to work? Stiglitz's critique of government intervention was spot-on because it pointed to an inevitable correlation between the transfer and some actions of the recipients or taxpayers. His critique had much less force in the case in which redistribution was due to some chance workings of the market, such as those caused by an unforeseen earthquake, plague, war, revolution, scientific discovery, or just about any other economic "shock" that is the daily reality of markets.

Free market types do not like to hear this, but the free market is constantly bombarded with inefficiencies due to chance redistributions of resources and opportunities. The good news is that, like a self-sealing tire, the market can patch itself up. The discovery of the automobile put the horse-drawn carriage industry out of business. The automobile's unexpected discovery acted like a reshuffling of the endowments of talent, and thus of wealth, that nature had handed out in a previous generation. The new opportunities for mutual gain between riders and mechanics that the auto's development presented led to a shift of resources away from the horse and carriage trade to the car trade.

We think of this as a normal market process and maybe that is so. It is also a demonstration of the second fundamental theorem of welfare economics. Chance redistributions of advantage are like lump-sum redistributions of income. They upset established market relations but eventually the tendency to equilibrium exploits all possible gains from trade and a Pareto efficient state is attained. Put slightly differently, because it is geared towards equilibrium, a market economy will exploit chances for improving economic efficiency as those chances arise. The "slings and arrows of outrageous fortune" may injure us when they strike, but the economy has a first-aid kit. Or more precisely, it is a self-correcting mechanism that takes change as a normal part of its daily routine and translates that change incrementally into a new and efficient system of social accounts.

It is in such novelty that advocates of the free market place their faith. They see in shocks to old wealth the impetus to discover ways of creating new wealth. Certainly the evidence of the last two centuries supports this view, but the first and second welfare theorems are mute on the question of whether a free market will lead to increasing prosperity.

These theorems are static representations of what is, and not of what may be. In a very circumscribed manner the theorems help us to understand that markets are not simplistic vehicles for the creation of wealth. Markets help people recombine resources after the upsets of chance in such a way that they find their most valued use.

Enter Pigou

THE MATHEMATICAL MODELING of free market equilibrium and its Pareto efficient properties captivated economists. It followed that the economy should be left to itself with the occasional correction of imbalances in wealth being the responsibility of government. What government should not do above all was to meddle in the workings of the market. There were dissenting voices however. There always are.

Cambridge economist Arthur Pigou, though a laissez-faire advocate, had doubts about efficient markets and was among the first to integrate the idea of market imperfections into a coherent economic model. He argued that markets were plagued by "externalities", such as pollution, which led certain products to be underpriced. Efficient equilibrium could be restored by a tax on those underpriced products. The Ford vehicle that sold for $1,000 was underpriced because in building it, Ford's Dearborn factory polluted the Rouge River. If the environmental damage, such as a reduced fish catch, was $100 per car, then a tax was needed to sensitize Ford to the true cost of the inputs to its production process. In an economic sense, the killing of fish was such an input. A tax of $100 a unit would restore Pareto efficiency by forcing Ford to take account of the cost it was imposing on anglers. Government could then compensate the anglers by transferring the tax to them.

Pigou did not reject market economics, nor the idea of a Pareto efficient equilibrium, but merely sought to devise some mechanisms by which government could patch up "market failures" that led away from Pareto efficiency. His protégé John Maynard Keynes went much further.

Keynes doubted that labor markets reached equilibrium in the demand for and supply of workers. An excess supply of workers, what non-economists call unemployment, may persist if wages do not fall in order to entice employers to hire idle hands. Workers might make irrationally high demands for salaries that could keep them unemployed for long spells. Government then had to step in, not to lower wages, but to stimulate demand for the excess labor through public works.

Keynes and those who followed him did not go so far as to completely reject the market model. They simply felt that markets could not respond to surpluses and shortages of output rapidly enough to keep the economy in equilibrium. Government had to intervene directly in markets and had to build "automatic stabilizers" into the economy that would stimulate private demand in times of recession and slow it in boom times. These ups and downs in the economy were signs of the inefficiency in markets. Governments needed to smooth them out.

Pigou and Keynes established the bridgeheads from which many an assault on the classical free market model would be launched in decades to come. Yet their assaults obeyed a sort of *Geneva Convention* of economic debate. Discussion took place within the social accounting framework of market equilibrium. So while free market skeptics launched assaults, they did so in a manner that generally respected the rules of intellectual engagement. These rules were based in the social accounting calculus of the mathematical model of market equilibrium.

Socialist free-marketers

WHILE FOR SOME time the Pigou-Keynes critique of free market economics became the dominant mode of thinking about social accounts, there was a short-lived but zestful assault launched on market equilibrium social accounting by a group of thinkers who called themselves "market socialists". They have largely disappeared as a coherent movement but their ideas continue to ripple through economics.

The label "socialist free-marketer" may seem apt as "puritan lecher" but it did have a certain logic. Their assault on free market thinking was less accessible to mainstream economists than the Pigou-Keynes assault, but in some ways it was far more devastating than the cannonades of Pigou and Keynes. Economists still struggle with the issues market socialists raised.

A prominent market socialist was Oscar Lange. In the 1930s he achieved the unlikely distinction of being a favorite of Stalin's while at the same time being a senior professor of economics at the University of Chicago. In two articles published in 1936, he argued that if planners in the central bureau of a socialist dictatorship had all the information they needed on supply and demand, they could dictate prices and people would produce and consume in such a manner as to bring about an efficient equilibrium. If the planners got the prices wrong they could check where there were surpluses and lower prices and increase them in markets where there were shortages. This was a straightforward transposition from the way free markets attain equilibrium to centrally planned markets.

Lange's articles were remarkable not just for their appropriation of free market reasoning to socialist causes, but also for their sarcasm towards the free market advocate Ludwig von Mises. In mock gratitude for explaining free markets so well that socialists could adapt them to their needs, Lange wrote, "Both as an expression of recognition for the great service rendered by him and as a memento of the prime importance of sound economic accounting, a statue of Professor Mises ought to occupy an honorable place in the great hall of the Ministry of Socialisation or of the Central Planning Board of the socialist state" (1936, 53).

Even Frank Knight, the great defender of free markets, who in the 1930s trained future Nobellists Milton Friedman and George Stigler, agreed with Lange. Knight wrote that "the place of marginal economics in a collectivist economy is not essentially different from its place in an economy of 'competitive individualism' … the problems of collectivism are not problems of economic theory, but political problems… A collectivist society of any type would necessarily confront the same economic problems, in the formal sense, as an individualistic one" (1936, 255–256). There was no surprise in similar views coming from differently minded scholars. They followed directly from the conception of the market as offering up prices that attracted consumers and producers to a fixed point in which supply equalled demand.

As Knight indicated, making the best use of resources subject to material constraints involves making trade-offs that move resources to higher value uses until a reshuffling of resources just barely exhausts the possibility for gain and so makes you indifferent to where you invest your last unit of resource, be that your labor, or your consumption. By the first welfare theorem, this is why competitive equilibria are efficient. The socialist view was that the logic of the welfare theorem could be inverted. Instead of allowing prices to emerge from supply and demand tensions in a decentralized market, socialists would deduce the correct equilibrium prices from their knowledge of the economy and allow these prices to guide people toward equilibrium.

Economists of a Freudian mindset might have surmised that socialists were suffering from "capitalism envy" because it seemed they were trying to inject elements of decentralization into a centrally planned system. After all, prices are indicators of the value of privately held and exchangeable property. Market socialists were not put out by this evident contradiction between central control and the need for prices. Their view was that a factory manager could follow a rule dictated from the center which said that if the value of the factory's product was above what it cost to pay its workers, then it should hire more of them until their value diminished to the point where their return just equalled their cost. It was not made clear why managers should do this without being compensated with some share of the company's profits, and thus *de facto* becoming shareholders, and thereby violating central control. Similarly, consumers could be given some "tokens", or money as we usually call it, and respond to prices set to equate demand and supply. Owning money was a violation of central control but it allowed central planners to "grope" towards an equilibrium by varying prices. Despite these violations of the central control principle, market socialists believed them to be trivial, and thought they had discovered a way of achieving economic efficiency without delegating authority to capitalists.

The absorption of free market equilibrium into socialist pre-scriptions for economic dictatorship took place many decades ago. Yet this appropriation left questions unanswered. How could socialist central control and capitalist free enterprise market equilibrium lead to the same result? And if they did, what was the whole debate between left and right all about?

Free market defender and future Nobellist, Friedrich Hayek (1945) argued that no central planning bureau could gather all the information on people's tastes and productive abili-ties. Without such particular "knowledge of time and place" it would be impossible to know demand and supply curves and thus to dictate efficient prices in a socialist centrally con-trolled economy.

Hayek argued that a free market dealt with this enormous quantity of information not by gathering it up in a central bureau but through the emergence of prices that moved up or down until supply and demand equalled each other without the aid of some all-seeing planner.

The equation of what people produced and what they con-sumed was a "coordination problem" of high order brought about by prices that adjusted to the particulars of everyone in the market, the realities "time and place". Market socialists countered that the central planner did not need knowledge of time and place. All the planner had to do was post a price, see if it resulted in a shortage, then increase the price until demand and supply equilibrated.

The stalemate between Hayekians and market socialists over the best way to coordinate the actions of large numbers of people lasted until the union of game theory and information economics in the 1970s. Nobellist Roger Myerson (2008), who helped pioneer this fusion into a field called "mechanism design", argued that there were some sorts of informational problems that in particular plagued capitalism and others that plagued socialism. In either system it is difficult to monitor how well managers perform their duties. Capitalist systems solve the problem by paying managers with company shares so as to align manager and firm interests without the need to constantly monitor what managers are up to. Socialism did not give managers shares in their factories and never quite figured out how to monitor performance. The result was that managers had power without responsibility. This is a recipe for what economists call "moral hazard". The widespread shirking of duties and looting of enterprises was one of the reasons the Soviet system collapsed.

Capitalism was not without flaws. It had a particular informational problem called "adverse selection". Job candidates for managerial posts may misrepresent their abilities in order to get hired. Or salesmen may lie about the quality of their product in order to make a sale. Socialism removes the incentive for misrepresentation by paying people in a manner that has little to do with their qualifications.

Mechanism design theory saw these strategic interactions between people as games that could be manipulated to make people act honestly and obediently once government implemented the proper rules and reward schemes. The only problem was that when government was designing the rules, the costs of getting everyone to behave could be higher than the benefits. Despite Myerson's diplomatic clarification of the types of informational issues involved, the socialist calculation debate still rages, driven on the socialist side by the feeling that capitalism is unjust, and on the Hayekian side by the overwhelming real-world evidence of the inefficiency and corruption of socialist economies.

Political equilibrium

MARKET EQUILIBRIUM IS not the be-all and end-all of social accounting. A great deal of spending is determined not in private markets but by government. Demand and supply analysis is not directly applicable to government because of a fundamental difference in the way that private markets and governments work. Private markets are based on the consensus of every single person involved in a trade. The "decision rule" for how private resources are to be used is one hundred per cent unanimity. If you do not like a certain car you do not buy it. No one can force you into the purchase nor can the dealer be forced to sell to you. In private market equilibrium, price brings about a unanimous consensus by equating how much buyers want with the amount sellers provide. Market equilibrium tools such as supply and demand are easy to apply to situations such as these because the objectives of all parties are clear. Consumers wish to maximize well-being subject to the constraint of income and prices, whereas producers wish to maximize profits.

That is not the way it works with government. Whether in a dictatorship or a democracy, most people have no direct say in what government buys on their behalf with their money. The reason is sometimes political and sometimes technical. The entire rationale for having a government which coercively removes money from your paycheck is the presumed existence of goods and services which everyone would be willing to buy, but for which private firms find themselves unable to charge. Think of street lighting. It has huge benefits for almost everyone except night prowlers and back-door men. Yet private firms do not have the incentive to build a network of lamps. It is technically very difficult to charge someone every time he or she walks under a lamp in a public street at night. Private citizens might start a charitable collection, but the lights might not get built if some citizens shirked their contributions in order to "free-ride" on the contributions of others. The result is that a project that is affordable and good for everyone might falter because some users do not pay their share of the costs. The free riders in this story cripple society's ability to coordinate itself for everyone's good. In the end, because the project does not get done, even potential free riders suffer.

Most economists really do not like to think too deeply about scenarios such as how to build street lamps. That is "public stuff". Their malaise stems from the lack of an accepted equilibrium model of group behavior to tell them whether the lamps will get built or not, or if they are built whether too many or too few will be installed. More generally, there is no accepted model of how groups of people will collectively decide how resources should be used. That does not mean there are no models. On the contrary, models proliferate. They blossom because no one can quite agree on what are the core incentives driving people who influence government. The field seems to be split into a naïve segment which takes government as a pure do-good institution serving the interests of the people, and a cynical segment which sees government as an impartial vehicle for a variety of extractive interests.

Duncan Black's celebrated 1948 Median Voter Model can be considered a naïve model of political equilibrium. It proves that under very specific conditions the wishes of the "median" voter, whose income is right in between the income of the poor and the rich, will be the voter whose wishes politicians try to please. Under even more specific conditions the political equilibrium that results will lead to a Pareto efficient level of street lighting and other similar "public goods". Black's model presumes a true democracy with rulers who count votes honestly.

Nobellist Gary Becker's 1983 model can be categorized as cynical. According to Becker, political equilibrium exists even in non-democratic societies. It arises out of a simple calculation that predatory interest groups and their taxpaying victims make: what return on my investment can I get by lobbying government? Becker's insight is that the gains to predators are linear, but the losses to prey are exponential, thereby stiffening the resistance of victims as the aggression of predators plods on without similarly increased vigor. Think of a gang of robbers taking half the crop from peasants. They then return for the second half. The gain to the gang of the second half cut is the same as in their first extortion. Yet for peasants to lose the last half of their crops means possible starvation and the certain loss of seed corn. They can be expected to resist violently, as they did in the Hollywood movie *The Magnificent Seven* and in the Japanese movie on which it was based, *The Seven Samurai*.

Black and Becker are but two of many contending modelers of political equilibrium. They are joined by Gordon Tullock, Nobellist James Buchanan, and others who have launched a new school of economic analysis called Public Choice. It is geared towards modeling equilibrium in politics. In this quest to decide what is the basis of political equilibrium, a system of social accounts remains the basic datum of interest. And ultimately Pareto efficiency is the quest.

The example of politics highlights that equilibrium is more than an economic concept. It represents some ideal, efficient point towards which societies strive. If the ideal is inferior, as in the case of the Soviet Bloc, then these societies become inferior and eventually crumble. The US bankrupted the Soviet Union in the arms race of the 1980s. It was able to do so because American society was based on a social accounting system that encouraged effort and innovation from its people.

The Russian system stifled initiative and failed to control looting of government resources on a massive scale by the very leaders who were supposed to guide the collective good. The social accounting of the free market was able to motivate Americans to produce arms far more efficiently than was the collectivist social calculus of communist Russia.

The dark matter of economics

DESPITE THIS STUNNING vindication of the benefits of decentralized control and the weaknesses of communist dictatorship, there is still much we do not know about how equilibrium arises. We may know what equilibrium is, but we have a harder time knowing how people attain it. This lack of knowledge makes it premature to judge based purely on economic theory whether a free market would have been better for Russia than a communist dictatorship.

We lack data that would allow us to make a comparison. In particular we lack the "counterfactual" experiment demonstrating what would have happened had Russia taken the free market path after 1917. Without such a comparison between what was and what might have been, we can at best use our models and notions to speculate on the superiority of one system of social accounting over another.

French writer Milan Kundera said much the same thing in his novel *The Unbearable Lightness of Being* in which he lamented that nothing could be learned from life because we could not rerun the experiment of our existence to see if different choices might have improved our lot. Soren Kierkegaard had a more statistical approach. He wrote that "Life has its own hidden forces which you can only discover by living." Both have a point.

These challenges to equilibrium should be seen as calls to a treasure hunt rather than as obituaries. One of the great and fascinating mysteries of equilibrium lies in the pre-conditions for its emergence. Efficient market equilibrium is difficult to achieve without property rights protected by the rule of law. Harold Demsetz pointed out in his 2002 article that such rights can only arise if the costs of elaborating and maintaining property rights are lower than the benefits they generate.

Once again we see that the narrow market equilibrium of demand and supply is nestled within a broader logic. The conditions have to be right for property rights to be created. Just what these conditions are and how a society might acquire them is an ongoing topic of research.

In his book, *Plagues and Peoples*, William H. McNeill hypothesizes that markets emerge from a lengthy evolutionary process that culminates in a symbiosis between human predators and their human prey. At first, roving bands raid villages for food and put them to the torch. Over time some bands learn that they can extract more wealth by a less destructive and more systematic form of extraction. Thus taxes are born. Then the rulers may learn that by providing services such as education and health care, their subjects become richer and so better able to pay tax. Through symbiosis, governments and the markets they foster may develop.

However, despite a great deal of fancy intellectualizing, as yet we have no way of understanding why only a very few societies make the transition to a market economy. Nor do we understand why most of humanity is stuck in other forms of equilibria that have little to do with markets: internecine strife; clan alliances; foraging and self-sufficiency; communities living in harmony without courts of law or formal property. These phenomena are not easily categorized within a standard equilibrium framework. Think of them as the dark matter of economics. Integrating them into a model of social accounts that is as yet a feat of grand unification we are far from performing.

References

Becker, Gary S. 1983. "A theory of competition among pressure groups for political influence." *Quarterly Journal of Economics,* volume. 98: 371–400.

Black, Duncan. 1948. "On the rationale of group decision-making." *Journal of Political Economy,* volume 56: 23–34.

Coase, Ronald H. 1960. "The problem of social cost." *Journal of Law and Economics,* volume 3: 1–44.

Demsetz, Harold. 2002. "Toward a theory of property rights II: the competition between private and collective ownership." *Journal of Legal Studies,* volume 31: s653–s672.

Knight, Frank H. 1936. "The place of marginal economics in a collectivist system." *The American Economic Review,* volume 26: 255–266.

Lange, Oscar. 1936. "On the economic theory of socialism: Part one." *The Review of Economic Studies*, volume 4: 53–71.

Makowski, Louis and Joseph M. Ostroy. 1992. "General equilibrium and market socialism: clarifying the logic of competitive markets." UCLA Economics Working Papers 672.

McNeill, William H. 1976. *Plagues and Peoples*. Anchor Press/Doubleday.

Myerson, Roger. 2008. "Perspective on mechanism design in economic theory." *American Economic Review*, volume 98: 586–603.

Palda, Filip. 2011. *Pareto's Republic and the New Science of Peace*. Cooper-Wolfling Press.

Pigou, Arthur Cecil. 1920. *The Economics of Welfare*. Macmillan.

Stiglitz, Joseph E. 1991. "The invisible hand and modern welfare economics." NBER working papers series 3641.

Varian, Hal. 1984. *Microeconomic Analysis, 2nd Edition*. W.W. Norton.

GAMES   7

G AME THEORY IS THE EVEREST of economics. It daunts
us with its seemingly bizarre view of how people interact and its irrefutable but mind-bending proofs of how
so much can go wrong in human relations. But to the few who
manage to understand its logic the theory makes sense of so
many seemingly chaotic behaviors. In his *Essay on Man*, the
late 1700s British poet Alexander Pope wrote, "All nature is
but art unknownst to thee; all chance direction which thou
canst not see; all chaos harmony not understood; all partial
evil, universal good." Those were the mysteries game theory
sought to penetrate. Its inventors felt it was needed because of
a shortcoming in classical economic theory. As John Harsanyi
explained in his Nobel lecture

> In principle, every social situation involves strategic interaction
> among the participants. Thus, one might argue that proper under-
> standing of any social situation would require game-theoretic anal-
> ysis. But in actual fact, classical economic theory did manage to
> sidestep the game-theoretic aspects of economic behavior by pos-
> tulating perfect competition, i.e., by assuming that every buyer and
> every seller is very small as compared with the size of the relevant
> markets, so that nobody can significantly affect the existing mar-
> ket prices by his actions. Accordingly, for each economic agent,
> the prices at which he can buy his inputs (including labor) and at
> which he can sell his outputs are essentially given to him. This will

make his choice of inputs and of outputs into a one-person simple maximization problem, which can be solved without game-theoretic analysis.(1995, 291).

The classical economics Harsanyi was talking about is based on the notion that people try to do as well as they can with what they have. The formal phraseology is that people maximize some objective, such as profit, or pleasure, subject to material constraints. For the consumer, income is usually a big constraint, and so are prices. For most of us, income and prices are fixed quantities. We have to take them pretty much as given. Most economists are content to see the world in this manner because this view makes sense of so much of what we see in markets and even in politics. But there are a few who believe that material constraints are not the whole story. They call themselves game theorists and what they call strategic interaction is really a form of decision making under a very special sort of constraint.

The constraint central to game theory is not material but rather mental. In 1953, von Neumann and Morgenstern illustrated these mental constraints by retelling the famous death chase between Sherlock Holmes and his arch-enemy, Professor Moriarty, the Napoleon of crime:

> Sherlock Holmes desires to proceed from London to Dover and hence to the Continent in order to escape from Professor Moriarty who pursues him. Having boarded the train he observes, as the train pulls out, the appearance of Professor Moriarty on the platform. Sherlock Holmes takes it for granted and in this he is assumed to be fully justified that his adversary, who has seen him, might secure a special train and overtake him. Sherlock Holmes is faced with the alternative of going to Dover or of leaving the train at

Canterbury, the only intermediate station. His adversary whose intelligence is assumed to be fully adequate to visualize these possibilities has the same choice. Both opponents must choose the place of their detrainment in ignorance of the other's corresponding decision. If, as a result of these measures, they should find themselves, in fine, on the same platform, Sherlock Holmes may with certainty expect to be killed by Moriarty. If Sherlock Holmes reaches Dover unharmed he can make good his escape (1953, 177).

In this death chase Holmes' best choice of an exit station depends on the station at which he expects Moriarty to disembark. This expectation in turn depends on the station Moriarty divines as Holmes' escape. The story has the structure of an economic problem in that Holmes must attain some objective (in this case preserving his life), but he is not like the consumer of products who must passively accept the constraints imposed upon him by the economic environment. In this example, the constraint Holmes faces is Moriarty's mind. That mind will conceive a strategy based on its anticipation of Holmes' strategy. This means that Holmes' own mind is shaping to some degree the constraints he faces. Unlike the passive consumer taking prices and making choices, Holmes' choices can influence his possibilities. Holmes is forced into a "strategic interaction" with his environment. He does not choose his outcome, but rather a strategy that may or may not produce the outcome he wants. By taking charge of his environment he also determines in large part what the "equilibrium" outcome of the game is.

Obviously Holmes had his brain-work cut out for him. Before game theory, so did researchers wishing to analyze similar situations in which people constrain each other through their anticipated behavior. Today, the analytical apparatus these researchers developed in order to crack the mystery of strategic interactions is gradually becoming a standard part of economic thinking. Some go further in their assessment of the importance of game theory. Nobellist Roger Myerson claims that game theory holds the keys to understanding how political institutions should be designed, and to answering whether capitalism is better or worse than socialism. Others, such as Bates Medal winner David Kreps are more tempered in their evaluation of the field. Despite these differences it is clear that here is a form of reasoning that needs to be learned by anyone wishing to embark on a mastery economics. The Holmes-Moriarty conflict captures the essential spirit of game theory and thus can be our low door in the wall to what you will come to understand is the wonderland of game theory.

The essence of games

THE PUTATIVE CONFRONTATION between Holmes and Moriarty can be boiled down to a few essential elements. Both are players with strategies that depend on the payoffs of any possible choice, and the way each player values these payoffs. Both must move "simultaneously", as in the game of rock-paper-scissors, or matching pennies. That is, each must disembark from their respective trains at the same instant, whether they are in the same station, or in different stations.

More generally, game theorists take this to mean that even before the game starts all players will have devised their strategies and will not deviate from these. The players might as easily stay at home and mail their moves to a referee who opens the envelopes to determine who won and so administer the prescribed rewards and punishments. The prize in question is Holmes' life, and his loss of it is as painful a prospect to him as it is pleasurable to Moriarty. This is called a zero-sum pay-off structure because the gain to one player is exactly matched by the loss to the other. You can think of a zero-sum payoff as the case where a pickpocket removes a $100 bill from your back pocket. His or her gain is exactly your loss. The game is "one-shot" in that it will be played only once. This means that some sort of reciprocity cannot develop and neither player can punish the other in the future for vicious attacks in the past. Neither player can communicate with the other. No contract can be written between Holmes and Moriarty to limit the damages to each other. The conflict between them is total and unconstrained.

If these seem painfully unrealistic assumptions then have patience. Understanding so simply contrived an interaction flummoxed some of the finest minds of the 20th century. There is ample opportunity after studying this example to very quickly complicate the picture.

Superior intellect of no use

So at which stations does each disembark? Conan Doyle has Holmes getting off at the first station (Canterbury), while Moriarty speeds by that station to alight at Dover, fooled by the maneuver. Conan Doyle's reasoning for Holmes' victory is absent. Game theory can fill the gap.

The first thing to note is that there is no way either antagonist can out-think the other to come up with a certain strategy that dominates every other possibility. If Holmes reasons that Moriarty will guess he wishes to escape at the first station, then Holmes must get off at the last station. But Holmes knows that Moriarty will know that Holmes knows, and so the right choice is to get off at the first station. Both antagonists can go on reasoning like this until both trains run off the end of the earth. Neither will be able to settle on a strategy, also called an "equilibrium", if they are engaged in an "infinite regress of reciprocal expectations".

There is no strategy Holmes can choose given his anticipation of Moriarty's strategy that Holmes would not wish instantly to change. Children know this game as "matching pennies". The idea is for each player to reveal either heads or tails to the other. One player wins if the faces match and the other wins if the faces do not match. As in the Holmes-Moriarty game, there is no certain choice any player can settle on in matching pennies. Game theorists call the absence of a complete, certain plan of action a "pure strategy". There is no fixed pure strategy in an infinite regress.

There is, however, a way out of the death-chase regress. That is for each opponent to flip a coin, or roll a die, to stop at Canterbury with some probability, and Dover with the residue of that probability. If you flip a coin, then you will get off at either station with a chance of fifty per cent. If you roll a die with Canterbury on one side, and Dover written on the five remaining sides, then you will get off at Canterbury with a one-sixth chance, and off at Dover with a five-sixth chance. Many such random possibilities are open to the players.

Why can playing randomly lead to a definite strategy whereas playing with a sure strategy leads to an indeterminate infinite regress? You are about to learn one of the greatest theorems of economics, so kindly put your seat backs up and remove all sharp objects from pant and shirt pockets.

Put yourself in Holmes' shoes with the broadened knowledge that you can pick a probability of getting off at Canterbury, with the residue of the probability being the chance you will get off at Dover. Now a vista of possible strategies opens. If you think that Moriarty will get off at Canterbury for certain and you chose a "degenerate" random strategy of setting your probability of getting off at Canterbury as zero then you can get off at Dover and you survive. But there is a potential downside. If Moriarty decides to get off at Dover you die. So your strategy of setting the probability of Canterbury as zero has a very wide range of possible rewards ranging from 100% certain death to 100% certain life. Now suppose instead you decide to get off at Canterbury with a 50% chance. If Moriarty's strategy is to get off at Canterbury this means your chance of death is 50%. If he gets off at Dover, once again your die with 50% chance.

So the two extremes possible to you are actually the same. Your 50% strategy gives you a 50% chance of survival no matter what Moriarty does. Now suppose you decide to get off at Canterbury with 100% certainty. If Moriarty gets off there then you are dead and if at Dover you live. What I have just done is examine three mixed strategies. The two extreme strategies of certain disembarkation at one station or the other give the widest range of possible "payoffs" to the game from Holmes' perspective. The middle strategy of flipping a coin gives the narrowest range of outcomes in an average or "expected value" sense.

In fact, I could have described a strategy of either 40% or 70% chance of getting off at Canterbury and would have found a range of expected values for Holmes somewhere in between his middle strategy and the two extreme strategies.

One can carry on this exercise until on a graph one sketches a "butterfly tie" of the range of possible payoffs to Holmes. Where Holmes chooses a chance of getting off at Dover of 100% the butterfly tie is at its widest since the certain strategies of Moriarty disembarking at either port present the stark possibilities of certain life, or certain death. The tie narrows to a point where Holmes chooses to flip a coin. At that point his expected value of the game does not depend on what strategy Moriarty chooses.

Of course in this exercise I have assumed Moriarty only has the possibility of choosing a pure, or rather non-mixed strategy of certain disembarkation at one station or the other. It is easy to show that if he plays various mixed strategies the butterfly tie retains its general shape, but the range of expected payoffs changes, except at one crucial point. The strategy of flipping a coin still gives Holmes the single expected value of 50% of surviving. And it is tedious but straightforward to show that if Moriarty adopts a coin flip he too will have a 50% chance of killing Holmes.

Is the 50% coin flip an equilibrium strategy for the two? It might be. What is clear is that with the coin flip there is no possibility of an infinite regress for Holmes because if he flips the coin there is no range of expected payoffs. A coin flip leaves Holmes indifferent to the strategy Moriarty adopts. Similarly the coin flip strategy leaves Moriarty indifferent to an infinite regress. We still do not have an answer. We need to ask whether either can do better than the coin flip knowing that the other is flipping. That is the test of whether an equilibrium is stable.

The answer depends on what "doing better" means. Which in turn depends on their preferences. Holmes might be extremely daring and not mind the risk of an extreme strategy of getting off for certain at Dover. In that case the coin flip is certainly not an equilibrium because a more daring strategy would seem more attractive. But what if Holmes is morbidly afraid of risk— so much so that he always tries to minimize the maximal possible loss that he can expect to realize?

We have all acted like this in our lives, though perhaps not always with pride. There are moments when we say it is better to take a course of action that will not give us the prospect of a brilliant success at the risk of great failure, but at least will put a floor on our losses. Some people approach marriage in this manner. Game theorists call these "minimax" preferences. They are also known as "absolute risk aversion" preferences.

If Holmes has minimax preferences then a coin flip is the mixed strategy he was born to play. It has the highest possible downside of all other possible degrees of randomness he might choose. Think of the bow tie. All strategies except at the knot offer higher possible expected gains but also lower possible gains than the knot. Moriarty faces a similar bow tie of expected returns on an up-down scale. He also faces a left-right scale of his chosen probability of getting off at Canterbury.

If you put the two horizontal probability scales and the unique expected value scale together (you can do that because this is a zero-sum game where returns are perfectly symmetric) then you get a three dimensional picture akin to a saddle. In fact the minimax solution of chosen probabilities and expected value can be found at the lowest part on the saddle where your rump would settle if you chose to mount the otherworldly beast that is the zero-sum game.

This is why the solution of such two-person conflicts is called a "saddle-point". At this point neither Moriarty nor Holmes have any incentive to deviate from their strategies given their expectations of what the other's strategy will be. To do so would be to expose oneself to a greater downside risk than at the saddlepoint. Each in a way has insulated himself from the other by seeking refuge in strategy that utterly minimizes the downside the other can impose on him. Not only is this strategy an equilibrium, but it is also a self-fulfilling equilibrium in an average, or expected sense. Each man' strategy settles at a point where the outcome he expects from his strategy is consistent with what the outcome is expected to be in a statistical sense.

If the payoffs were somewhat less symmetric than in this example, with the greatest possible loss to Holmes in pure strategies being from getting off at Dover, then you might find Holmes' minimax probability of getting off at Canterbury as being perhaps 60% and that of Moriarty as being 40%, but this really just an aside that need not derail us as it were from the point of this exposition. The point being that equilibrium in this game emerges from payoffs and preferences, the view each of Holmes and Moriarty have of how the other plays the game, and the possibilities for randomizing your play.

Having just scaled one of the greatest intellectual tours-de-force of the social sciences a breather is called for in which we gaze over the landscape we have traversed. In the death chase there is a clear set of rewards and losses, players that have well-defined preferences, and an equilibrium concept. In the death chase this type of interaction will lead to strategies such that each player has the same expected payoff no matter the station of egress. The word "expectation" here is used in a mathematical sense. Getting off at a station has two possible payoffs. The expected value of these payoffs is the sum of each multiplied by its probability. Having the same expected payoff no matter what others plan is the consequence of strategies geared toward avoiding the worst possible outcomes in an average sense.

The minimax theorem

JOHN VON NEUMANN proved in 1928 that games such as the death chase have an equilibrium in mixed strategies and showed how to calculate the probabilities each player uses to determine his or her move. More generally, he proved that any two-player game in which the payoffs were of a zero-sum or constant-sum nature, and in which players had minimax preferences, had an equilibrium of the sort that no player had any incentive to change his or her strategy given his or her expectations of the other player's strategies. This is the fundamental theorem of game theory and arguably one of the great intellectual accomplishments of the social sciences.

While this reasoning dazzled game theorists, it rested on an unusual view of how people interact. In von Neumann's world, people play games as if they understand his theory and bow to it. One of the most difficult and subtle parts of von Neumann's analysis is that even though players decide their strategies before the game starts, without knowing what the others will do, knowing the rules of the game and others' preferences in effect allows each player to divine the mixed strategies of others. There is no direct interaction between the players, and they do not have the chance to learn from experience because the game is one-shot. If that were not strange enough, a one-shot game can have many different stages at which players move simultaneously, not in reaction to what the others do, but in reaction to what the others were anticipated to do before the game even started. Even with many stages each player could write down his or her strategy for every contingency, mail this in to the referee, and wait to hear whether he or she had won or lost.

The equilibrium from this one-shot game represents a set of strategies for which it is not profitable for any player to change his or her planned game given the anticipated strategies of the others. So knowledge of what others might do arises out of people knowing not only how the game is played, but how equilibrium emerges. More technically, knowledge of other people's strategies is "endogenous" to the model. The endoge-neity of expectations about other people's behavior means that equilibrium is on average self-fulfilling. If it were not, people would change their strategies to exploit what they believe are incorrect views held by others. As Myerson explains, "… by his emphasis on max-min values, von Neumann was implic-itly assuming that any strategy choice for a player or coalition should be evaluated against the other players' rational response, as if the others could plan their response after observing this strategy choice" (1999, 1072). This non-stop rumination about other peoples' strategies is what leads everyone to converge to mixed strategies such that their anticipations of the game's outcome are in line with what that outcome will be on average.

The self-fulfilling nature of equilibrium remains one of the most troubling aspects of game theory. Equally troubling is von Neumann's proof that at least one equilibrium mixed strat-egy exists for every two-person zero-sum game with minimax preferences (mixed strategies involve people throwing dice to decide their moves). It was also possible that multiple equi-libria might exist and that researchers could not tell which one people would choose. Von Neumann bought the certainty of equilibrium at the price of admitting randomness in the strategies of the players. The only path to a certain strategy, or strategies in his model was to admit an uncertain outcome. It became curiouser and curiouser.

The Nash Supremacy

WHEN VON NEUMANN was developing game theory the field was moving too quickly for people to be worried about subtle-ties such as multiple equilibria. Early researchers, those from the dark ages of game theory, wanted to prove there always would be an equilibrium to games of the most varied sort. What the games were saying about real-life problems was of less interest to them than proving that solutions to such games existed. Mathematical reasoning reigned. Economics was relegated to a corner in the sense that integrating game theory into current economic models was a subject of intense neglect.

Von Neumann was only able to prove that at least one mixed equilibrium would exist for zero-sum, two person non-cooperative games. Remarkable as his analysis was, it did not really cover much ground. A few years later John Nash proved that minimax preferences and zero-sum rewards were not needed to prove the existence of equilibrium. There was always an equilibrium mixed strategy for any game, be it non-zero-sum or games in which the outcome could favor both players, or so called "non-constant-sum non-cooperative games", and for any preferences.

His result was held to be revolutionary, but in fact it followed from a very simple, very clever restatement of the von Neumann problem. The key to Nash's ability to prove existence far more generally than von Neumann lay in his definition of equilibrium. According to Nash (1951, 287) "an equilibrium point is an n-tuple such that each player's mixed strategy maximizes his payoff if the strategies of the others are held fixed. Thus each player's strategy is optimal against those of the others." This is the most important two line passage written in the social sciences. It has been paraphrased and reparaphrased much as the theme song from *Casablanca*. What it boils down to is that if everyone believes that his or her actions cannot be changed to improve his or her wellbeing given the actions of all others, then we have Nash equilibrium.

Just putting the problem in this framework allowed Nash to employ a high-powered mathematical tool called *Kakutani's fixed point theorem* in his 1950 paper, and a variant upon it in his 1951 paper called *Brouwer's fixed point theorem* to prove that there had to exist at least one set of mixed strategies that mapped back into themselves for non zero-sum games, namely, a set of strategies that did not call for a shift in strategies that could improve payoffs.

The fixed point theorem was a natural way of proving this because it showed how a continuous mapping of a surface into itself always has a fixed point. In nature, wind is a continuous transformation of the atmosphere from one part of the earth's surface back to another part of that surface. Wind shifts molecules of air in a flowing manner from some position on the earth back into another position. This is the meaning of a continuous mapping of a surface onto itself. The fixed point property of such a transformation explains the fact that the wind cannot be blowing in different directions all over the earth. There has to be at least one point of calm on the globe from which the wind starts to take direction.

By adopting mixed strategies, people transform a limited set of options based on coarse pure strategies (an aggressive advertising campaign; a friendly campaign) into an infinity of options based on subtle gradations of probability (a campaign that could be aggressive or friendly with an infinite number of different probabilities). This is what produces a continuous mapping of strategies into other strategies, and this extravagant widening of options is ultimately where an equilibrium, or a fixed point, is to be found.

Hunting for stag

DESPITE THE ELEGANCE of the Nash proof it is not really clear that he added anything conceptually to von Neumann's formulation of the basic game equilibrium concept. What we were left with was an unusual way of looking at how people interact and an unintuitive master proof guaranteeing that if they did as theorists said they should a mixed equilibrium would be guaranteed to exist. It was not a guide to finding equilibria, but merely an assurance they would exist. And it suffered from the von Neumann assumption that people would play the game according to the analysts notion of how it should be played. What might happen if Holmes had not read Nash's memo and had simply fallen asleep on the train? This was never considered in the theory.

The result of this first round in the development of game theory was a mix of enthusiasm and reticence. Mathematicians respected the Nash-von Neumann results. Economists did not understand the maths and were distressed by the tendency of Nash equilibria to proliferate. For instead of pulling a single rabbit out of a Nash equilibrium hat, game theorists sometimes pulled a rabbit, a guinea pig, and a rat—so-called multiple equilibria. Game theory can be either a miserly or a promiscuous generator of equilibria. That is undesirable from the practitioner's point of view because it means the theory either can determine nothing or determines so many possibilities as to be useless as a guide to what the outcome of a game will be.

The parable of the stag hunt, first described by Jean-Jacques Rousseau, shows what is troubling about multiple Nash equilibria. Two hunters, Brimoche and Rompenil, wait quietly behind a bush for a stag to show up. Both must cooperate and pounce together or the stag escapes. Yet after a long wait, with still no stag in sight but one suspected to be lurking in the distance, both at the same time observe the chance to each catch one of two rabbits. Each can individually catch a less nutritionally satisfying rabbit, but if only one hunter does so while the other maintains his watch, the stag in the distance is alerted by the commotion and escapes. The one who waited then gets neither rabbit nor stag.

Here we have a classic simultaneous game in which the rewards are not zero-sum but allow some scope for concerted action based on mutual interest. From Brimoche's perspective, waiting to catch the stag if he expects Rompenil to go for the rabbit is not a Nash strategy because he ends up with an empty belly, whereas he could increase his payoff by also catching a rabbit.

The same reasoning is true for Brimoche. So that leaves two possible Nash equilibria in pure, that is, non-random, strategies. If Brimoche expects Rompenil to focus on the stag, then his Nash strategy is also to focus on the stag. He cannot improve his outcome by deviating from this strategy. If Brimoche expects Rompenil to hunt rabbit, then he too must hunt rabbit, and again this is a Nash strategy because deviating from it will worsen his condition by landing him with an empty belly.

There is actually a third, randomized Nash equilibrium which we do not really need to illustrate to make the point. And this point is that the cast-iron logic of Nash equilibrium makes many people want to scream in frustration at being the mental captives of so fine a theory. We want to shout at these hunters from our ivory tower and tell them to cooperate. Doing so allows them to bag the biggest game. It is even a Nash equilibrium! But what can we say when the hunters call back that chasing rabbit is also a Nash equilibrium and they are stuck in it? We must draw the curtains and remain mute. For by itself the Nash equilibrium concept is not able to say which pure equilibrium will be observed. It can only say that both are viable because each is a situation in which deviating from the strategy lowers one's payoffs given what one expects the other to do.

The Schelling Point

THE INABILITY OF the Nash equilibrium concept to rule out equilibria that were clearly inferior to all parties suggested that Nash equilibrium was a necessary but not sufficient condition for how games would play out. What was this sufficient condition? Among the first to propose an answer was Thomas Schelling, who in 1960 published a highly readable, non-mathematical treatise entitled *The Strategy of Conflict*. He suggested that when there are two or more Nash equilibria possible, and one is clearly better than the others for all involved, then people should place their hope in a "focal point" that allows them to coordinate their behavior in a way that guides them to the superior solution. The problem in the stag hunt game was one of expectations. If you had a dim expectation of your fellow man or woman, and he or she had the same of you, then you could all settle into an inferior equilibrium. But if you both believed in the village elder's sermon about the duty to be cooperative and helpful, then you could coordinate your actions around this belief to achieve a superior result. Focal points in the stag hunt throw some light on why societies in which the two main groups of citizens are deeply divided can, through some leap of faith, or belief in a wise man or woman, move almost overnight from an inferior Nash equilibrium to a superior one. Nelson Mandela's transformation of South Africa from apartheid to democracy in 1992 comes to mind.

This kind of reasoning has an immediate and intuitive appeal. How many of us have not sensed upon driving from the small town to the big city that we have left behind a certain culture of driving and entered a different culture? Traffic situations resemble games in which simultaneous choices have to be conditioned on our expectations of what others will do. In the small town, a Schelling focal point may attract people to cooperative solutions, while in the large city the focal point may be one of disregard for others. The same person, transplanted from one setting to the other, will have to rationally change his or her behavior in response to the closest focal point. The function of the focal point in each case is that it gives people some means of coordinating their behavior based purely on expectations and not upon any communication or commitment mechanism such as a contract.

If we consider society as a collection of people in need of some efficient way of coordinating their actions, then the challenge becomes that of moving to ever more efficient focal points. These thoughts can be applied to a comparison of the US and Europe. As trivial as it may sound, the US is united by focal points such as baseball, hotdogs, and American English. Europe, which is of similar size, had focal points of such variety and number that in the 20th century it gained the dubious honour of being the most ultra-violent, racist, genocidal society in history. The recent calm that has befallen that continent is perhaps due to post-war efforts to create broad focal points such as a common market, a common currency, a common soccer league, and the *Eurovision* song contest. Whether these attempts at homogenization are successful, or a return is made to older, less appealing focal points is a question haunting the policies of France and Germany, the main architects of Europe's present stability.

So how do you move from a bad focal point to a good one? In Myerson's view "pathological social expectations can be changed only by someone who is perceived as an authority or leader and who can identify a better Nash equilibrium for them" (2009, 1114). The challenge here is that everyone has to accept that the leader is properly identifying the Nash equilibria. If we go with Schelling's way of solving the problem of multiple Nash equilibria, we are reaching into an old philosophical bag of tricks. Plato had explained the need for wise men who could perceive the fundamental forms of reality lying below the surface appearance of things. The ordinary flock of mortals would then rally around these super-sensory paragons. Myerson's essay in honour of Schelling expounds on this point and even suggests that oracles interpreting divine messages can act as focal points (2009, 1116). I kid thee not.

Subgame perfection

SCHELLING'S CRACKER-BARREL SOLUTION to multiple Nash equilibria failed to impress John Harsanyi and Reinhard Selten, who eventually shared the first Nobel Prize for game theory with Nash in 1994. They may have been troubled, if not appalled, by the fix Schelling was proposing for perceived deficiencies in the Nash program. Instead of assuming some focal point for all their theoretical problems, they wanted to probe Nash's austere generalizations to see if, by thinking inside the box Nash had built, a technique for eliminating bad equilibria might not be found. They wanted to work within the frontiers of the theory and not assume the *deus ex machina* of a focal point. Schelling was then, and still remains, an outsider to the game theory purists who insist that equilibrium solutions to games must follow from the theory and not be imposed upon it from without.

Part of the problem giving rise to multiple Nash equilibria was that some games had to be played over stages. There is a first move, a second move, and so on. Von Neumann, and later Nash, showed that we could compress all such moves into a "strategy" that could be determined even before the game had started to be played. This made extended games look like one-shot games. In a strict technical sense, they were, because under the von Neumann-Nash approach, no player learned anything new about the other player at intermediate stages. Knowing the way the game was played, the incentives, and how equilibrium worked, each player could figure out all the possibilities beforehand, send in their moves by mail to an arbiter and pay the fine or collect the reward at the end. In such multi-stage games you might find absurd Nash equilibria similar to those we discussed in the one-stage stag hunt game.

Future Nobellist Reinhard Selten thought the compressed, or "normal form" Nash representation of these games hid the possibility that the Nash equilibria which seemed not-credible to all players could be eliminated. He said that the only credible equilibria were those in which each "subgame" was itself a Nash equilibrium. A subgame was a strategy chosen for the last stage of the game, or the two last stages, or the three last stages, and so, on. Basically a subgame perfect strategy had the feature that if you lopped off earlier plays and forgot about what had preceded, then your ensuing strategy would remain unchanged. It was strikingly similar to Richard Bellman's "principle of optimality" in the totally unrelated field of dynamic optimization. If you strung together the sequence of such "subgame equilibria" you would have found the only credible strategy over the whole game. To even begin to grasp what all this means we desperately need an example.

Formally the example is known as the incumbent-challenger game but I like to think of it as the Fanucci-Corleone showdown. It takes place in New York around 1915 when an aspiring gangster by the name of Guido Corleone starts committing robberies on the Brooklyn "turf" of the older Don Fanucci. There are two stages to this game. In the first stage Corleone decides either to stay off Fanucci's turf or continue robbing there. In the second stage Fanucci either fights or does not fight. If Corleone stays out and Fanucci does not fight, then Fanucci gives him a small weekly bribe of $100 while himself pocketing $500. In the other branching of this game Corleone decides to enter the turf. If Fanucci fights both die, and if Fanucci allows him to compete for criminal earnings, both get $200 a week. There are two possible Nash equilibria in this game, only one of which is subgame perfect.

Remember that a strategy is a complete specification of what a player plans to do given every contingency. One strategy leading to a Nash equilibrium is for Fanucci to fight if Corleone enters. If Corleone thinks this is Fanucci's strategy then he will simply choose to accept the $100 bribe because the alternative is to die. It is a Nash equilibrium because neither player sees an advantage in deviating from this strategy. If Corleone deviates by fighting he gets killed along with Fanucci. If Fanucci deviates and does not plan to fight, his earnings go down to $200. Yet this is not a subgame perfect equilibrium because one of the subgames in it is not a Nash equilibrium. If we consider the final stage in isolation, no matter what Corleone has chosen in the first stage, it never makes sense for Fanucci to fight. If he does he dies. If he does not then at least he gets $200.

The other Nash equilibrium is for Corleone to enter and Fanucci not to fight. In this case both get $200. Neither wishes to deviate because then all get killed. This game has a Nash equilibrium in each subgame. It would never make sense in the subgame of the final stage for Fanucci to fight. And if Corleone knows this, his optimal strategy in the first stage is to enter the market. So the larger subgame including both stages is also a Nash equilibrium.

The number of parents tormented by the logic of playing this sort of game with their children over the aeons is hard to quantify. A firm strategy of abandoning your child at roadside will, if credible, calm any backseat agitations by the most inveterate of young miscreants. Yet children are aware that the final stage of this game is not a credible equilibrium and intuitively solve the game according to Selten's logic.

As you can surmise, subgame perfection was around long before economists "discovered" it. What Selten contributed however was to prove under very general conditions that for games with some finite span, by picking their way backwards through all the payoffs each player would rule out non-credible choices by other players. By this method of backward induction players could exclude "some cases of intuitively unreasonable equilibrium points for extensive games" (Selten, 1975, 33). Put more precisely "every finite extensive game with perfect recall has at least one perfect equilibrium point." Economists later called this "sub-game perfect equilibrium". By producing a method for how people would play sequential games Selten showed how to winnow out non-credible Nash equilibria. No reliance on some mystical focal point *a la* Schelling was required.

Much of the subsequent work in game theory has emulated Selten's program of finding "refinements" to Nash equilibrium which allow the researcher to rule out non-credible behavior arising from the predictions of a model.

Yet what they mean by refinement is really a restriction. The more "refined" an equilibrium concept becomes the less general it is, and in some cases is the sign of the researcher's effort to impose equilibrium on what he or she perceives as an inefficient and inappropriate outcome to the game. So for "refinement" think "ruling out".

What Selten was ruling out was in fact the enormous efforts people go to in making their threats credible. If Corleone had thought Fanucci "crazy" enough to fight even though it deviated from the Nash equilibrium, Corleone's best strategy would have been to not enter Fanucci's turf and Fanucci would have benefitted from a better Nash equilibrium than he did by backing down. As he matured into a Don, Corleone would become very interested in whether his opponents were "men of stomach", meaning that they might well play strategies that Selten would rule out as being non-credible. These men of stomach ended up getting their way in most conflicts because of their fearsome reputations, but sometimes they met a similar opponent and the result was a very inferior Nash equilibrium for both.

An excess of stomach is thus a way to attain equilibria outside the Selten framework but also can be the path to occasional disaster. On a clear and calm day in 1976 the British Navy frigate *HMS Mermaid* and the minesweeper *HMS Fittleton*, both functioning without impairment, crashed into each other while on a standard exercise in the North Sea. The sea is a big place and crashes between big ships on clear days might seem unlikely. In fact they are not. In 1899 the first class warship *HMS Collingwood* drove straight into the side of cruiser *HMS Curacoa*. Examples abound. Sea captains are unusually tough specimens, used to getting their way, mainly because they have to in order to be effective. Was there some excess of toughness, needed to garner the credibility to attain higher Nash equilibria that led in these instances to tragically inferior Nash equilibria? Such questions define a broad swath of human interactions, ranging from relations between neighbors to relations between nations. Selten's work gave us at least some basis for thinking about the outcomes of these treacherous interactions.

The Harsanyi Renaissance

SELTEN WAS CONCERNED about multiple equilibria, but another problem plagued the Nash agenda. Everybody in the game had all the information about their opponents and their opponents about them. Von Neumann–Nash games were games of perfect information in a very specific sense. Even though you did not know how the game would pan out, you knew what your opponent's payoffs and motivations were and thus what their strategies would be. In other words, you had the complete background picture. You might not be able to predict the outcome due to mixing but you would know how the game would be played.

But what if on the train ride from Victoria station to Canterbury, Holmes believed it possible that Moriarty might fall asleep between Canterbury and Dover, but that only Moriarty knew for sure how tired he really was? This was an added wrinkle. Fatigue could come on for reasons that had nothing to do with any strategizing by the players. The risk of fatigue multiplied the possibilities Holmes had to consider. Only Moriarty knew the real answer. One could even imagine a sprite, or an unpredictable Greek deity, or as Harsanyi called it more prosaically "Nature" being a third player in this game. Nature revealed only part of her hand to any one player, and only that player would know how nature's quirks had influenced the potency of his or her strategy. From the point of view of the opponent without inside knowledge, nature split the effect of one strategy into as many different effects as nature had faces. Only the affected player knew the truth and the others had to guess the truth by forming an impression of the average potency of the other's strategy. This average was more technically called an expectation.

John Harsanyi invented this sort of reasoning in the 1960s. He called his solution a "Bayesian equilibrium" in honour of an 18th century British cleric who showed how to include prior beliefs about your environment into measures of probability, though this is not really what his equilibrium concept was about. In Harsanyi's equilibrium each player's strategy maximizes his average or "expected" payoff, given his or her equilibrium beliefs about the probable influence that nature will have on the effect of whatever strategies others will choose.

Bayesian equilibrium is the key tool for taking account of the hidden information people have about how nature has touched them, or more technically about what "types" they have become. Using this tool Harsanyi was able to create an equilibrium concept that is really nothing other than a souped-up version of Nash equilibrium, and as such, along with Nash equilibrium, has the property of being self-fulfilling, at least in an average sense. As game theorists D'Asprémont and Gérard-Varet put it in 1995, in Bayesian equilibrium, "the players' 'conjectures' about their mutual behavior are confirmed by the decisions taken by each on the basis of their private information." This mutually confirming state is the analogue of the Nash equilibrium, so looking at things this way guaranteed at least one Nash equilibrium.

"And so what?" you might rightly ask, as did some economists fatigued by the endless and seemingly pointless theorizing of game theory. Yes, the theorems were interesting, and the field seemed full of promise just as did the newly created field of genetic engineering. But despite big promises, game theory seemed just as incapable as genetic engineer of "delivering".

Great visions abounded. But applications seemed as scarce as sightings of a yeti. It was important at this stage not to blink. For indeed the yeti was about, lurking just within reach of those in the intellectual hunt for relevance in game theory.

Fusion of game theory and information economics

WE HAVE SEEN so far that game theory took off in a blast of theorizing on the existence of equilibria in mixed strategies. In the 1940s and 50s von Neumann and Nash were the pilots at the helm of this mental rocket. Then came a period of consolidation in the 1960s by Reinhard Selten, who sought a theoretical means of ruling out equilibria that game theorists found not credible in games played over stages. Another consolidator was John Harsanyi who showed how to solve games with asymmetric information. Harsanyi's work was the most important innovation in game theory since Nash, but this did not become evident until the 1970s. Then, from left field as it were, arose a new generation of young economists bent on questioning the hallowed presumptions of the theory of markets and perfect competition. Their approach had nothing to do with game theory. They were concerned with good old-fashioned equilibrium and welfare economics. They brought attention to two problems that plagued markets: lying and cheating.

You would think economists would have noticed the nuisance these darker sides of human nature posed for markets, but for some reason economic minds were otherwise occupied during the first seventy years of the 20th century. The new kids on the economic block were more street-wise than their predecessors. They were concerned about showing how lying and cheating, or more technically, "adverse selection" and "moral hazard", harmed commercial markets and threatened the integrity of social organizations such as businesses, and even governments.

You can see that when you start talking about deception, notions of strategic interaction calling for game theoretic reasoning are not far away. What then exactly was the relation between information and game theorists? The answer was fairly simple. Information theory fixated on the consequences of deception. Game theory focused on the degree to which people would try to deceive each other in the quest for some prize. One studied the consequences, the other the processes leading to bad behavior. Despite these varying objectives both information theorists and game theorists soon realized they were dealing with asymmetric information. Information theorists understood the consequences of asymmetric information for market efficiency. Game theorists understood how much asymmetric information would emerge from market interactions. This mutual recognition of common ground led to the next stage of developments in game theory.

In the first part of this next stage information theorists learned how to use the techniques of Bayesian games to understand particular problems of adverse selection and moral hazard that were bothering them. This was the era of "signalling", as discovered by Nobellist Michael Spence in 1973, which will be discussed at greater length later on.

Second, and more remarkably, game theorists used their knowledge of Bayesian solutions to transform games of lying and cheating into games where everyone was honest and obedient (which, as you might quickly grasp, is no game at all). Put differently, they created a sort of "reverse game theory" in which government manipulated the rules and rewards of games to neuter all strategic comportment. It was as if someone had invented the jet engine and then a team of engineers figured out how to dampen the sound by attaching speakers that sent waves of sound to perfectly counter the engine's roar. Roger Myerson, David Kreps, Bengt Holmstrom, Thomas Mroz, Jonathan Ostroy, Sherwin Rosen, Theodore Groves, and about a dozen others who in greater or lesser degree came up at around the same time with the idea that games with Bayes equilibria could be hemmed about by incentives which made people tell the truth. There is no other precedent in economics for such a simultaneous eruption of discovery. The convergence of this intellectual pullulation, known as the "revelation principle", is only now starting to be appreciated.

Ex ludis probitas et oboedentia

BEFORE GETTING INTO how information and game theory merged we need to learn a few terms from information economics and appreciate why some researchers bothered to invent them. Then we need to see how Spence's informational model of signalling led to the fusion of game theory and information economics. We want to grasp how this fusion led to the neutralization of games through inverse game theory. In other words, we want to understand how by setting the rewards and rules of games to act as incentives for behavior, we can make people behave honestly and obediently. A Latin scholar would describe this situation as one of *ex ludis probitas et oboedientia*. Through games, honesty and obedience. What other science can boast such a motto?

Information economics is about lying and cheating. Lying is called adverse selection. Adverse selection arises when people misrepresent themselves in order to gain access to some group in a way that profits them at the expense of everyone else in the group. Academic plagiarism is a manifestation of the quest of some to obtain real credentials based on false achievement so that they might insinuate themselves into businesses, churches, or academia. Once ensconced, they draw a weekly check while riding upon the superior efforts and abilities of their fellow workers. Resentment and ultimately the demise of the institution which they populate may result.

At its heart, adverse selection is a problem of honesty. Dishonesty can bring down insurance companies. Some people want to hide the fact that they are high-risk types because they would have to pay higher premiums than low-risk types. An insurance company that fails to devise and enforce a contract that separates people into different risk categories may go bankrupt through a subtle process of in-migration of high-risk types to its policies and out-migration of low-risk types. To see this, consider that when high-risk clients sneak into a low-risk insurance pool by pretending to be low-risk, suddenly claims on the pool increase. Then premiums must rise to ensure the solvency of the pool. The premiums are still lower than what high-risk types would pay in their own pool, but higher now for low-risk types than what they would have paid without the added risk burden of helping to prop up high-risk clients. These premiums may drive some low-risk types to seek companies that better control adverse selection, leading to higher premiums for the people still remaining in the pool which chases out further low-risk types until all that are left are high-risk people in the market for insurance.

The separating equilibrium problem plagues used car markets where lemons and sound vehicles are difficult to distinguish before purchase. Without a market mechanism, such as credible inspection certificates and 30-day guaranteed return policies, a separating equilibrium may not emerge. Instead, some people with sound vehicles will prefer to take them off the market because the presence of lemons depresses prices. As this process continues, soon most of what is left in the market are lemons. Of course there will always be gems to be found, but these are the exception rather than the rule in markets plagued by adverse selection, or "lemonitis".

Adverse selection also afflicts social organizations where team effort determines some collectively sought-after result. Think of managers at a government health ministry. They work together to help the ministry provide efficient health services to citizens, but pointing to and then rewarding the output of any single manager is difficult, if not absurd, despite "performance management plans" that may be implemented.

The difficulty of measuring individual contributions exposes the ministry to the influx of managers who overstate their abilities and qualifications. When too many such managers are hired, the burden on good managers rises. They may leave and the ministry may fall into disrepute. To protect itself from such adverse selection, the ministry may invest hundreds of thousands of dollars to find a qualified manager.

The fundamental problem in all of these examples is that of finding a separating equilibrium based on the credible communication of information. In other words, how do we guarantee honesty so that our organizations do not topple under the burden of carrying light-weights? The problem may go beyond the honesty of applicants to include the honesty of employers who may accept bribes to let in under-qualified candidates. One of the reasons Napoleon's armies clobbered the armies of continental Europe and Britain was that during *La Revolution*, the French instituted a system of officer selection based on merit. In Britain and on the continent, aspiring officers could and sometimes had to buy their commissions. The dishonesty here lay not with the applicant, but with the army, which by admitting inferior officers betrayed the trust of the people.

As if adverse selection were not a sufficiently daunting challenge to social organizations, a further problem known as "moral hazard" follows upon admission to the organization. Even if a separating equilibrium exists in which low-risk people pool uniquely with each other for insurance, they might be tempted to be lax about taking risks, or might even take risks on purpose in order to profit from some important payout.

Consider insurance and the old joke of the farmer who tells his friend he has just bought crop insurance against fire and hail. The friend scratches his head and says, "Well, I understand about the fire insurance, but how do you make it hail?" The point is that for insurance in which people cannot influence the outcome, moral hazard is not a problem for either the insured or insurers.

A wedge of suspicion slips between the two in cases where the insured party controls what theorists call a "self-protection variable", meaning the ability to take precautions that minimize risk or to expose themselves to needless risk. Suspicion and obfuscation can arise when the self-protection variable is difficult for the insurer to observe. Then the prospect of manipulating this variable for their own gain acts as a hazard to the morals of those buying insurance.

Armen Alchian and Harold Demsetz (1972) showed that moral hazard is not just a problem for insurance markets but also for companies. Once they have passed through the filters of the hiring process, even highly qualified and talented managers may decide to "free-ride" on the efforts of others. When such free-riding becomes endemic, as it seemed to be in *East Bloc* countries at the end of the 1980s, an entire system of social organization may collapse.

Whereas adverse selection arises from the individual misrepresenting his or her risk type or skills, moral hazard arises from the difficulty of observing the individual's manipulation of his or her self-protection variable. Thus both adverse selection and moral hazard are problems of information that individuals withhold to the detriment of the group. These problems arise from an asymmetry of information. Wherever such an asymmetry exists, so does the possibility of a Bayesian game.

The Spence Signal

AMONG THE FIRST to notice that Bayesian games and adverse selection were a fit, was future Nobellist Michael Spence in 1973. How do businesses know whom to hire and how much to pay? If businesses could properly assess the contribution of an employee to the bottom line, then the business could easily pay less to the less productive worker. The problem is that it can be very hard to know how much employee number 32,715 has contributed to the value of a complex output such as a jet plane. In the absence of a clear metric of performance, companies may remunerate workers based on their abilities. Often they judge these abilities by the certificates of qualification workers acquire before they enter the market. The problem businesses encounter by using this technique is that official qualifications are an imperfect, or noisy, signal of worker aptitude. Despite this difficulty it is imperative for companies to pay according to some reliable metric of worker contribution to output. And it may even be possible for the payment to elicit from workers a clear signal about their potential contributions to output!

To understand this imperative, consider a team of employees devising a new braking system for a luxury automobile. If the sum of salaries reflects the value the team of workers contributes to a company, then a policy of equal pay to workers making unequal contributions can provoke unrest among the achievers. The policy of equal pay is a clear transfer of money from achievers to non-achievers. This zero-sum burden may incite competent workers to leave the company in search of employment where they do not have to carry incompetents on their backs. As competent workers flee, fewer competent workers are left. The burden of the incompetents on them increases, and soon a mass exodus may lead to the firm's collapse. The risk that these free-riders pose is acute because they impose zero-sum costs on their fellow workers. Their gain comes strictly at the loss of others. In the end, bad workers chase out the good ones. The challenge to the firm lies in getting workers to themselves reveal to it their abilities.

Spence's achievement was to provide a rigorous example of a case in which employers could use their compensation strategies to elicit honest revelation from workers. He postulated a Bayesian game between the firm in a competitive job market and the potential workers it must choose from. The reward is the salary the firm chooses to pay based on education. The game is Bayesian because only the worker knows if he or she is competent or incompetent, whereas the firm knows only the general proportion of worker types in the economy. If fifty per cent of workers are known to be competent, the firm might just take its chances, engage the worker, and pay the high salary. But the firm would like to do better. It would like to somehow separate the two types. In this, its interests are aligned with competent workers who want to be believed about their type, and opposed by the incompetents who wish to misrepresent themselves.

There might be some way of having the truth come out if the competent worker could send a credible "signal" to the firm of his or her type. The firm knows that in general, fifty percent of workers are competent. Then upon observing a credible signal, the firm would increase its perceived probability that the worker is competent to perhaps sixty per cent. This credible signal would lead the firm to offer potential workers who send it a higher wage. An even more credible signal would lead to an even higher wage. But what would lead to a completely credible signal, one that contains full information about the types?

For a signal to be credible, it must be costly to send, and the competent potential hire must have lower costs of sending it than the incompetent one. Talk cannot be cheap. The firm must be careful not to set the wage for strong signals too high or the incompetent worker could be induced to bear the extra costs of sending the signal in order to get the job. Recall Muceus Scaevola, a Roman who snuck into the enemy Etruscan camp to assassinate its leadership. He bumbled, was caught, and in defiance of his captors held his right hand over a flame until it caught fire, all the while extolling Roman virtues and his defiance of the Etruscans. So impressed were the Etruscans by his bravery that they set him free. Because there was no anticipated reward in sight, Muceus' gesture was a costly and credible signal. But if instead he had been promised his freedom and a bag of gold then the motives for his bravery might have been questioned. The inept job candidate who sees great qualifications may be moved to great efforts to attain them, perhaps through bribery, if the salary is right. What ideally happens is that the employer sets a wage premium for the better job only just high enough to make it profitable for the able worker to send the signal but not for the inept worker.

The result is a Bayesian equilibrium because the employer does not know worker types but only their spread in the economy. As Spence explained "... an equilibrium can be thought of as a set of employer beliefs that generate offered wage schedules, applicant signalling decisions, hiring, and ultimately new market data over time that are consistent with the initial beliefs" (1973, p. 360). The signal Spence had in mind was education. In his view, education could help employers separate competent from incompetent workers, even if the education had contributed nothing to the student's abilities and knowledge. If all workers recognize that getting a degree will help them land a job, but it costs competent workers less time to get a *BA* than it costs incompetent workers, then given the right spread of wages, the degree would separate the two groups and serve as a perfect signal for competence.

Take, for example Isolde who is a competent potential job candidate and can do her weekly studies twice as fast as Tristan, who is an incompetent potential candidate. This means that over her years at university, Isolde can work more hours part-time earning money, and thus reduce more than Tristan the foregone income from not working full-time over the course of her education. These foregone wages are the opportunity cost of an education. If the salary difference between competent and incompetent candidates is $20,000 over the career, and Isolde's opportunity cost of education is $19,000, then she goes to university. If Tristan's opportunity cost is $21,000, he does not go to university. All the Tristans and Isoldes in the economy reason this way and thus there exists a "separating equilibrium" wage which sorts high skill workers into firms that need them and shuttles low skill workers into low skill jobs. It remains for the firm to divine this wage, perhaps through trial and error as Spence suggests, though the actual process is secondary to the game-theoretic solution of this problem.

This example is almost trivial because it makes no direct use of the firm's knowledge of the proportion of worker types in the economy. If incompetent workers had varied in their opportunity costs of getting an education, a simple separating wage might not have been obtained. Instead some incompetents at the low range of education costs of their type might have completed their *BA*s and so slipped into the firm. In this case fuller use of the Harsanyi solution concept for Bayesian games would come into full play because this concept was designed to apply to a spectrum of player types. This game also may have no solution if the costs of education are very high and the differences in abilities of Isolde and Tristan are small. In that case, the cost of the signal is large and potentially discouraging, especially if there is little by way of differences in education costs to distinguish the two candidates.

It is difficult to emphasize what an important turning point in game theory Spence's analysis was. The signalling game differed from the games that had preoccupied earlier theorists because in it one or more players can control the rewards. In the stag hunt and Sherlock Holmes games, the rewards were given and players had only their choice of a move or a probability to work with. The signalling game is often much easier to solve than those other games because one or more players has the freedom to alter the conditions of the game until the best possible solution for each appears. In the case of education, the potential worker can decide how much to invest in education. This affects his costs and potential rewards. The firm decides how to vary the wage to elicit the desired signal. The reason Spence got his Nobel prize for writing one significant article in economics was because he showed that information theory and game theory could be united in a way that did away with lying in equilibrium. He was a pioneer of reverse game theory.

The signalling game also differed from previous research in that it actually had something to say about public policy.

After three decades of arid theorizing some practical result was a development that came as a welcome relief to applied economists. If it were true that education had a strong signalling function, say at the university level, how should this guide government funding for undergraduates? The traditional economic argument had been that markets fail to appreciate the "externalities" or "spillovers" that an educated person generates on his or her path through life. Spillovers might be participation on hospital boards, organizing food aid, and civic spirit. Some argued that these positive manifestations should be more frequent in the person whose sensibilities had been trained up in places of "higher" learning. Even if education cost more than the amount by which it increased job productivity, the extra value of these spillovers to society would justify the government subsidy.

Spence's signalling game raised a contrary point. If government lowered the cost of an education through subsidized tuition and generous bursaries, then incompetent potential employees might start to think it was worthwhile to get an education. As they left the ranks of academe clutching their degrees, they would march onto the job market where they would elbow out some of the more competent workers and spend years mooching off the efforts of their fellow workers. Some indication that the signal from an undergraduate education had indeed been corrupted by "degree inflation" was the search for a remedy in the rapid spread of professional schools offering professional degrees for graduates. Degrees such as the *MBA* were not subsidized and because they would then attract only those truly interested in investing in demonstrating their competence might serve as an appropriate signal for generating separating wages.

So where did Spence's analysis fit in a broader picture?

Spence had suggested a means by which the deception inherent in Bayesian games could be eliminated. In his signalling game, revelation came about by the choice a potential employee made to invest his or her time and money in an education. Because the cost of education is related to the competence of the person, education would then serve as a credible signal of the student's likelihood of turning out to be a competent employee. It is up to the firm to elicit this signal by controlling the rewards to investing in education, namely, the salary. The way to short-circuit the game lies in paying the correct salary to elicit the correct signal.

There are other games of asymmetric information where one player, usually called "the principal", cannot tell if the signal is true, and where the other player or players, called the "agents", have no means by which to send a credible signal. The idea in these games is to elicit the truth from people by setting up the rewards of the game in such a way that it makes truthtelling the most profitable action. Instead of investing money to *elicit a signal*, money is invested to *elicit truthful behavior*.

The Vickrey auction

THE TRICK FOR doing this was first noticed in 1961 by William Vickrey. He is credited with discovering how to elicit the truth from a few non-competitive suppliers trying to sell services to a government marketing agency at exaggerated prices. What Vickrey had in mind was some government marketing agency that wanted to buy from different suppliers and resell to consumers in such as way as to mimic what a free market would do.

Government presumably feels the need to intervene for fear that suppliers would organize themselves into a cartel to artificially boost prices. In this role as middle person, government is subject to the potential lies of suppliers complaining they need a high price because of supposedly high costs. On the other end of matters, consumers may pretend that their willingness to pay for the product is lower than it really is. The example seems contrived in the present age, where government has curtailed its direct role in managing private markets, but as we shall see, Vickery's idea is widely applicable to many other forms of government intervention. How exactly does the truth-revelation scheme work? Let us speak of firms. The idea is similar for consumers.

First, let us consider a non-Vickrey solution to this problem and see where it goes wrong. That will better help us to understand Vickrey's insight. In deciding what a reasonable bid is, the government does not know the individual cost of any particular firm, but may have some general idea of the proportion of firms with high and low costs. Using this "prior" information it could play the Bayesian game by developing some notion of the probability that a firm is telling the truth, given the known distribution of firm costs in the economy. The government could decide whether to believe and award the contract, not believe and exclude the firm, or to randomize by flipping a coin to determine which firm or firms get the contract. The problem is that the resulting equilibria might satisfy the Nash condition, but could be quite bad if, by randomization, government chose the high-cost firms exclusively.

Vickrey saw that government could do better by avoiding randomization and game-playing. It could neutralize the game by manipulating its conditions so as to get full revelation of cost information by firms. The term used in his day was "anti-speculation". The modern term for this sort of reverse-game is "mechanism design". Thinking of a truth revelation scheme Vickrey noted that, "one method, though an expensive one

... [is] to arrange to purchase the commodity from suppliers and to sell it to purchasers on terms that are dependent on the reported supply and demand curves in such a way that the suppliers and purchasers will maximize their profits, individually at least, by reporting correctly, so that any misrepresentation will subject them to risk of loss" (1961, 10).

One way to make firms tell the truth is to make them aware of the cost of lying. To do this Vickrey suggested government ask them all to submit information on their production costs (which is the same thing as a supply curve in a competitive market). The government has no way of telling now or in the future if these costs are real or fictitious. What the government can do is tell one supplier, call it Baal Telephone, that it will consider as truthful the reports of all other suppliers. Government will then calculate on the basis of these presumably true-cost reports from the other firms what their free-market level of production should be. Then it will look at Baal Telephone's supply report and calculate how much extra free-market production that would merit. Recall that the government is trying to calculate the optimum free market level of production by all firms. This optimum involves contracting to firms with the lowest costs the greatest amount of production.

In addition, for this extra production, government will pay to Baal the premium that consumers would have been willing to pay for it over the free-market price. The idea here is that consumers seldom pay exactly what they were willing to pay. Often the price they pay is below their maximum hold-out price. So now Baal must consider that if it pretends costs are too large, government will calculate that its production should be small and Baal will lose out on collecting juicy consumer premiums in the form of government handouts. If Baal low-balls its costs, it will be ordered to produce beyond what consumers are willing to pay and falling into this negative zone will curtail its profits as well.

If each firm is given this sort of choice, will all firms be ultimately led by the government payoff scheme to produce the correct competitive quantity? This is a question of the Nash equilibrium that would emerge. If Baal Telephone believes all others are going to pretend they have high costs, this is just fine by Baal, because that reduces what they get to produce and gives Baal a large segment of the market to indirectly milk through truthfully reporting and getting government subsidies. Others see the danger and try to thus get more output by being more truthful. Everyone being truthful is a Nash equilibrium because no one could deviate from it given the strategies of the other players and come out ahead. The final quantity that results from this game will be efficient in the sense that it has exhausted all possibility for furthering productive exchanges between producers and consumers. It turns out that this is also a Pareto equilibrium.

Vickrey's mechanism does not work in all cases of asymmetric information. It only makes sense to look for a Vickrey mechanism when there is some sort of alignment of interests. In other words, the game in question may be non-cooperative but must not be zero-sum. The essence of the Vickrey mechanism is that one player is paying off another, albeit indirectly, in order to get a better outcome. You can only pay someone off and come out ahead yourself if there is a concordance of interests. In the Holmes-Moriarty death chase, no bargaining is possible because one man's gain is precisely the other's loss. This is why a zero-sum interaction precludes the implicit bargaining behind the Vickrey formula. The concordance of interests in the telephony example was between Baal Telephone and the government acting on behalf of consumers. The government's truth revelation mechanism was motivated by the creation of wealth in society that such a mechanism might induce.

Mechanism design and the size of government

VICKREY MADE A case that government is needed to prevent rapacious oligopolists from milking consumers of a private good and that mechanism design was the way to reverse engineer the Bayesian game in favour of economic efficiency. Government achieves this objective by devising a reward structure for truth. This structure is characterized by "incentive constraints". As Myerson explains, "These incentive constraints express the basic fact that individuals will not share private information or exert hidden efforts without appropriate incentives" (2009, 587). The constraint is devised to be "incentive compatible", a phrase signifying that being honest and obedient is compatible with your private, selfish objectives. Ten years after Vickrey, a swarm of economists used his insights to argue that government may also fruitfully apply mechanism design to government spending.

Suppose government must decide between building a hospital or creating a national park, each of which will cost the same amount of money. How does it know which one to finance? It could ask voters how much they are willing to pay above the per-person cost to see their preferred project go through. The project for which people are willing to pay the most would be the one creating the most wealth in society. If you expected only to pay this cost, you would be tempted to overstate the value of your choice because by doing so you could skew the government decision towards your desired position without a concomitant increase in your personal cost. Here we have a commonality of interest in that the government is seeking to create the most value in society. There is also the problem of asymmetric information because government has no way of knowing whether people are telling it the truth about their valuations. This is a Bayesian game ripe for conversion to a truth-telling equilibrium through the application of an incentive-compatible mechanism. The revelation principle at work.

The mechanism is similar to Vickrey's and is generally called a Vickrey-Clarke-Groves auction. It works by asking each person what the net benefit to him or her is above the per-person cost of providing the preferred alternative. You add up the dollar votes for the hospital and if the sum is greater than that for the park, the hospital gets built. But there is a catch. As well as getting charged the per-person cost of building the hospital, any voter who was "pivotal" in forcing the decision will pay an extra cost equal to the loss of net benefit to the other voters who did not see the park get created. "Pivotal" means that by announcing a high valuation on a certain outcome, it was you who tipped the political balance in its favour.

As Tideman and Tullock explained, "A nontruthful response cannot benefit the respondent, and it carries a risk of making him worse off than he would have been with the truth. If he understates his value, he may pass up an opportunity to obtain the result he desires at an attractive price. If he overstates his value, he may wind up paying more than it is worth to him to have his choice" (1976, 1148).

Correctly revealing your preferences is a Nash equilibrium because if everyone is expected to tell the truth, there is no profit for any single person to deviate from the truth. If we lie to get our way and others are telling the truth, we will be punished with an extra tax. If we lie by understating our preferences while others are honest, the compensation they pay will be proportional to our understated loss and thus not really enough to compensate us for our true loss of not seeing our preferred alternative go through.

Centralized (Vickrey-Clark-Groves) vs. decentralized (Spence) mechanisms

ENTHUSIASM FOR MECHANISMS that reveal voter preferences was quite high among researchers during the 1970s, but it eventually waned. The catch with the Vickrey-Clarke-Groves scheme is that the money collected by the government has to be literally destroyed. If you give the money back to voters through a transfer scheme, then the impact of the user-fee revelation scheme on truth telling is blunted. Even if money is used to pay off the national debt, or build a road somewhere, people in general will still feel that some of it is coming back to them through lower future taxes needed to pay off the debt, or increased services through the use of roads. There are similar revelation schemes that pay voters to tell the truth but these can rack up large deficits, as Groves and Ledyard (1977) proved.

Enthusiasm also waned because the schemes being proposed were not only bewildering but also impractical. The difficulty and impracticality of Vickrey-Clarke-Groves mechanisms stemmed from trying to elicit truth-telling through complicated reward schemes and the use of a multi-stage arbitration process by some impartial government figure. Mechanism designs of this type relied on a central authority to make them work, because individuals had no way of by themselves proving that they were telling the truth. Only a straightjacket of rewards or punishments designed by the government could squeeze the truth out of them. In contrast, the signaling games that Spence discovered allowed individuals to make private decisions to invest in say, education, to send a signal to employers that was credible because it was costly. The employer did have a role in eliciting this signal through the salary, or more generally some reward. The ability of the other parties to send signals gave Spence's theory a degree of latitude that made it simpler to understand and to see at work in the real world.

Compare, for example, the contortions required by Vickrey-Clarke-Groves mechanisms to elicit truth from voters. Compare it with the way politics seems actually to be done via the use of costly signals. Voters who want to honestly express their preferences may do so by bearing costs. Campaign contributions are a signal of preferences, as are the lobbying efforts and the efforts of those who organize rallies and letter-writing campaigns.

As in the case of job-market signaling, politicians, like employers, do not want to over-reward investment in signals. Too strong a reward dilutes the value of the signal by encouraging everyone to invest in sending the signal. Employers then lose the means of divining the type of person they are considering for a job, and politicians have trouble trying to decide which interest groups should get a grant. This is why laws that restrict campaign contributions, and which award start-up money to budding interest groups may actually interfere with the duty of a democracy. For without credible signals from the people, politicians have little to go on in deciding how to spend money.

In societies where voters are not able to send credible signals by their own efforts, some attempt to coax the truth from them must be made. Vickrey-Clark-Groves mechanisms are one such possible attempt. They do not rely on signals but rather upon enticements to elicit the truth about voter preferences. As such, they have to be imposed from the top. In sum, if we do not allow mechanisms to work whereby individuals may send costly signals to politicians, we may need to rely on schemes that politicians concoct to bribe the truth out of us.

The mechanism zoo

BY GETTING PEOPLE to reveal the truth and act honestly, Vickrey-Clark-Groves schemes and signaling games make people coordinate their actions in a mutually fruitful manner.

Each mechanism took a different path. Vickrey-Clarke-Groves was in a centralist tradition. Spence offered a decentralized solution to lying and cheating. Of mechanism designs in the Vickrey-Clark-Groves approach, Nobellist Eric Maskin noted that, "The theory of mechanism design can be thought of as the 'engineering' side of economic theory. Much theoretical work, of course, focuses on existing economic institutions. The theorist wants to explain or forecast the economic or social outcomes that these institutions generate. But in mechanism design theory the direction of inquiry is reversed. We begin by identifying our desired outcome or social goal. We then ask whether or not an appropriate institution (mechanism) could be designed to attain that goal" (2008, 567). True. But there were other mechanism designs that worked in a decentralized manner. Spence's signaling model was one such example. There were others.

In fact there was an entire zoo of mechanisms for getting people to behave and coordinate their actions towards a mutually profitable outcome. Game theorists Claude d'Aspremont and Louis-André Gérard-Varet explained that, "game theory can ... propose a solution: some cooperative transformation may be introduced creating a new game with equilibria having better welfare properties. Such a transformation can come about through a 'regulation,' a 'mediation' or an 'audit.'

It may be obtained by 'repeating' the game, by adding a 'communication scheme,' or by 'contractually' modifying the original payoff structure" (1995). To most people, the term "cooperative transformation" would be gobbledygook, but having come this far we are in a position to understand it effortlessly. The cooperative transformation these authors speak of is a means of converting liars and cheats into honest, obedient folk. Vickrey-Clark-Groves did this through a "mediation". Spence did this through a "communication scheme". One mechanism we have not explored was discovered by Roger Myerson and Mark Satterthwaite (1983) who focused on how the expected payoffs could be modified by manipulating the probabilities of success. There is a proliferation of other schemes, but to best round out our survey we can be satisfied with looking at the "repeating the game" phrase from the above paragraph. What does a mechanism like that look like?

Repeated interaction is perhaps the only game theoretical idea that non-economists seem intuitively comfortable with, perhaps due to the 2005 French historical movie *Joyeux Noël*. In the first Christmas of the European conflict of 1914-1918, soldiers in opposing trenches dialled down their aggressive acts, knowing that a night raid or a mortar lobbed on the heads of lunching enemies would provoke an outraged retaliation. Those making these decisions were low-level people, junior and non-commissioned officers on opposing sides of a line across which higher-ups tolerated no communication except the roar of guns and the thrust of bayonets. Yet using primitive signals, soldiers managed, through repeated interactions in no-man's land, to implicitly agree to a neutral posture. So complete was this informal truce that on Christmas Day 1914, French, Scottish, and German soldiers came out of their trenches to play football and exchange trinkets.

The emergence of peace from war is captured in the repeated play of a game called the "prisoner's dilemma". It is one of those rare games where you do not need a Nash solution concept to see where matters are heading because one solution clearly dominates all others. To stay with the warfare analogy, imagine two soldiers on either side of the barbed wire, armed with grenades. If the French soldier throws and the German does not, then the German dies, and vice versa. There are two other possibilities. If both soldiers throw simultaneously then the blast of two grenades partially neutralizes their effect but both soldiers still get some injuries. If neither throws, then neither is injured. What to do? If you are only playing this game once, then there is only one option. Throw your grenade. This is a "dominant" strategy because no matter what the other guy does, your best decision is to throw. For if the other throws and you do not, then you die. It is better to throw if you think this is going to happen. If the other does not throw and you do, then he dies. Better to throw in this situation, too. In other words, no matter what the other guy decides, it is better for you to throw. But because he is thinking in the same way, then he throws too. What you get is an inferior equilibrium in which both are injured. If only they could have somehow communicated and then committed to not throwing, then both would be unscathed. Repeated play allows both players to communicate in the sense that if someone throws this time around and you do not, then you will punish him next time by throwing.

Computer simulations have shown that this sort of game can converge to a cooperative equilibrium, although game theorist David Kreps (1990) has also shown there are many other possible equilibria to this repeated game. The point for game theorists is that repeated interaction is a way of signaling intentions and coordinating actions in such a way that the game "converges" to a cooperative interaction. We may think of many societies where government is not present as experiencing such convergence between isolated pockets of individuals living far away from a mechanism-minded law-giver.

Are free markets better or worse?

THUS WE COME to the end of game theory. The first half of the subject consists of learning how people play games. The second half consists of learning how to neutralize these games to prevent lying and cheating. *Ex ludis probitas et oboedentia.* Out of games, honesty and obedience. We have examined three main categories of neutralization techniques (though others exist): Vickrey-Clark-Groves mechanisms, signaling mechanisms, and repeated game play. All seek to fruitfully coordinate behavior by enticing people to reveal their personal information. Understanding what leads to communication and coordination between groups of people may seem like thin gruel to those who struggle through the basics of game theory and mechanism design. David Kreps (1990) and Roger Myerson (2008) urge us not to despair. Despite some frustrating features, game theory enables us to understand what forces are at work in some of the really big questions of political economy.

One of these big questions is whether private markets are more or less efficient at coordinating people than is control by a central authority. In the 1930s this was known as the "socialist calculation debate" because knowing how to calculate what people needed and what factories could produce seemed like the essence of the debate between free marketers and socialists. Louis Makowski and Joseph Ostroy (1992) describe how socialists cleverly turned free-market logic against capitalism. So-called "market socialists" argued that a government that controlled all resources could find an economically effi-cient way of producing by imitating the free market. The gov-ernment needed to know the value people attached to con-suming some product and at what cost firms could produce. Willingness to pay and ability to produce at low cost are the essence of demand and supply relations. In free markets a price is supposed to emerge that equates consumption and output in such a way as to unite consumers who are willing to pay the most with producers who are able to produce at the lowest cost. A government that knew consumer needs and producer capa-bilities could manipulate prices until an equilibrium emerged.

Friedrich Hayek accepted the socialist premise that a cen-tral planner could ape the free market provided it had all the relevant information on needs and abilities. But according to him this presumption of knowledge was a "fatal conceit". In his 1945 article, "The Use of Knowledge in Society", he argued that each person holds private information about his desires and abilities, information of "time and place" that he or she is either unable or unwilling to share with the central planner. If, instead, the individual may own his or her own property, then through a process of competitive bidding for this property and its fruits, people reveal personal information. The equilibrium price that results is a compression into one number of all the dispersed economic data needed to guide the economy to an efficient equilibrium. Socialists countered that by allowing fac-tory managers to experiment with prices in their local markets, they could also arrive at the "knowledge of time and place" that Hayek said was only available to private individuals.

The debate became a stalemate that lasted for forty years. It seemed neither side was really speaking the same language as the other. This is not surprising, as the language needed had not yet been invented. What was needed was a better understanding of the informational problems that prevent coordination between people. By fusing game theory and information economics, mechanism design provided the language, or framework, in which both socialists and free marketers could compare the merits of their arguments.

It seemed that socialism and capitalism were good at different things. Socialism suffered from cheating, or "moral hazard", more than capitalism because it did not allow company managers to own shares in their own companies. In socialist systems managers would readily sell raw materials needed by their firm on the black market because the manager had no part in the ownership of the company. By way of contrast, in capitalist economies, allowing managers to own shares in their firm discouraged them from slacking or corruptly selling at too low a price. This aspect of private property provided managers with the "incentive constraint" necessary to make them behave honestly. Knowing that the manager would not be pilfering the company stockpiles gave outside investors the confidence to coordinate their financial support with the entrepreneurial drive of the company managers. Of course Soviets were not blind to the moral hazard problem. They dealt with it by investing in propaganda that would inculcate a sense of public service in managers. Failing that, there was the gulag.

The flip side of the cheating problem in socialism is the lying or "adverse selection" problem in capitalism. If potential firm managers are either good or bad, but telling them apart is difficult, bad prospects will lie to become a part of the firm. According to Roger Myerson, "a potential advantage of socialism … is that a socialist state's monopoly of capital can facilitate honest communication, as bad managers cannot gain from imitating good managers if neither type gets any profits from entrepreneurial management" (2008, 600). He argues that, "society does not need to pay anything more than the manager's normal cost of time, and the manager has no incentive to lie about his type to get the project funded because he gets no special benefit from managing it" (2008, 599).

Myerson's view of the socialist calculation debate can be disputed. Makowski and Ostroy (2001) use a subtle argument about who gets what in capitalism to suggest that perfect competition with "full appropriation" of the social contribution everyone's production makes is an incentive compatible system.

Getting deeper into this debate is not our objective. The important thing to understand is that the old questions of how people use information to coordinate their actions is very much alive in present research on game theory and mechanism design. Coordination is really where everything "is at" in game theory, just as this is the preoccupation of classical economics, where strategic interactions between individuals do not figure.

The apprenticeship of game theory

GAME THEORY IS an abstract vision of how people formulate strategies against others contesting some valuable resource. It fits into the logic of economics because it postulates a rational individual maximizing some objective subject to constraints. Yet it differs from most other branches of economics in that the constraints are not material, but mental. Material constraints do not allow for strategic interaction. As discussed, the consumer has no control over prices or income. These are givens that emerge from the competitive jostling of masses of people looking to buy or sell. In their numbers they are either anonymous to each other, or have their behavior prescribed by the rules governing the exchange of property. In the interplay of supply and demand, no one exerts control over how resources are to be divided.

The situation changes when people confront each other over control of a resource and have either no interest in striking a bargain with each other, or no reliable way of entering into one. In that case, personal intentions rather than impersonal parameters such as prices become the constraint against which every person must make his or her calculations of how to make the best of the situation, though of course behind intentions there may be a backing force. The subject matter of game theory is thus hostility and antagonism, though elements of common interest may sometimes be present. Antagonism is rife because either the rules governing the transfer of property are not well defined, or because the owners of property interact in a non-competitive setting where buyers do not feel the pressure of other potential bidders to force them to reveal their true valuation of a product.

Hostility is present because the resource in question is up for grabs. For some thinkers, the view that everyone is out to "get you" is a paranoid and unrealistic stance that relegates game theory to irrelevancy. They believe that through trial and error the masses strive to replace unpredictable and potentially catastrophic game playing between individuals with rules. An ordered society allows people to disengage from the fabricated constraints of hostility and focus their attention on dealing with the immutable constraints imposed by limited physical resources. This critique of game theory misses the point that a theory which explains behavior that never takes place is not useless. The US and Russia did not drop atomic bombs on each other but the military expense of that era was a reaction to game theoretic forces. In the same vein, even if a society finds a fix for the problems that lead to gaming, the structure of the games in question allow us to understand whether these fixes are the best possible.

Becoming a game theorist is a life-long quest, but mastering its essentials is within reach of almost anyone. To figure out how people will interact in a strategic encounter only three pieces of information are needed. One must know what the prize in question is, how the game is played, and how a resolution, or equilibrium, is reached. All critiques of game theory must center on questioning the validity of any one of the assumptions we make about these three necessary pieces. David Kreps's simple yet brilliant exposition of game theory exposes these three pillars to a critique in Chapter 5 of his 1990 book.

Starting from this base you can obviously come up with any sort of game your imagination may conceive, but game theorists have come up with only a handful that they believe are at the basis of human strategic interaction. In this vein, Myerson explained that, "… the task for economic theorists in the generations after Nash has been to identify the game models that yield the most useful insights into economic problems. The ultimate goal of this work will be to build a canon of some dozens of game models, such that a student who has worked through the analysis of these canonical examples should be well prepared to understand the subtleties of competitive forces in the widest variety of real social situations" (1999, 1080). These "canonical" games are really just stories told with a high degree of precision and consistency.

The consistency and logic of game theory are its strengths. Yet by setting itself the lofty task of understanding interactions between individuals, it runs up against the "curse of dimensionality". Originally used to express problems in dynamic programming, this term now describes situations in which a wealth of categorizing and assumptions leads to an explosion of possible outcomes such that no solution or equilibrium is evident. Game theory's most basic lesson may be that as we shift focus from crowds (supply and demand) to individuals, general insights cede their place to a proliferation of stories and possible outcomes known as "multiple equilibria."

References

Alchian, Armen A. and Harold Demsetz. 1972. "Production, Information Costs and Economic Organization." *American Economic Review*, volume 62: 777-785.

d'Aspremont, Claude and Louis-André Gérard-Varet. 1995. "Collective choice mechanisms and Individual Incentives." First published in French as "Théorie des jeux et analyse économique 50 ans après" in *Revue d'Economie Politique (Special Issue)*, 1995, volume 4: 529–733. Published in English in Christian Schmidt, ed., 2002. *Game Theory and Economic Analysis: A Quiet Revolution in Economics*. Routledge. The edition cited is the 2004 e-library PDF published by Taylor & Francis e-Library and as such no page numbers can be referred to in the present text.

Groves, Theodore and John Ledyard. 1977. "Optimal Allocation of Public Goods: A Solution to the 'Free Rider' Problem." *Econometrica*, volume 45: 783-809.

Harsanyi, John, 1967. "Games with Incomplete Information Played by 'Bayesian' Players: Part I. The Basic Model." *Management Science*, volume 3: 159-182.

Harsanyi, John C. 1995. "Games with Incomplete Information." *American Economic Review,* volume 85: 291-303.

Hayek, Friedrich A. 1945. "The Use of Knowledge in Society." *American Economic Review,* volume 35: 519-530.

Kreps, David M. 1990. *Game Theory and Economic Modelling.* Oxford University Press.

Makowski, Louis and Joseph M. Ostroy. 1992. "General Equilibrium and Market Socialism: Clarifying the Logic of Competitive Markets." UCLA Economics Working Papers 67.

Makowski, Louis and Joseph M. Ostroy. 2001. "Perfect Competition and the Creativity of the Market." *Journal of Economic Literature,* volume 39: 479-535.

Maskin, Eric S. 2008. "Mechanism Design: How to Implement Social Goals." *American Economic Review,* volume 98: 567-576.

Myerson, Roger B. 1999. "Nash Equilibrium and the History of the Economic Theory." *Journal of Economic Literature,* volume 37: 1067-1082.

Myerson, Roger B. 2008. "Perspectives on Mechanism Design in Economic Theory." *American Economic Review,* volume 98: 586-603.

Myerson, Roger B. 2009. "Learning from Schelling's Strategy of Conflict." *Journal of Economic Literature*, volume 47: 1109-1125.

Myerson, Roger B. and Mark A. Satterthwaite, Mark. 1983. "Efficient Mechanisms for Bilateral Trading." *Journal of Economic Theory*, volume 54: 265–81.

Nash, John F., Jr. 1950. "Equilibrium Points in N-Person Games." *Proceedings of the National Academy of Sciences of the United States of America*, volume 36: 48-49.

Nash, John F., Jr. 1951. "Noncooperative Games." *Annals of Mathematics, Second Series*, volume. 54: 286-295.

Schelling, Thomas C. 1960. *The Strategy of Conflict*. Harvard University Press.

Selten, Reinhard. 1975. "Reexamination of the Perfectness Concept for Equilibrium Points in Extensive Games." *International Journal of Game Theory*, volume 4: 25-55.

Spence, Michael. 1973. "Job Market Signalling." *Quarterly Journal of Economics*, volume 87: 355-374.

Tideman, T. Nicolaus and Gordon Tullock. 1976. "A New and Superior Process for Making Social Choices." *Journal of Political Economy*, volume 84: 1145-1159.

Vickrey, William. 1961. "Counterspeculation, Auctions, and Competitive Sealed Tenders." *Journal of Finance*, volume 16: 8-37.

Von Neumann, John. 1928/1959: "On the Theory of Games of Strategy." English translation of von Neumann's 1928 German article in A.W. Tucker and R.D. Luce, eds. 1959, *Contributions to the Theory of Games*. Princeton University Press, 13-42.

Von Neumann, John and Oskar Morgenstern. 1953. *The Theory of Games and Economic Behavior, Third edition*. Princeton University Press.

CONTROL
8

THERE EXIST SPECIALIZED BUILDINGS THAT float in shallow pools of mercury. The mercury absorbs tremors from the earth so that delicate scientific instruments within the building can conduct experiments without interference. The measurements sought are ones that might show a link between a stimulus and a response. If you have set up a machine that vibrates a chemical mixture with a certain frequency and amplitude in order to see how this affects the chemical reactions within the mixture, you do not want vibrations from the earth added. If vibrations from the earth can subtly join with vibrations from the machine, you will not know what really caused the strength of the chemical reaction. Was it the machine, was it the earth, or was it both? By removing possible earth tremors from the stimulus part of the experiment, the mercury pool allows the scientist to establish a clear link between a cause and an effect.

And that is what science is about. Science is not about people in lab coats, peering through thick-rimmed spectacles and scribbling on clipboards. It is about separating the signal from the noise, the wheat from the chaff, so that clear linkages can be established. You create an area—a laboratory—where you control the environment so that no vibration, or noise, or electric shock, or speck of dust can interfere in the link you are trying to measure between a cause and an effect. The key word is control.

Along with physicists and other scientists, economists strive to show a link between cause and effect. Was foreign aid to Senegal responsible for the improvement in the farm yields of poor villages? Is the low salary of minority workers in a company the result of racial discrimination? Does the minimum wage hurt the employment opportunities of the young? These are questions about cause and effect.

Yet as you might have noticed from the examples, human events do not unfold in a controlled laboratory setting. In a laboratory all other confounding influences can be eliminated by controlling the environment in which the experiment takes place.

The economist enjoys no such control. Nature is the laboratory and it does not care about concepts of control. The economist must accept that perhaps it was fine weather instead of foreign aid that improved the yield on Senegalese farms. Perhaps the company pays minorities less because they have different educational qualifications from non-minorities. Perhaps youth employment fell not because of a rise in the minimum wage but because the economy weakened. The "perhapses" gather, making it harder to see how one thing is linked to another. What is an economist without a laboratory to do?

The Dark Ages of econometrics

ALTHOUGH THEY LACK a laboratory which would allow them to exclude outside interference from causal experiments, what economists do have is an abundance of imagination with which to analyze the numbers the economic environment generates. They might not be in control of the "data generating process", but they certainly are in control of how they can interpret the data. That is one freedom experimental physicists rarely have.

In physics, once the laboratory experiment is set, the numbers generated generally speak for themselves.

An experiment allows for only one interpretation of events. In contrast, for economists, interpretation was until recently the main method they had of making sense of the data. Nobel Prize winner Christopher Sims explains that, "Because economics is not an experimental science, economists face difficult problems of inference. The same data generally are subject to multiple interpretations. It is not that we learn nothing from data, but that we have at best the ability to use data to narrow the range of substantive disagreement. We are always combining the objective information in the data with judgment, opinion and/or prejudice to reach conclusions" (2010, 60). To understand what this means, we have to go back to the 1930s and the dawn of "model building" in economics.

A "model" in economics is some simple statement of the relation between important quantities, also known as variables. During the 1930s, John Maynard Keynes developed a theoretical model of the whole economy. He connected all the important macroeconomic dots such as national income, interest rates, investment, and inflation in his 1936 book *The General Theory of Employment, Interest, and Money*. A year later in 1937, his protégé John Hicks worked Keynes' verbal descriptions into mathematical equations in which consumption by everyone depended on national income, investment on interest rates, and vice versa, and so on. There were few real-world numbers in *The General Theory*. It was mostly, well, theory.

At the same time that Keynes was building his model, Dutch economist, physicist, and statistician, Jan Tinbergen, was confronting the problem of how to precisely measure the relation between these variables by using real-world data and their evolution through time, so-called "time-series". His problem was that to relate, for example, investment to interest rates, it was not enough to simply see how they moved together through time and claim he had found a causal link. Other factors could be influencing investment, such as investor confidence in the future, or more technically, the anticipated marginal value product of capital. Randomness could also contribute to the final effect. You had to account for these other forces or you might end up thinking you had found a causal link where none existed. Accounting for these forces meant isolating each of their individual effects on investment so that you did not attribute to interest rates an effect that was really due to anticipations of returns to investment.

The method for isolating these effects and distinguishing them from random forces that could influence the dependent variable is a tool called linear regression. Think of linear regression as a very directed means of searching through a spreadsheet or database for the independent effect that each of many possible causal or "independent" variables has on a single target or "dependent" variable. The types of effect to look for are not left to the discretion of the computer, but rather are specified by the researcher. If you think that the overall level of investment in the economy should move in some constant but unknown relationship to interest rates and other possible causal variables, regression will only search for proportional, or "linear" links in the data.

The word "regression" was coined by British scientist Francis Galton in the 19th century. He wanted to see the relation between the height of parents and the height of their children. Using the linear statistical technique which he called regression he found that taller than average parents tended to have smaller children than they, and small parents tended to have taller children. In other words, child height "regressed" to the mean of the population, which is a good thing, because otherwise the world would be covered with giants and ant people.

A physical analogy that might help explain what regression does, concerns the famous chord that opens the Beatles' song, *A Hard Day's Night*. For decades people thought it was a combination of bass and guitar. Then Canadian mathematician Keith Devlin used Fourier analysis to decompose the waves that combined to make up the chord, while at the same time filtering any randomness or "noise" from the recording that could obscure his search. The logic is similar to regression analysis. By restricting his search using the method of Fourier analysis to sift the "data" of sound waves that make up *A Hard Day's Night*, Devlin was able to discover that a piano was also striking notes and contributing to the final sound.

Regression is a powerful statistical tool for isolating the effect of all causal variables on some target variable of interest but there is a catch. Regression is an apt tool provided all causal variables are fed into the regression formula. If you are missing important variables that move with, or are "correlated" with the ones you include, then the effect of these "omitted variables" may get folded into the ones included, thereby giving the latter a possibly false importance in the causality one is trying to establish.

A rough analogy exists in sprinting where a tailwind of greater than a certain speed, or the presence of steroids invalidates world record times. You cannot say that the sprinter was the sole "cause" of the record because the tailwind was "positively correlated" with his or her forward motion. To credit the sprinter as being the sole cause of the record in such cases might be to bias attribution of success to his or her person and away from other causal variables such as wind and illegal drugs.

I say "might" because the other causal variables might work to cancel out each others' effects. To protect themselves from such bias researchers may become overcautious and include a great many variables, with the risk that some have no business being in the regression at all. If you feed irrelevant variables into the regression formula this does not bias results, but it makes finding a causal link between relevant variables less likely. The problem is similar to applying to a dating service. The more criteria you specify, the less likely you are to find a partner.

Finally, the best specified regression may not show you any causal link if the random forces affecting performance are too great. To carry on with the sprinting analogy, if the wind buffets from many sides it will make it hard to judge whether the sprinter's result is better or worse than it would have been without wind. Buffeting wind creates "noise" that obscures the link we are trying to make between effort and performance.

The role of models

To HELP HIM cope with what variables to include in his regressions, Tinbergen did what generations of economists have done in imitation. He used a model as a best guess guide to selecting regression variables. Here is where *The General Theory* came to the rescue. If you believed in its soundness you could use its theoretical equations as a prescription for the practical search of cause and effect through regression.

Theory limits the choices of so-called explanatory or causal variables, and it can also limit the range within which you should look in your data for links and trends. Through the marriage of regression and the *General Theory*, the field of econometrics was born.

David Hendry summarizes the ideas described above as follows:

> ... econometrics commences an analysis of the relationships between economic variables (such as quantities and prices, incomes and expenditures, etc.) by abstracting the main phenomena of interest and stating theories thereof in mathematical form. The empirical usefulness of the resulting "models" is evaluated using statistical information of supposed relevance, and econometrics in the narrow sense (used hereafter) concerns the interpretation and analysis of such data in the context of "established" economic theory (1980, 388).

Now we can better understand the earlier quote by Sims that, "We are always combining the objective information in the data with judgment, opinion and/or prejudice to reach conclusions." Without a laboratory the economist is not learning uniquely from the numbers the way a physicist might, but is rather imposing on the numbers a certain range in which he or she believes beforehand a causal relation should exist.

Such an approach is contrary to the popular view of the scientist learning about causality through experiments. By stating *a priori*, that is, beforehand, what form the relationship between investment and interest rates should take, the economist is making an hypothesis about the form which causality might take. The regression technique he or she uses is just a recipe for finding patterns that seem to associate investment and interest and any other causal or "control" variables within the range specified by theory. In a different passage, Sims observes stoically that, "The best we can hope for is that econometricians are trained to confront the complexities and ambiguities that inevitably arise in non-experimental inference."

How do economists justify this peculiar approach to analyzing data? They take the practical view that the world is not a laboratory where you can always control the environment to isolate the relationship between a cause and effect that might interest you. But that does not mean that useful information is absent from data the world generates. You just need to know how to look at the data. Looking at the data means having a lens that filters out what in this abstract discussion might be called glare, and other unwanted forms of light. Polarized lenses clarify a scene by allowing only light of a certain polarity to pass, eliminating scattered light which is not polarized, and even eliminating other forms of polarized light that interfere with the aspect of a subject you wish to examine. The economist takes the data and says, "My lens on the world is based on the notion that people make choices that maximize their well-being subject to constraints they face on their incomes, their time, and the limits placed on them by the law."

Some call this prior view of the world a model. Others call it ideology. Whatever name one chooses, the economist's approach presumes a relationship between investment and interest rates, advertising and smoking, the minimum wage and employment, or taxes and investment based on logical models of human behavior. A prior model narrows the search the economist needs to undertake by telling him or her which control variables to use. With the control variables in place, the economist can now use the regression technique to measure the quantitative impact of the causal variable of interest on the target variable. The problem is that if the economist's model is incomplete or just plain wrong, the causal impacts measured may turn out to be meaningless or even misleading. This problem is akin to designing a lens for your glasses that either fogs up, or presents the world in too rosy or too dismal a color.

Despite these misgivings, Tinbergen and his colleagues were so gifted and visionary that their approach to data research dominated economics until the early 1980s. Then, in rapid succession, bad-boy econometricians Christopher Sims (1980), David Hendry (1980), and Edward Leamer (1983) launched what James Stock has described as a "scathing critique of contemporary econometric practice" (2010, 83). Leamer famously wrote that, "This is a sad and decidedly unscientific state of affairs we find ourselves in. Hardly anyone takes data analyses seriously" (37). Hendry wrote that, "It is difficult to provide a convincing case for the defense against Keynes' accusation almost 40 years ago that econometrics is statistical alchemy since many of his criticisms remain apposite" (402).

The critiques were all based on the problems of finding the correct variables to put into the regressions. Each researcher suggested in his own manner that researchers needed to be less demanding of the data. Instead of insisting on finding the precise effects of certain economic forces, we might do better to settle for knowing some broad range into which these effects might fall. We also might not wish to disentangle causalities that ran both ways, but rather try to relate both variables to some fundamental feature of the economy. For example, interest rates could influence investment, but as machines were built and the economy became more productive, investors might demand more loans and this could drive up interest rates. Disentangling the effects of investment and interest rates on each other was so difficult that we should settle for understanding how each depended on some feature of the economy outside this causal loop.

These were difficult suggestions to understand and particularly to implement, but they had the merit of uniting economists in the belief that some simple, incontestable, non-subjective, that is, scientific way of analyzing data was needed. This realization led in the 1990s to what Joshua Angrist and Jörn-Steffen Pischke have described in a defining survey of the field as a "credibility revolution" in econometric work (2010, 4). The revolution was based not on fancy statistical theorizing and complicated formulas, but upon finding a way to simulate in economics the sort of controlled laboratory environment that physicists and other scientists take for granted. Let us examine why this development is so remarkable.

The credible path to control

TO THE SCIENTIST, control means that you block out any force, other than the one you are studying, from having an effect on the target of interest. Science does this by building laboratories that insulate their experiments from vibrations and other contaminants. Economists and, to be fair, other social scientists such as psychologists, figured out that there was a way to mimic the laboratory. What you needed to do was find two groups of people who were similar in all ways that mattered to the target variable of interest. Then you subjected both groups to a different set of circumstances and then checked whether over time the target variables for each group differed. Then you attributed the difference between the two to the causal variable that differed between the groups.

Twins separated at birth were an early example of this procedure. Some were put into the care of rich families and others into the care of poor families in the same town and the same district. If the rich twins did better in life, you could assume that it was due to being brought up in luxury and not because of any mental or physical advantage over the other twin. Nurture, not nature, was responsible for the evolution of the target variable, which in this case is income. The twins example, taken from psychology, illustrates the point that similar groups may evolve differently if subjected to different influences. The differences in the performance of these groups can then be causally traced to the different circumstances in which they evolved.

Economic examples abound. Suppose you want to measure the effect of foreign aid on crop yields in Senegalese villages. You could just hand over the money and do a before and after comparison of yields. The problem is that you would not know if it was the aid or some other factor, uncontrolled for in your analysis, such as good weather, that influenced the change in yield. To avoid this confusion, before giving the aid you divide the villages into two groups. Each group has similar numbers of people, plot sizes, proximity to large towns, tractors, access to fertilizer, weather, and any other factor you think might influence the crop yield.

Now you give aid to only one subgroup of villages that in all other respects are similar to the remaining subgroup, and call it the treatment group. You do not give aid to another group and call it the comparison or "control" group. You wait a year, then measure how crop yields changed in each group. The difference between the yield chance of the group that received the aid, the treatment group, and the group that did not, the control group, gives an idea of the effect of the aid program. If both groups are the same in every respect except for the fact that the treatment group is the only one to receive aid, then the result of the treatment group will be the same as the result of the control group to which it is similar, augmented by the fact it received aid. If you subtract the increase in crop yield of both groups, then the influence of their similarities on yield cancel out and all you are left with is the effect of the only factor that differs between them: aid. Believe it or not, fortunes in aid dollars were spent, some under the guidance of economists trained in econometrics, without such an experiment ever being run, as the devastating exposé *The Idealist* by Nina Munk reveals. Norms for best practice are changing, but we will get to that a bit later.

For now, what we need to understand is that by creating similar treatment and control groups, you assure yourself that a part of the performance of each group will be similar because it is determined by the factors they share in common proportion. When you subtract the results of the control group from those of the target group, you filter out these common effects. All that is left is the net effect of what was different between them—in this case, receiving or not receiving aid. By subtracting the results of similar groups, economists filter out confounding effects to distill a unique cause. Thus they mimic the physicist's laboratory where environmental control blocks out confounding effects.

The beauty of this method is that you do not need some complicated regression formula to tell you if foreign aid is having an effect on yields. All you need to do is know how to compare averages. Everyone understands averages. As long as you believe the experiment was properly carried out, then the results are understandable and credible. This is the revolution in data analysis that Angrist and Pischke are talking about, or almost.

Randomness cannot be controlled but can be measured

OUR DISCUSSION IS not complete because there is an important difference between the efforts of economists to control outside factors by filtering them out of their results and the control over the laboratory environment that physicists favor. The difference is that there is one effect economists can never filter out. Most people call it chance. Economists also call it randomness, stochastic shocks, or non-systematic influences. It is some force that acts differently on each member of the treatment and control groups, which the researcher cannot observe, and which would continue to act differently were the experiment run again. This is why it is sometimes called a non-systematic influence, as opposed to the systematic influence of factors such as age or education which presumably dispose the test and control subjects to a consistent level of performance.

The problem that chance poses for the economist is that it weakens his or her ability to conclude whether or not a government program was a success. Suppose the program whose effect you are trying to measure really increased the performance of the treatment group above that of the control group, yet by some unlikely quirk people in the control group were feeling good, or alert, or in some fleeting, unrepeatable way were "on". Then the control group could end up having a better performance than the treatment group simply because luck favored it on that day. The consequence is that despite the logical beauty of filtering out other systematic effects by creating similar groups, economists must sort out whether the difference between groups they observe are due to a government program or due to the non-systematic effects of chance.

Physicists do not face this problem on anything but the smallest of atomic scales. What are economists to do? They have only one choice. They must try to quantify how certain they are that the net difference in performance between groups is not due to chance but rather due to the causal variable of interest, such as foreign aid to a village, or employment subsidies for workers.

257 THE APPRENTICE ECONOMIST

Enter applied statistics, one of the least understood and most widely detested subjects imposed on generations of students. That it is so detested is a shame because applied statistics is about nothing more than getting a feel for how certain we are about something. More technically, it tells us the probability something will happen, or perhaps just how much more likely one event is than another.

Knowing how likely it is that something will happen can be of inestimable value. No wonder then that statistics had its origins in the calculations of gamblers who wanted to know the odds of dice, card games, and lotteries. The French philosopher Pascal formalized the insights of gamblers by creating the mathematics of probabilities, also known as the probability calculus. He too was a gambler of sorts, interested in the biggest bet a person could make. Should you devote your life to the worship of the Christian God? Pascal used probabilities to argue it was a rational bet to do so, and lived his life accordingly.

Later mathematicians used Pascal's probability calculus to show that almost all of applied statistics could be developed from an understanding of one of the simplest games of chance: flipping a coin. The coin flip is known as a "binomial trial". For a large number of coin flips you can use the mathematical formula for something called the "normal distribution" to approximate the likelihood of a long run of luck with heads. A distribution is simply a device for cataloguing how frequently some event takes place. In a thousand coin flips, the normal distribution can tell you how likely it is that you will see twenty heads, or three hundred heads, or even a thousand heads. Each of these is one event out of many possible events that could emerge from a large number of coin tosses. The normal distribution seems to pop up all over statistics. In addition to predicting binomial events in large numbers of trials it can also be used to predict runs of luck from games about whose odds of different outcomes we know little to nothing.

This discovery was made in the 19th century and came to be known as the *Central Limit Theorem*. You will not hear about it on science documentaries, but it is one of the most astounding intellectual discoveries. It says that if you take an average of the performance of many people, say on a driver's exam, and so do not really know anything about the likelihood of how any one person will perform, the average performance will have many people who are very close to it and a few others who are further away.

More remarkably, the spread of the average will increasingly conform to a normal distribution as the number of people increases (this is quite different from the "law of large numbers"). So, starting without any knowledge of the chance acting on an individual unit, you can build a coherent picture of the chance acting on large groups of these units.

Hearing through the noise

WHAT DOES THIS have to do with treatment and control groups? Recall that a normal distribution is just a device for telling us how likely an outcome is. So if we see that the treatment group exceeds the control group by fifty per cent on average, we can refer to the normal distribution to see how likely a fifty per cent difference would be if only chance where generating it. If it is highly unlikely that chance alone was the generating force behind the difference, then the economist can conclude, with "statistical confidence" that the government program in question, instead of chance, had some role in the enhanced performance of the treatment group.

If this reasoning seems difficult then rest assured that you have used it all your life. Think of judging whether a coin is honest or not. You already know the statistical distribution behind the flip for an honest coin. It is fifty-fifty for heads and tails. If you flip it twice and see two heads, you cannot really deduce anything is out of order because there is a one in four chance of that happening. But if you flip the coin twenty times and observe twenty heads, then intuitively you know it is highly unlikely that an honest coin would behave in this manner (in fact, the probability calculus can help us find that the chance is slightly more than one in a million). So you would conclude with confidence that the coin has been tampered with.

The same logic applies to treatment and control groups. If you know they started out similarly but see a very large difference between their performance after one group gets government help, then you can use the normal distribution to give you a probability that such a difference could be generated solely by chance. If this probability is low, you can conclude it was not chance but the government program at work, just as with the coin you can conclude that tampering and not chance is responsible for the extended run of heads.

The main shortcoming of the normal distribution is that if you want to use it to assess probability you need to know some detailed facts about the true average of the population and how it spreads out, or its variance. These population averages and spreads are called parameters and they are usually costly to find because you need to gather a lot of information about the whole population. Through decades of study costing millions of dollars we know what the average and variance of IQ scores are in North America. When it comes to farm yields in Senegal we draw a blank. There is a low rent alternative to the normal distribution that does not require a knowledge of population averages and spreads but simply of sample averages and spreads. Here is what you do.

Take the average performance of your two groups and divide their difference by an approximate measure of its spread called the estimated standard deviation. An estimated standard deviation is the square root of the average of squared differences between each individual score and the average score. The difference in the average performance of the two groups divided by the estimated standard deviation of this difference gives you a number called a t-statistic.

This t is basically a signal-to-noise ratio. You have experienced this sort of dilemma when listening to a fuzzy radio signal. Was that a voice you heard or was it just static? In trying to understand whether foreign aid increases crop yields, the "signal" in this case is how big the difference is between the performance of the treatment and control villages. The "noise" is how spread out the results are around the average. If the ratio of signal relative to noise is high, then the t is high. Large t's are very unlikely if only noise is responsible for differing crop yields. If differences are due purely to chance, then we would expect these to largely cancel each other out and we would observe very little average difference between yields. A large difference in yields means that there is a strong probability that there really is a signal rising above the noise.

The surprising aspect of the t-distribution is that the only information you need calculate the probability that the t-value derived from the difference between your treatment and control group was due entirely to chance, is the number of people in your sample. You do not need to know population average or variances. This is why the t-test is called a non-parametric test. A parameter is a value that goes into some equation to determine how inputs to that equation bleed out into results.

What is the catch? Statistics, like economics is a science of trade-offs. Because the t distribution requires less information than the normal distribution, it also yields less information about the nature of the differences between groups. Suppose the t-value we calculate based on the difference between groups and their spreads, has a one in ten probability of being observed if only chance were responsible for creating the difference, and not some systematic force like government aid. But if we had sufficient background information to use the normal distribution we might be able to say that the chance of observing such a difference purely by chance is one in a hundred. In other words, when there is a difference between groups generated by something other than chance, the normal will let you see that better than the t. The catch is that you need more background information on the distributions of the experimental and control groups in order to use the normal. To use the t you do not need this information. The good news according to statisticians is that if you are dealing with groups of more than thirty individuals, or farms, or whatever is your unit of analysis, then the t-distribution starts "converging" to, or being almost as good as, the normal in telling you whether a difference is due to chance or to some systematic effect.

To summarize, there are rules that govern chance. By applying these rules economists can quantify their belief that a certain cause had a certain effect. Once we have assured ourselves that both control and treatment groups have similar measurable, consistent characteristics, statistics steps in and allows us to assess how much of the remaining result is due to chance and how much to the government program. If statistics tells us that the probability that chance was responsible for the difference is very small, say five per cent, then economists speak of a statistically significant result.

The message that can get lost in this discussion of statistics is that there is a logical model for establishing that one independent factor or variable, such as a government program, influences some target or dependent variable, such as crop yields or poverty. This logical construct has nothing at all to do with statistics. It simply says that you should start with two similar groups. You expose the treatment group to a stimulus, such as a government program to get the destitute back to employment. You compare that group's average result to that of a similar group of the destitute. Any difference you note could then be due to the program because the influence of all other possible factors will cancel out due to the similarity in the two groups.

Statistics enters because any inferences you draw from the comparison of averages needs to be qualified. You can make comparison groups that have similar ages, sex, education, and so on, but you can never eliminate the chance factor that will tilt individuals one way or the other. While you cannot eliminate chance, you can use statistics to tell you how probable it is that the differences you observe are due purely to chance. If, say, there is only a one-in-a-hundred chance that the differences between the control and treatment groups would be generated by chance, then you deduce with this statistical confidence that the program had an effect.

Finding similar groups

THE LOGIC OF finding causality depends on starting with similar treatment and control groups, subjecting the treatment group to, say, a government program, and subtracting the subsequent enhancement in the performance of both groups to arrive at a net effect for the government program. All of that is fairly straightforward except for "similar groups". What does that mean? We need to look at some early attempts to put the idea of similarity into practice.

During the recessions of the early 1970s and then again in the 1990s, welfare rolls swelled with chronically unemployed but able-bodied people. Previous research had shown that the longer a bout of unemployment lasted, the less chance any given person had of finding a job. Their skills might degrade, their motivation could wilt, and employers would start asking pointed questions. To pull the unemployed out of this welfare trap governments devised short-term programs that paid private employers to hire them. All the unemployed person had to do was volunteer for the program and agree to be interviewed at six-month intervals for several years afterwards to see how he or she was getting on after the end of the subsidized job. The group of volunteers was, in effect, the treatment group.

Researchers had access to data on each person pertinent to how well he or she might be expected to perform in the labor market. Age, sex, education, and length of previous bouts on welfare were among these available data. Yet more information was needed. To gauge the success of job subsidies, researchers could not simply look at the job market record of participants after the program. If many succeeded in remaining employed after the program they might have done so because the economy was improving, and not because of the experience they had gained during their subsidized spell of work.

Researchers decided to create a control group. But where to get it? The answer was to search through diverse government databases. There they found unemployed welfare dependents who had not signed up for subsidized jobs, but who were an exact match in the factors deemed to be important for job market performance. Age, sex, education, and the list of regular suspects were criteria used to make matches. The color of socks one wore was not, presumably because that had no influence on job market success.

Because they were identical in the characteristic that mattered, this control group of non-participants would presumably react to general economic conditions in the same manner as the participants. Once you subtracted the employment performance in the period after the program from the success of participants you would filter out the influence of the all other factors except the subsidy and chance. Other studies using this methodology, which came to be known as "quasi-experimentation", found that government programs where people volunteered to participate had strong and undeniably positive effects.

Enthusiasm with such findings deflated after economist Robert Lalonde (1986) pierced them with a critique. He argued that the programs were showing an effect that was not due to the government program but rather to some elusive, yet very real difference between groups. Perhaps the volunteers who comprised the treatment group were more motivated to find work than were non-participants. If you do not match treatment and control groups on motivation, then the apparent success of the program may not be due to government subsidies but rather to motivation. Incomplete matching is the same thing as lack of control, which is also the same thing as a failure to filter potentially confounding effects out from the result. In the case where people choose by themselves to participate in a program, this confounding effect is called "self-selection bias". In practice, Lalonde found this bias so severe that it cast doubt on causal inferences drawn from all experiments where people had a say in whether they would be part of the treatment group or would not participate. His critique was similar to that launched against Tinbergen's regression agenda. In regression, leaving some important variables out of the formula can bias your estimates of cause and effect.

Despite these critiques, economists felt they were on the right track. They just needed to prevent people from biasing the experiments. Since this bias arose from the choice to either participate or not participate, the answer seemed clear. Create treatment and control groups without reference to people's wishes. This could be done by adopting a long-established practice from biology and multi-billion dollar pharmaceutical research, called randomization. As the name implies, it is the whim of chance, and not the determination of the individual that guides the group, treatment or control, to which he or she is assigned.

Randomized experiments

RANDOMIZATION IS SO ridiculously simple that you can perform it in your living room. Suppose you want to test whether hanging paintings on the walls of otherwise drab hospital rooms speeds patient recovery. Go to a ward and get a list of the numbers of the hundred or so rooms they have there. Write each room number on a piece of paper and put all papers in an urn, a bucket, or even a gym bag. Put on a blindfold, dip into the container, and place the first slip you grab on a pile called "treatment". Place the next slip on a pile called "control". Do this a hundred times and you will have a list of who will be in your treatment group and who will be in the control group. You have just laid the basis for a randomized experiment. What you will find after your selection is that the characteristics of participants and non-participants in the experiment tend to be very similar, provided you have more than a few dozen in each group.

People in rooms to be assigned a painting and those to be left without one have similar average ages, education, number of children, afflictions, and other factors that could influence their "performance"—in this case, the speed of recovery. The similarity arises because chance does not dictate you will pick rooms with women for the treatment group with any greater frequency than you will pick them for the control group. The same holds for other characteristics of the people being studied.

When people say that chance is blind, what they are really trying to express is that it is impartial (by the way, this was a true study, and it found that, with high statistical confidence, the presence of paintings on the walls sped up recovery; I have had an impressionist on my wall ever since). The reason randomization is a credible way of setting up experiments is that, being impartial, chance will allocate participants and non-participants equally, not simply on the basis of their observable characteristics but also on their unobservable characteristics.

If welfare recipients had been allocated randomly to either participate or not participate in subsidized jobs, self-selection bias might have been avoided. Chance would dictate that both treatment and control groups would have similar levels of motivation, or morale. Being able to match groups on unobservable characteristics is the main reason for using randomization to create treatment and control groups.

Here, as in the case of opting for the t-statistic instead of the normal distribution, there is a trade-off to be considered. The price you pay for matching fairly closely on unobserved characteristics is that control and treatment groups are close, but do not have exactly the same average features on the observed characteristics as was the case in quasi-experiments. The small differences that remain could bias your results. Recall that differences in characteristics other than participation in the program can influence differences between the performances of the two groups.

This is a trade-off many are willing to make. Many are willing to accept a small exaggeration, or possibly obfuscation of the result (bias can run both ways), due to imperfect matching, instead of being deceived by a very large bias resulting from perfect matching on characteristics we can observe in quasi-experiments where people chose to participate or not rather than having chance determine participation.

A few examples

ONCE YOU UNDERSTAND the basic logic of randomized experiments you need not be an economist to tap into a rich flow of studies on the effects of public policies. All you need to understand is how to compare averages. Even to economists versed in the mysteries of econometrics this approach is a welcome relief from the nuanced and highly subjective attempts at analysis using non-experimental data to which they are accustomed, or even inured.

Consider the question of whether private schools provide better education than public schools. The average performance of students at private schools generally exceeds that of students at public schools. However, is this due to better quality of education or simply because the students who tend to go to private schools come from richer families that have more resources outside classes, such as private tutoring, to improve their children's academic performance? Simple comparisons of public and private schools tells us little about their relative quality because these comparisons lack control. You need to compare similar students in public and private schools.

As educational scholar Paul Peterson and his colleagues describe, such a comparison was accomplished in a 1997 randomized experiment by the School Choice Scholarships Foundation (SCSF) in New York City. The foundation invited parents to apply for "1,300 scholarships worth up to $1,400 annually for at least three years to children from low-income families then attending public schools. The scholarship could be applied toward the cost of attending a private school, either religious or secular. After announcing the program, SCSF received initial applications from over 20,000 students between February and late April 1997" (2003, 109). The researchers then randomly chose 6,000 names of the 20,000 who had applied: 3,000 received the scholarship and 3,000 were the control group. Similar experiments were conducted around the same time in Washington, DC, and Michigan. Non-African-Americans saw no improvement in their test scores, but for African-Americans the result was different. According to Peterson and his colleagues, "Overall, the effects of attending a private school on student test scores are moderately large ... black students who switched to private schools scored, after one year, 0.18 standard deviations higher than the students in the control group. After two and three years, the size of the effect grew to 0.28 and 0.30 standard deviations" (2003, 121). In statistics, when you rise 0.30 standard deviations above the average, you find yourself roughly in the top third of students.

While randomized studies of this sort can cost millions of dollars, a little imagination can lead to fascinating findings without the researcher experiencing sticker shock. Economist Joel Slemrod and his colleagues analyzed data from a Minnesota Department of Revenue experiment to enhance tax compliance. They write that, "in 1995 a group of 1724 randomly selected Minnesota taxpayers was informed by letter that the returns they were about to file would be 'closely examined'. Compared to a control group that did not receive this letter, low and middle-income taxpayers in the treatment group on average increased tax payments compared to the previous year" (2001, 455).

These are the types of easy-to-understand studies that are responsible for the "credibility revolution" in economic data analysis. All the work goes into making sure that confounding forces are controlled and that randomness is neutralized through large sample size. The rest is just a comparison of averages to reveal whether some program had any effect.

Natural experiments

THE LOGIC OF randomized controlled experiments carries over to so-called "natural experiments". A natural experiment is one in which some clearly understood random process determines the manner in which a cause, such as government intervention, is applied to a target population. The random aspect of who participates or when people participate helps to create similar groups in precisely the same manner as did the experimental randomization described earlier. This abstract idea is best understood through examples.

Sebastian Galiani and his colleagues studied the military draft lottery in Argentina to see if military service makes men violent even after they have left the army. Since the lottery is random it creates nearly identical groups of young men who are chosen for the army and others who do not perform military service. They put their idea of a natural experiment as follows: "In order to identify the causal effect of conscription on crime, we need to identify a variable that affects participation in conscription but does not affect crime through any other mechanisms. The draft lottery in Argentina offers an opportunity to address this question. The lottery randomly assigned eligibility of all young males" (2011, 121).

Here was a natural experiment in the sense that Argentina's draft lottery was intended purely as a recruiting device and not as an experiment in the effect of military life on subsequent criminal behavior. The authors found convincing evidence that "participation in conscription increases the likelihood of developing a subsequent criminal record, particularly for crimes against property and white collar crimes ... conscription has detrimental effects on future job market performance" (2011, 119).

Then there is the case of US food aid to Africa. After the famous 1985 *Live Aid* concert that raised funds to send food to starving Ethiopians, no one dared question the usefulness of such gifts. Twenty or so years later professors Nathan Nunn and Nancy Qian from Harvard and Yale used a natural experiment to show that food aid could have negative side effects. They wrote, somewhat obscurely, that their "paper examines the effect of US food aid on conflict in recipient countries. To establish a causal relationship, we exploit time variation in food aid caused by fluctuations in US wheat production together with cross-sectional variation in a country's tendency to receive any food aid from the United States" (2012, 1).

For decades aid researchers had wondered whether food aid was given in response to conflicts in recipient countries or whether food aid caused conflicts. It was quite possible that there was a circular relationship between aid and conflict. Aid could enhance conflict, which could enhance aid. Most people call this a vicious circle. Economists called it a positive feedback relation, or a simultaneous equation relation. No one seemed to be able to disentangle one effect from the other.

The ensuing ambiguity fuelled conflicts between researchers and policy-makers with opposing views on the merits of aid.

To break out of the "causal loop" between aid and conflict, Nunn and Qian made use of the fact that in the US when there is a bumper crop of wheat, by law some of the surplus is put aside to be sent to needy countries the following year. The legally mandated nature of this aid created an automatic mechanism that broke the causal loop. Chance fluctuations in weather may lead to a US bumper crop. Because chance is at work, this crop will have no relation to whether some conflict is taking place in some far-off country. This independently determined aid surplus is then sent off to Africa. Nunn and Qian were astute enough to track the surplus aid and they then attempted to associate it with conflicts in the recipient areas. They concluded that, "an increase in US food aid increases the incidence, onset and duration of civil conflicts in recipient countries … increasing food aid by ten percent increases the incidence of conflict by approximately 1.14 percentage-points" (3). For every ten dollars of food aid there is a one tenth increase in war conflict.

Computer experiments

THE CREDIBILITY REVOLUTION in econometrics applies mainly to so-called microeconomic phenomena. Did a quota, attributed by lottery on the minimum number of women to serve as head of town councils in India, lead to improved road and water quality? Does a subsidy to employers help get workers back into the market? Answering these questions in a credible manner depended on some variant of randomized experiments. But how do you conduct a randomized experiment when you want to see if a collapse of the housing market leads inevitably to a widespread economic depression? For macro-economic phenomena, experimental methods are not helpful. In his 2010 essay on experimental methods, Nobel Prize winner Christopher Sims called the application of experimental methods to determining causality in macroeconomics "nonsense".

In the face of such intellectual broadsides some researchers retreated, quite literally, into their own imaginations. Their idea was to forget about establishing causality by using statistics and an experimental approach to data. Instead, they decided to build a mathematical model of the economy with pencil and paper. The model had to show how investment influenced national income, how interest rates varied with investment, how labor supply rose and fell in response to wages, and how consumption and savings and income changed. Especially, it had to be consistent with past economic reality. You could explore different scenarios with such a model. What if government lowered taxes on corporate profits? What if there arose an unexpected improvement in the technology for extracting petroleum? Finn Kydland and Edward Prescott (1982) outlined how such a *Gedankenexperiment* should proceed in their foundational article on what has since come to be known as "real business cycle theory."

The first step in building a model that would allow you to simulate the economy was that you had be guided by some sense of economic history. If you look at economic growth in developed economies you see a long upward trend with many small deviations and then a few very large ups, which represent booms, and downs, which represent depressions. You also see that investment spending is much more volatile than personal consumption.

These contrasting variations suggest that a mathematical model capturing the evolution of the economy over time requires two components. First, it should have a some inner core which produces baseline trends. This is, in fact, what the theory of equilibrium in a certain world provides. Most versions of equilibrium theory says that in a certain world there should be no booms or busts, or even minor deviations from the long-term upward trend in income. If they have perfect certainty, investors continue pouring money into machines until a saturation point is reached at which the rate of return from investing in "capital" is equal to the cost of an extra dollar of investment, the interest rate on borrowed money. Once an economy reaches this "steady state" its growth rate remains constant, and income grows at this steady rate forever. There are no booms or busts, simply convergence to a steady state.

The second feature of the *Gedankenexperiment* should add booms and busts to the baseline trend in growth. One way to get booms and busts is to spike the certainty model with so-called "random economic shocks" (though one can also generate cycles by assuming that preferences for consumption in different time periods are so tightly wound up with each other that their effects rebound on each other in a manner that creates waves).

Kydland and Prescott did not invent this idea. In 1937 Eugen Slutsky discovered that by adding a randomly generated number to a simple "difference equation" relating future income to past income you could generate ups and downs resembling economic cycles. What Kydland and Prescott contributed was to insert these random shocks within the context of a model of consumers and producers optimizing their well-being and profits.

In their model a new technological discovery might push up the productivity of investments. In response, firms quickly increase their investments above their long-term trends to take advantage of the new opportunities. Once these one-time new opportunities are exhausted, businesses once again lower their investment spending to the original long-term trend. Investment is fuelled, in part, by workers who also find extra cash in their pockets because the boom in business opportunities leads to an increased demand for their services. Because they do not like to live in either feast or famine, they save some of their unexpected cash windfall, which banks then lend out to investors. This is why consumption has a muted response to surprise changes in productivity while investment reacts much more suddenly. It does so in order to take advantage of fleeting opportunities. The triumph of the real-business cycle model was that when you dropped random shocks into it, trends consistent with the stylized facts of economic growth emerged. This model of the economy allowed Kydland and Prescott to simulate what would happen if government tried to stimulate the economy by lowering taxes or increasing spending.

Yet an enormous question mark hangs over this approach to understanding how the economy works. The equations in the Kydland-Prescott model spit out their predictions based on two types of information fed into them. One type of information is the value that variables will take. A variable is just that. It varies. Taxes, or investment are variables. Then there are things that do not vary and they are called parameters. A parameter is a number that translates the impact of an increase in wealth into increases in savings. If each dollar increase in wealth increases savings by half a dollar, the impact parameter is 50 per cent.

Kydland and Prescott had to choose impact parameters such that their mathematical model was backwardly consistent with preceding economic trends. Put differently, if you had data from 1900 to 1980 on national income, investment and so on, then your model had to be able to generate these numbers.

It turned out that many different combinations of impact parameters were consistent with past historical trends. When you picked a set of parameters you had "calibrated" to be consistent with the past, you were never quite sure whether they were the right ones. Naturally that influenced your ability to evaluate the future effect of changes in government policy. I say "evaluate" because the Kydland-Prescott framework was not really about prediction as most people understand it. It was about simulating the very narrow impacts of changes in the economic environment. To appreciate this we need to look more closely at what prediction in economics really means.

What about prediction?

ALL THIS DISCUSSION about statistics generally gets people interested in the question of predicting the future. One of the most annoying and embarrassing questions an economist can be asked is "so if you are so smart with your economics *Ph.D.* why aren't you rich?" At the heart of this reproach is the sentiment that with all their fancy models of the economy and their high-powered data analysis, economists should be able to predict how stock prices will move, or when the economy will crash. At the very least, they should be able to tell us where society is heading in the long-term.

These assaults on economists are understandable. From the 1930s to the 1960s, data analysis in economics was dominated by scholars who were either originally physicists or who had a strong training in that discipline. The earliest and greatest triumph of physics was the ability to predict the course of the planets and even stars. That power is based in part on Newton's first law, which says that an object in motion tends to stay in motion, thereby allowing one to trace a future trajectory based on the preceding trajectory.

Yet anyone who has studied physics closely will tell you that, with the exception of rocket trajectories in the vacuum of space, prediction is a challenge. The best physical models of the atmosphere cannot predict the weather with any useful accuracy for longer than a week. What prediction really means in physics is that you can tell how an entity will react when acted upon by another entity. Prediction is based on a knowledge of how the components of the system interact. Then you can calculate how some components will change when others change.

Predicting the effect on one variable of a change in another is also the essence of prediction in economics. This does not mean that a model which predicts behavior will tell you how people will behave in the future. Did you get that? Few people do, though the point is not difficult to grasp.

Suppose you have a model which tells you that when the price of movie tickets rises people will go to fewer movies. You go back over the numbers and look to see if attendance fell when prices rose. If it did, then your model is said to be able to predict the effect of a rise in ticket prices on the level of attendance. But this is very different from claiming that the model can tell you how attendance will evolve over the next three years.

Economic models are not crystal balls. They are a statement of relations between variables. This is why economic models are at their best when being used to analyze the result of a government intervention, such as the imposition of rent control. A ceiling on rent discourages landlords from providing rental properties because landlords conform to the economic prediction that supply falls when price falls. Rent control disturbs an economic system previously in equilibrium. Theory tells us how variables in the system, such as apartments for rent, will change when the system is disturbed.

But ask an economist to tell you where the economy will be next year and you will draw a blank. The models may be sound but the economist can only predict if he or she knows how the inputs into these models, such as interest rates, inflation, technological change, will vary over the next year. These changes are disturbances to the economic system which neither the economist nor any other individual has the ability to predict systematically. The point is that we must understand that economic models "predict" in a very different manner from what people understand the term to mean. It is the prediction of change in a system when subject to a particular disruption.

If this line of reasoning sounds like a dodge to you, then perhaps you might be convinced that some economic values cannot be predicted because of the very logic of the economic models used in the attempt to predict them. People anticipate future developments in the economy and this makes their current decisions inscrutable in a necessary sense. Suppose someone could anticipate your every move and reaction to future economic developments. He or she could then exploit you. To thwart being exploited humans have built into their decisions a certain degree of randomness. Game theorists call this a "mixed strategy". Humans generate uncertainty and unpredictability of necessity, as a protective measure against exploitation by other humans. We are all squirting ink and muddying the waters, which vastly complicates the efforts of economists who wish to map the human heart, whilst mixing metaphors.

Even when we are not playing games with others we absorb information in such a way as to invalidate the economist's efforts at prediction as the case of stock markets shows. If people make the most of the available information, then the past trend in stock prices should be no guide to the future trend. If it were, then you would buy more of an upward rising stock, thereby pumping up its price in the present and by this anticipatory purchase wiping out the remaining anticipated increments to its price. Since past trends are of no use, the only valid information to act upon is that which nature reveals at its whim. News that the CEO will retire may precipitate a fall in the stock price. The reaction is immediate. And being immediate, it makes stock prices look random. New information is revealed randomly and is immediately folded into stock prices, making these resemble what Burton Malkiel described as a "random walk".

In regards to government interventions, Robert E. Lucas Jr. showed in his celebrated 1976 essay that simply relying on past relations between, say, consumption and government spending, would not tell you how consumers were going to react to new government attempts to stimulate the economy. Consumers based their decisions on how long they believed the government stimulus would last. The new government plan or "rule" for increased stimulus became part of the consumer's decision problem. This invalidated any past relations that might have been established by econometricians between government spending and private consumption because those past relations were based on a different government stimulus rule. More technically, the method of regression analysis suffered from "specification bias" by not taking into account how consumers reacted to the new policy and so failed to integrate the "parameters" of the government policy into the "decision problem" of consumers, thereby making any estimated regression relation between consumption and government spending incomplete and therefore potentially biased.

Perhaps the only predictions we can bank upon are those relating to government interventions whose effects we measure through controlled experiments. The controlled experiment does not suffer from bias, but the lessons it teaches are circumscribed by the nature of the experiment. Discovering that lessons in crop rotation increase village agricultural yields does not mean that it is a good idea to extend all sorts of help to villages. Experiments tell you only what you ask of them. The lesson is that the predictive power of economics is closely related to the questions one asks. The more specific the question, the better the prediction, but the more specific the question, the less widely applicable is the lesson. In prediction as in all of statistics—and economics—trade-offs rear their unpleasant heads, reminding us that there are no free lunches.

Summary

STATISTICAL CONTROL CAN be summarized first in a word, then in a sentence. In a word, control means filtering. In a sentence, statistical control is a method for isolating the influence of a variable of interest, such as a government effort to help the unemployed, on a target variable, such as unemployment, by removing the contribution to unemployment of all other possible "control" variables.

Control should be a part of every educated person's mental arsenal because control is a concept that can help us easily uncover false ideas we encounter every day. If you read in the morning news that video games make children socially inept because a new study shows that one goes with the other, then the idea of control allows you to poke through the essential flabbiness of the stance. Video games may not cause social ineptitude, but rather, social ineptitude may lead children to play video games. To determine whether video games cause social ineptitude you would have create two similar groups of children and allow one group to play video games and forbid the other from doing so. Then you would test them to see whether the gamers became less socially adept. In doing so, you would have eliminated all explanations for why gaming and ineptitude go together, with the exception of chance events. If you find the gaming group more socially inept by a small margin, you could use statistical analysis to tell you how likely it was that chance created this difference.

Control allows you to draw a clear line between a causal and a dependent variable. Statistics then lets you say with what likelihood the link you are seeing is the result of chance. Control is part of every scientist's way of reasoning. Yet economists have done perhaps more than any other group of thinkers to broaden the applicability of control to respond to three types of data. The worst data, from the economist's standpoint, are those that the economy generates without any reference to the economist's research needs. Economists responded to this unhelpful state of affairs by inventing econometrics, the science of the study of causal relations between economic variables. To make up for the uncontrolled nature of the data they invented elaborate statistical techniques. These techniques were pattern-searching algorithms that relied on the economist to provide a model. The model narrowed the range of the pattern search.

By the 1980s the grossly subjective nature of these exercises became obvious to most economists and a cry went up for a "credibility revolution" in economic data analysis. The answer was to focus far less on developing fancy statistical techniques for reading patterns in economic tea leaves, and to instead focus on creating a second type of dataset that could be analyzed by the simple comparison of average performances between treatment and control groups.

Controlled experiments are costly, so economists also focused on finding a third type of dataset which arose from what they called "natural experiments". Government interventions that resembled lotteries were the best type of natural experiment to analyze. A government lottery to participate in some initiative creates similar groups of participants and non-participants. Similarity allows you to subtract the results of the treatment from the control group. What you are left with is the net effect of the program. Which is all the news that's fit to print.

References

Angrist, Joshua D., and Jörn-Steffen Pischke. 2010. "The Credibility Revolution in Empirical Economics: How Better Research Design Is Taking the Con out of Econometrics." *Journal of Economic Perspectives*, volume 24: 3–30.

Galiani, Sebastian, Martín A. Rossi, and Ernesto Schargrodsky, 2011. "Conscription and Crime: Evidence from the Argentine Draft Lottery." *American Economic Journal: Applied Economics*, volume 3: 119–136.

Hendry, David F. 1980. "Econometrics—Alchemy or Science?" *Economica* , volume 47: 387–406.

Hicks, J.R. 1937. "Mr. Keynes and the Classics—A Suggested Interpretation." *Econometrica*, volume 5: 147–159.

Keynes, John Maynard. 1936/2007. *The General Theory of Employment, Interest and Money.* (London: Macmillan).

Lalonde, Robert J. 1986. "Evaluating the Econometric Evaluations of Training Programs with Experimental Data." *American Economic Review,* volume 76: 604–620.

Leamer, Edward E. 1983. "Let's Take the Con Out of Econometrics." *The American Economic Review,* volume 73: 31–43.

Lucas, Robert E., Jr. 1976. "Econometric Policy Evaluation: A Critique." *Carnegie Rochester Conference Series on Public Policy,* volume 1: 19–46.

Munk, Nina. 2013. *The Idealist: Jeffrey Sachs and the Quest to End Poverty.* Doubleday.

Nunn, Nathan, and Nancy Qian. 2012. "Aiding Conflict: The Impact of U.S. Food Aid on Civil War." NBER Working Paper No. 17794.

Peterson, Paul, William Howell, Patrick J. Wolf, and David Campbell. 2003. "School Vouchers. Results from Randomized Experiments." In Caroline M. Hoxby (ed.). *The Economics of School Choice.* University of Chicago Press: 107-144. Available at http://www.nber.org/chapters/c10087.

Sims, C.A. 1980. "Macroeconomics and Reality." *Econometrica,* volume 48: 1–48.

Sims, Christopher A. 2010. "But Economics Is Not an Experimental Science." *Journal of Economic Perspectives*, volume 24: 59–68.

Slemrod, Joel, Marsha Blumenthal, Charles Christian. 2001. "Taxpayer Response to an Increased Probability of Audit: Evidence from a Controlled Experiment in Minnesota." *Journal of Public Economics*, volume 79: 455–483.

Slutsky, Eugen. 1937. "The Summation of Random Causes as the Source of Cyclic Processes." *Econometrica*, volume 5:105-146.

Stock, James H. 2010. "The Other Transformation in Econometric Practice: Robust Tools for Inference." *Journal of Economic Perspectives*, *volume* 24: 83–94.

EPILOGUE

9

THE SEVEN STEPS TO MASTERING economics are actually not all that difficult to ascend. The difficulty lies in deciding what to do when you get to the top of the staircase.

Economics can be a hobby or it can be a way of looking at the world. A light reading of this book will give you an idea of what the fundamental issues in economics are. The concepts of moral hazard, adverse selection, Nash equilibrium, equalizing differences, time-inconsistency, permanent income, mean-preserving spreads, efficient frontiers, Pareto efficiency, mechanism design, randomized controlled experiments, and many more will no longer be strangers to you. But while individually interesting, these islands of thought form part of larger archipelago. For what unites all of economics is a quest to establish a science of social accounting. In this pursuit the many ideas we have discussed have an important place. The method of social accounting into which they fit is known as Pareto-efficiency.

Provided that decisions on how to use resources are taken in a context that encourages Pareto-efficiency, societies will be able to experiment with new ways of using resources without risking the wellbeing of the many. Pareto-efficiency puts a floor on the losses from social interactions involving property because any Pareto-improving exchange must benefit at least one person without harming anyone else. The result of this economic error-correction protocol is a society in which social accounts tend to be balanced. What people believe they are getting out of the "system" is at least as large as what they think they are putting into it.

Such a belief can be the bedrock of a stable society of people who live together in large numbers but may not even know who their neighbors are. The need to understand whether the system of social accounts under which we labor is stable or will lead to ruin makes of economics a science to be taken seriously, explained with intent, and appreciated for its solemnity.

The Apprentice Economist is no book of quips, or witty anecdotes. It is a guide to mastering some of the most important ideas that govern the individual and society. When faced with material crises governments do not call upon historians, anthropologists, political scholars, or psychologists. They call on economists. These have developed the most coherent and convincing description of how society organizes itself through a system of accounting amenable to precise analysis. Mastering this analysis is the challenge of the apprentice economist.

Also available by Filip Palda

PARETO'S REPUBLIC AND THE NEW SCIENCE OF PEACE

"Palda offers a novel and interesting perspective" Nobel
Prize winner James M. Buchannan

available at www.amazon.com
also go to www.paretorepublic.com

Made in the USA
San Bernardino, CA
10 September 2014